AN ISLAND PARISH

In pursuit of a dream...

A photographer turned baker who's now trying his hand at running a pub. A schoolteacher who gave it up to become a master brewer.

A German foot model, who's arrived to be the islands' vet and moonlights as a tour guide.

A flower farmer who's discovered his talents really lie in painting landscapes.

And the bishop's chauffeur, and former farm labourer, who followed a calling to become Chaplain to the Isles.

These are just some of the inhabitants of the Isles of Scilly—28 miles to the west of Land's End— who writer and broadcaster Nigel Farrell encounters when he spends a summer discovering what life is really like for the two thousand islanders who belong to England's most remote parish.

AN ISLAND PARISH

A Summer on Scilly

Nigel Farrell

BBC LARGE PRINT

First published 2008 by
Tiger Aspect Productions
This Large Print edition published 2008
by BBC Audiobooks Ltd
by arrangement with
Headline Publishing Group

UK Hardcover ISBN 978 1 405 64997 1
UK Softcover   ISBN 978 1 405 64998 8

British Library Cataloguing in Publication Data available

Printed and bound in Great Britain by
CPI Antony Rowe, Chippenham, Wiltshire

Nigel Farrell is an author and broadcaster who for many years has been exploring and writing about remote and aspirational communities.

His adventures setting up a home and a new life in the south of France became a long-running televison documentary series, *A Place in France*, for Channel 4. He has also chronicled the day-to-day joys and dramas of a Hampshire village over an eight-year period, which became *The Village* for BBC2. Later he wrote and produced *Country House*, following the aristocrats Lord and Lady Tavistock at their country seat of Woburn Abbey, in Bedfordshire, and *A Seaside Parish*, which charted two years in the lives of the villagers of the old fishing port of Boscastle, in north Cornwall. He has been staying on the Isles of Scilly, the stars of *An Island Parish*, for the last year—his wildest, remotest, and most intriguing destination to date.

Sadly, Nigel can't afford to live in any of these lovely places, so is based in a very small flat in north London, where he spends much time looking with envy at neighbours' gardens.

CONTENTS

Map of Isles of Scilly   viii

Acknowledgements   xii

Introduction   1

Chapter 1: A Chaplain To The Ales   17

Chapter 2: All The Way From Bavaria   37

Chapter 3: The Long Journey North   48

Chapter 4: Standing On The Edge Of The
            World   71

Chapter 5: Chocolate Eggs And Wedding Bells   89

Chapter 6: More Woes For The Vet   111

Chapter 7: The Return Of The Bobby   126

Chapter 8: The Biggest Weekend Of The Year   141

Chapter 9: The Entrepreneurial Spirit   160

Chapter 10: Storm Clouds Gather   178

Chapter 11: A Tragedy Engulfs The Islands   195

Chapter 12: Bounty from the Butcher   220

Chapter 13: The Sun Seems to Know When to
            Put his Hat On   235

Chapter 14: An Indian Summer to the Rescue   252

Chapter 15: The Waves Hit The Air Too   270

Chapter 16: A Shore Always To Return To   286

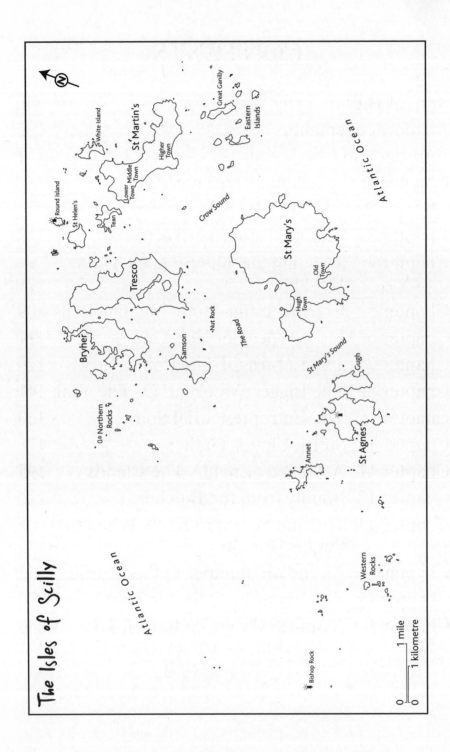

The Isles of Scilly

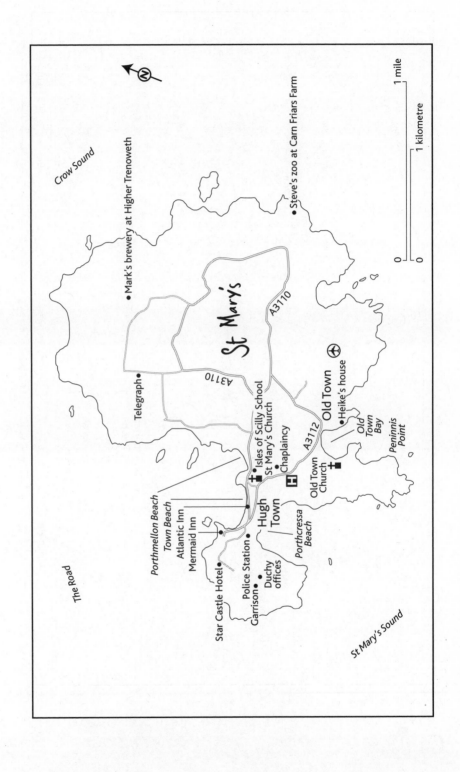

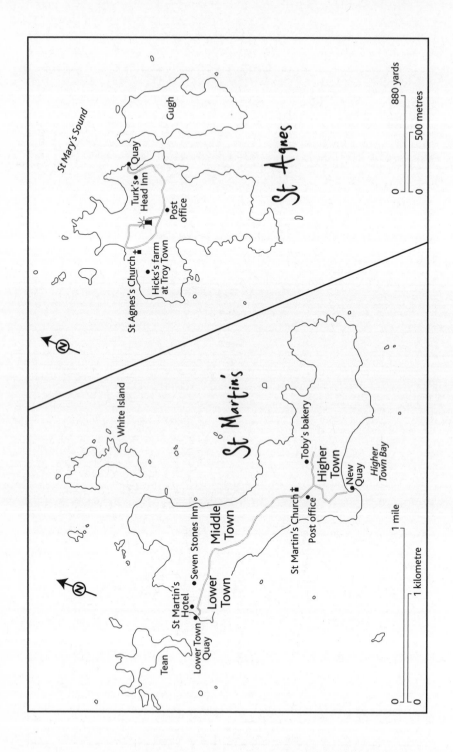

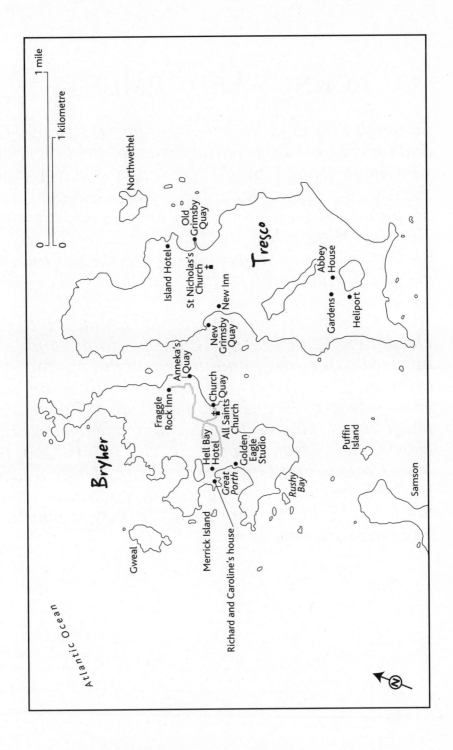

Atlantic Ocean

Gweal

Bryher

Merrick Island

Richard and Caroline's house

Fraggle
Rock Inn

Anneka's
Quay

Hell Bay
Hotel

*Great
Porth*

Golden
Eagle
Studio

Church Quay

All Saints
Church

*Rushy
Bay*

New
Grimsby
Quay

Island Hotel

St Nicholas's
Church

Old
Grimsby
Quay

New Inn

Northwethel

Tresco

Gardens

Abbey
House

Heliport

Puffin
Island

Samson

N

0   1 kilometre

0   1 mile

ACKNOWLEDGEMENTS

So much thanks to the many big-hearted islanders, and others from less civilised parts of the kingdom, who have helped in the creation of An Island Parish, including Mark and Susie Groves; Clive Mumford; Fraser and Julie Hicks; and Jeremy Dowling, Bishop Bill, and the Diocese of Truro for all their help and support. An extra special thanks goes to Marian and Charlie Bennett.

Also thanks to Gordon Wise; Emma Tait at Headline; Adam Kemp, Eamon Hardy and all involved at the BBC; and the wonderful production team at Tiger Aspect, especially Paul Sommers, Elaine Foster, Luc Tremoulet, David Lawrence, Hugh Fairs, Martin Blythe, Johnny Wagener, Ed Harris, and Simon Cooper. Special thanks, too, to Noel Coward and Gilbert O'Sullivan, whose music strangely provided long periods of inspiration; and the lovely Sally Ann for being so very supportive and long-suffering.

Introduction

It's billed as an utterly exotic journey, maybe on a par with the Orient Express to Istanbul or the famed Trans-Andean mountain railway in Peru—your own cabin on the overnight sleeper from Paddington to the Cornish Riviera, and thence by steamer to the remote and beautiful Isles of Scilly, way, way out in the Atlantic Ocean. This is the safest, cheapest and, allegedly, the most romantic way to make the journey.

Things seemed to get off to a promising start. Under the beady-eyed gaze of the statue of the station's famous Victorian designer, Isambard Kingdom Brunel, I arrived on Platform One in good time, half an hour before the train was due to leave at midnight, and was greeted by a broad-beamed, jovial First Great Western train conductor, who addressed me as though I were a frightfully important VIP traveller, clearly a proper gentleman and no doubt well-off enough to offer a respectable tip at the end of the line. Apart from the lack of billowing steam and a deerstalker, I could be a Holmes or a Watson about to set off on a great adventure somewhere deep in the provinces.

I followed my genial conductor onto the train and down a dimly lit corridor that was exactly the width of his backside to my allocated cabin. It was incredibly narrow, but looked cosy. There were coat-hangers cleverly sunk into recesses in the walls and at the foot of the bunk were a little sink and a small linen bag containing a tiny toothbrush,

1

tube of toothpaste, flannel and comb.

'I hope you'll be comfortable here, sir,' he said with an ingratiating smile. 'Mr Sopers will be with you soon. What time would you like tea?'

'Mr Sopers?'

'The gentleman you'll be sharing the cabin with,' he said, snapping down a second, hidden bunk folded higher up the wall with a flourish and handing me a small steel ladder, which he appeared to have been hiding behind his back.

'Since Mr Sopers hasn't arrived yet, it's your choice, sir: top deck or down in the bilges, as you wish.'

To my knowledge, I have never shared a bedroom with a complete stranger, especially a room as tiny as this, and the prospect filled me with instant horror. What were the conventions of such an arrangement? There certainly wasn't room for both of us to stand simultaneously, let alone undress.

I made my way through two carriages to the bar (which I noted with relief was open all night), quickly downed two large Plymouth gin and tonics and returned to the cabin, resolving to get into my bunk as fast as possible, before Mr Sopers arrived. Inevitably, just as I had started to remove my shirt, and with my trousers at half-mast, there was a rap on the door and there stood a small, bald but very dapper man wearing a pinstripe suit and starched collar. He could have been a High Court judge.

We awkwardly introduced ourselves and he politely backed out into the corridor for a moment while I clambered hastily under the sheet and blanket of the lower bunk and pretended to be lost in a book. After a respectable pause, I heard Mr

Sopers re-enter the compartment and start to shuffle about. I was quite unprepared for this: did one pass the time of day, discuss developments in the Test Match or simply ignore each other? Eventually, I could stand the silence no longer, so decided to engage in a little tentative conversation by asking him if his destination was also Penzance or an earlier station. But just as I turned from my book and started speaking, I realised he was completing the process of removing his underpants. He being a small man and just a few inches away, I found my field of vision almost completely blocked by a sight that, after my schooldays, I'd assumed—indeed hoped—I'd never see again.

I slept badly as the train rattled through the night, across Wiltshire, down through the Somerset flats and on to the West Country, creeping through shadowy stations lit only by what looked like the odd, misty gaslight. Just as I'd got used to the rocking rhythm of the wheels, we would suddenly slow or stop completely, in order to stretch the journey so that we wouldn't arrive at 4 a.m., and every now and then Mr Sopers would grunt or sleep-talk. Just after we left Taunton, he took me aback by releasing a short, high-pitched fart. It was certainly a relief to reach the end of the first stage four hours later.

Later, in the early gloom of Penzance, I made my way around the harbour and on to the old *Scillonian*, a ferry built in 1977, but really a throw-back to a bygone age, newly painted white with a bright-yellow funnel and a strong smell of diesel on each deck. It's quite a small ship, but can take six hundred people at a push and a surprisingly large amount of cargo. Cars and square blue containers were being loaded aboard by a derrick, and a surge of well-wrapped, beaming passengers crowded up the gangway.

It was a breezy morning, but not stormy, and as we set sail across the bay and past St Michael's Mount, I was surprised to see large piles of seasick-bags stacked in every corner of the deck. The surprise didn't last long. The *Scillonian* has a very shallow draft, so that she can get into St Mary's at low tide, and no stabilisers. The ship was heaving a little as we passed the monochrome silhouette of the old lifeboat house at Penlee, a sad and lonely reminder of that terrible night in 1982 when the lifeboat went down with the loss of all hands. On we went, past the cute, comfortable harbour at Mousehole and the dramatic steppes of the Minack Theatre, cut into the sheer cliff and apparently about to topple down into the sea. Then, when we were steaming into a westerly and rounding the headland out towards Land's End and the Seven Sisters, where four conflicting currents collide, almost all my fellow travellers sitting close by suddenly vomited simultaneously, rather like a volley of medieval cannons, some even projecting into the wind so that it was whipped back on to us like a heavy blanket of gravy. There was absolutely no shame. The scene was like a Hogarth cartoon, with every single passenger I could see doubled-up or leaning over at crazy angles. A middle-aged fellow opposite really did turn green, throwing up over and over again into an overflowing bag. I have absolutely no doubt that had I handed him a loaded revolver at that moment, he would gladly have blown his

4

brains out. Soon the open deck was awash with a kind of multicoloured custard.

Two hours later, we staggered into the lee of St Mary's Harbour and the ordeal was over for most of us, although for day-trippers the nightmare of the return journey would be underway in just over four hours. It is amazing how quickly humans recover from the near-death experience of seasickness. It was like one of those war films, when the all-clear has just been sounded after a particularly heavy Blitz raid: everyone was grinning, aware that a future to their lives did, after all, still exist, as tributaries of colour began to trickle back into cadaver-like cheeks.

I took a deep draught of the salty, damp air. The sun was beginning to break through the gloom, casting pasty shafts of light onto the gentle sheen of sand which spread out like an apron in front of the terraced houses squeezed onto the low spit separating Hugh Town and the Garrison from the rest of the island. In contrast to the activity on the quay, there was little movement in the harbour. In the lee of the westerly, there was an almost eerie stillness. On Town Beach, a solitary fisherman was lifting dozens of black lobster pots onto an overloaded dinghy and ferrying them precariously back to the beach from an ancient, pale-blue lobster boat, which even had a tatty little mizzen sail on its stern to steady it at anchor. Apart from that, the place looked like a photograph.

It was hard to take in, but this was still England. Yet the journey had taken an exhausting twelve hours, at a total cost of £230. It would have been cheaper, faster and considerably more comfortable

5

to have flown to Singapore or New York.

*   *   *

From the quay at the main island, St Mary's, you can usually see three of the other four inhabited islands quite clearly; indeed, the water between them is so shallow that the circular archipelago looks like the tips of the vast crater of an extinct, subterranean volcano. At very low tides on dark and gloomy days, these rocky outcrops turn the topology of the place into something akin to a bleak lunar landscape; but when the sun is up, the sea, spread so lightly over the granite bed below and weighed down with semi-transparent plankton, sparkles with ribbons and shafts of azure-blue so rich and dazzling you could be among the mermaids of the Aegean, kissing a Caribbean equator or discovering some uncharted corner of the South Seas.

During the summer, the waters between St Mary's and the off-islands are constantly criss-crossed by a motley fleet of assorted and multicoloured ferryboats, hauling bubbling white wakes that mirror the vapour trails lingering in the skies above from transatlantic jumbo jets. Some of the older, open ferries were converted from old Royal Navy liberty boats used in the Second World War; one was allegedly used in the evacuation of Dunkirk. On bright and busy days, they are packed with hundreds of fresh-faced holidaymakers on day trips to explore other islands, who set off excitedly unaware that once out into the Road or over Crow Bar, they stand a fair chance of a complete soaking, an ordeal most will bear with frozen grins set in granite.

On this day, though, most of the ferryboats were beached, in various stages of repair, renovation or repainting, beneath the empty, windswept terrace of the old Atlantic Inn, formerly the Old Customs House and the first port of call for visiting sea captains. The long winter lay ahead, and with it was a chance to take stock, savour the sea air once again and begin the process of renewal. Some of the trees in Church Street were being pollarded. Rotting window-frames were being replaced in a guest house on the Strand. New furniture was stacked outside the slip bar at the Mermaid. The whole place had the air of the morning after the night before.

Apart from one fleeting visit a quarter of a century before, when I first arrived I knew virtually nothing about Scilly, apart from ancient memories of black-and-white television reports featuring a tubby Prime Minister Harold Wilson, clad in baggy, knee-length shorts and ghastly plastic sandals, standing on the sand and puffing away at a pipe in front of a large group of pale-faced Fleet Street reporters with heavily Brylcreemed hair, sweating away in suits. I'd come across various, often madly unflattering, opinions of Scilly: the place was like something out of the Middle Ages and was claustrophobic, inward-looking, inbred and inhabited by misogynistic reactionaries who were deeply suspicious of strangers. Well, well . . .

I have an odd fascination with remote and aspirational communities, and have spent the last twenty years writing and making television documentaries about some of them, from life in a hamlet on top of a mountain in the primitive

7

Ardèche region of southern France, to the struggles of the villagers of the beautiful old fishing harbour of Boscastle in north Cornwall, which was devastated a few years ago by a flood of biblical proportions. The Isles of Scilly, where I was now filming a new series for the BBC, promised to be the most intriguing yet.

So of course I was curious. There seems to be something deep within most of us that must occasionally wonder about island life or dream of living it. I love boats and the sea, yet have spent most of my life commuting to and from dark and sweat-stained city centres. I was again ready for a taste of the wild, the remote, the extraordinary. I had booked a tiny room in the turrets of the moated Star Castle Hotel, the miniature Elizabethan fortress on the highest point of the main island of St Mary's, overlooking the harbour and the south-westerly approaches to the islands. From the little desk with its Bakelite radio, I would plot my aim: to chart a detailed, personal record of one full summer season on Scilly, from the stirrings of early spring to the first golden touches of autumn, spanning the year's two dramatic equinoxes, when huge high and low tides reconstruct the entire landscape of the islands, and the toil of a community whose fortunes depend utterly on the success or failure of a few short months.

Armed with a list of 'useful contacts' I had compiled, literally, on the back of an envelope, I set about organising my exploration of the remotest parish in England.

The words on the envelope read as follows:

'Troytown Farm, voted the most beautiful

campsite in Britain by the *Independent* (aspirational?).'

'Toby Tobin-Duigan Esq., baker and noted photographer (Society?).'

'Island butcher Steve "Griff" Griffin, who can't bear to see animals slaughtered.'

'On her way from the forests of Bavaria, Dr Heike Dorn, eccentric German vet.'

'Richard Pearce, successful artist whose great grandfather was personally praised by Mussolini.'

Spoilt for choice, it was hard to know where on earth to start.

*　　*　　*

The one island you can't see from the main quay is the smallest and most exposed: St Agnes, population just sixty-four, due south-west across the only deep-water entry to the archipelago, St Mary's Sound, a short but often very lumpy journey into the teeth of the prevailing Atlantic winds.

The wiry-haired, weather-beaten St Mary's boatman Fraser Hicks had agreed to take me over to St Agnes 'directly', a quaint Cornish term I'd heard a few times on the mainland, but never been able to define accurately, and which he pronounced as 'dreckly'. When I asked Fraser exactly what 'dreckly' meant, he replied tersely, ' "Mañana", but without the urgency.' Fraser, who is married to the island school secretary Julie Hicks, introduced me to two other boatmen, his brothers Steve Hicks and Alex Hicks, and then his cousin Paul Hicks and uncle Alfred Hicks, also boatmen. Fraser Hicks's father, Mike Hicks, is a

9

retired boatman, as was his grandfather, Gee Hicks. Meeting so many Hickses seemed an odd coincidence, since I was off to see a farmer on St Agnes called Tim Hicks, but in time I realised this was no coincidence at all.

Fraser took me across the channel to St Agnes on the *Wizard*, one of three new high-speed, all-weather, small, rigid, inflatable jet-boats that have revolutionised travel in Scilly, and which tend to be the only means of getting around the islands off-season, when the big, old, timber ferryboats are laid up. There was only a gentle swell, so it took less than ten minutes. Fraser muttered away about this and that, rarely looking me in the eye, like most of the boatmen. It's a habit they've picked up to avoid conversations with the holidaymakers and the list of identical questions that will inevitably follow, such as 'How do you get all the boats at anchor to point in the same direction?' and 'Does all the water go over to the other islands at low tide?'

There are no cars on St Agnes, so Tim Hicks was there to meet me on a quad bike caked in mud and cow dung. It was a bumpy ride, and I gripped his hard, bony shoulders as we went up the little track and across the island to Troytown Farm. En route, Tim helpfully pointed out the houses of various neighbours: Westward, home to Mike and Christine Hicks; Osbert and Pam Hicks's Castle View; Tamarisk Farm, run by Johann Hicks; and the majestic and now sadly disused seventeenth-century lighthouse on the highest point of the island, home to Francis and Carol Hicks. When we passed the Old Parsonage I asked tentatively, 'Do Hickses live there?' and Tim said curtly, 'No, of

10

course not, it's the Beresford-Smiths.'

Troytown is the most south-westerly farmhouse in England, and the origins of its name, as so often on Scilly, are bizarre. A short walk along the enchanting coast path through an ancient, prehistoric field system spattered with huge granite outcrops, you'll find a spiral circle of stones, about two metres across, that's been there for at least three hundred years, although nobody knows why. It's based on the design of the walled defences of ancient Troy, a brilliant military concept whereby there is only one, very defensible entrance to the circle and to reach the inner citadel at its centre any invading force must make a long and perilous journey round and round the spiral. It was the first of a myriad weird but wonderful discoveries I was destined to make in the months to come.

Most islanders must do at least two or three jobs in order to survive. They were multi-tasking long before the term was invented, driven by a creativity and invention born out of necessity. Tim Hicks's family has been farming dairy herds on the island for generations. He still supplies St Agnes with fresh milk, and is off at 8 a.m. sharp on the quad, with a cartload on the trailer, round the island's one circular track, dropping off at the little Post Office, the only shop on the island; the Turks Head, the only pub, with a breathtaking view across the Sound to the Garrison; and finally the island primary school—one teacher, four pupils.

The farm income is supplemented by the small campsite, which overlooks the crumbling medieval quay of the tiny harbour and the church, with a graveyard full of Hicks graves, and beyond the

11

treacherous Western Rocks and that towering tribute to the ingenuity of Victorian engineering, the Bishop Rock Lighthouse, the tallest in the country and the first piece of Britain to be seen by ships arriving from across the Atlantic. The next landfall beyond Bishop Rock is a place Tim Hicks's more distant ancestors never knew existed: America.

Standing in Tim's empty campsite, staring out over 3,000 miles of ocean, I felt my stomach suddenly tighten and my heart quicken, as if in a flutter of panic; it really feels as though you are standing on the edge of the world.

To help make ends meet, Tim is also a member of the St Agnes fire brigade, which consists not of a fire-engine, which would be too ungainly and totally unsuitable for getting across the island's tracks and fields, but a fire-*tractor*, which tows a creaking trailer loaded down with old hoses and ladders. It's wheeled out at fire practice every Tuesday evening, complete with siren and blue flashing light, even though there is no other traffic and its maximum speed is about three miles per hour. I asked Tim when the fire-tractor had last been used in earnest, and he scratched his head and said he seemed to remember a small gorse fire a few years ago. Most of the men don't have driving licences, of course, so when they're out on a 'shout' they must be sure to display an L-plate on the tractor's windscreen.

But now even the fire brigade, farm and campsite weren't enough. For years, Tim and Sue had harboured a dream, which had suddenly— maybe—come within their grasp.

On the way back to St Mary's, Fraser took

Wizard right under the ramparts of the old Garrison and the Star Castle, where I was staying, its union flag almost ironed flat by the growing south-westerly breeze, and explained how it had been the last centre of Royalist resistance after the victory of the Parliamentary forces in the Civil War. While the entire English mainland fell to Cromwell's control, the Isles of Scilly, under the command of Sir John Granville, defiantly continued to fly the Royalist flag and harass Parliamentary shipping, along with any Dutch ships that happened to be passing. The Netherlands, allies of Cromwell, were outraged and in 1651 declared war on the islands. Shortly afterwards, Scilly fell to the Parliamentary forces, but a peace treaty was not signed until the anomaly was noticed over 300 years later, in 1985, by a local historian. The Dutch embassy confirmed the story, and the next year the Dutch ambassador came to the islands and signed the peace treaty with a flourish.

'Odd thing,' chuckled Fraser, staring fixedly at the duckboards, 'to think that for much of my life Scilly was at war with Holland.'

As the days went by, I soon began to understand that almost everything and everyone on Scilly is inter-connected and inter-dependent. This is both the price and the strength of a successful self-contained community. It also means that adultery and divorce are a constant danger. During the season, most people are working around the clock, seven days a week, to pull in the cash, but in the winter one can imagine there's little else to do but contemplate swapping partners, which makes Christmas over here rather more exciting than you

13

might expect. What also takes getting used to is the fact that daily routine is dependent not on the clock, but on the weather and the tides. The shops and pubs regularly run out of certain types of goods and food, and the post can arrive at any time, or not at all.

*   *   *

From my modest headquarters in the turrets of the Star Castle, I made contact with a character who will undoubtedly make a dramatic impact on the introverted world of Scilly. There has been much chatter about the appointment of the new island vet, Dr Heike Dorn, who lives in the heart of the Bavarian forest, forty minutes drive north of Munich.

The islands had been without a vet for six months, and along with the euphoria caused by her appointment were whispered fears that once she absorbed the financial reality of her position, she would pull out, as several others had already done. But it was clear from the first moment of speaking to her that this was a woman made of pure Nordic steel.

She was in the process of packing up her belongings when I phoned, and had already booked the pantechnicon that will carry everything she owns right across Europe to Calais. From there, it will be transported by boat to Dover, then loaded onto lorries and taken to Penzance, and thence by ferry to St Mary's, finally coming to rest in the little terraced vet's house overlooking Old Town Bay, which the Duchy was even now in the process of renovating.

I noted that her English was very good, as she had worked at riding stables and a stud farm in Berkshire for three years, where she met the Queen (an intriguing image) and at the age of thirty-eight had a fling with a twenty-three-year-old Chilean polo player, which resulted in a son, Sammy, now five years old.

She was lucky to be coming at all, she explained. Heike nearly died from a brain haemorrhage after she'd taken four aspirins for a bad migraine. In fact, she had mistakenly taken massively powerful equine aspirins, collapsed and been rushed to hospital, to where her parents were summoned from Germany and told that she stood an eighty per cent chance of dying. As a result, this was a woman who clearly intended to live life to the full. It was my guess that her arrival would hit the islanders like a firestorm.

'One final thing before I must go,' said Heike, in her powerful, fizzing, no-nonsense voice.

'Yes?'

'What is it really like living on Scilly?'

I didn't know where to start.

*　　　*　　　*

It was hard to find anyone prepared to admit it, because it's hardly great public relations, but it seems that the summer before was a poor season. According to the records, on August Bank Holiday, one of the traditional benchmarks for the season, there were only 151 day-trippers on the *Scillonian*, which can take over six hundred passengers; most of the new yellow buoys for visiting yachts in St Mary's harbour swung empty;

15

many of the beaches were deserted. Annual visitor numbers to Scilly reached a peak of 145,000 in 2002 in the wake of the Twin Towers disaster in New York, when many travellers were wary of travelling 'abroad' and correctly deduced that Scilly was unlikely to be the target of a major terrorist attack. Since then, and in the face of the relentless march of low-cost air fares, each year has seen a steady decline in numbers. Since the income of virtually every islander below retirement age depends on the holidaymakers, in one form or another, this is an unsustainable trend. Something must change, or the islands will enter a slow, terminal decline. So it was no surprise that everyone here was awaiting the arrival of the new season and the gifts or disasters it may or may not bring, with a quiet, unstated sense of trepidation.

So ahead of me, with luck, lay one long, lanquid, engaging and revealing sunny summer in England's remotest and oddest parish. But in order to understand the mechanics of the busy half of the year, it is necessary to follow the seeds of the upcoming season as they develop from the bleak months of winter.

Which is why my story really starts at the very dawn of the New Year.

1

A Chaplain To The Ales

I'd been warned that New Year's Eve was a Big Event on the Isles of Scilly, but nothing could have prepared me for the extraordinary scenes which were to unfold. By 6 p.m., everyone—and I mean everyone—is in fancy dress, and since the islanders come out on to the streets and strut up and down like fashion peacocks in a dusky Italian piazza, there are some memorable scenes to be enjoyed: Nazi officers sharing jokes with mermaids, pirates and scarecrows linking arms with Mr Blobby, Superman smoking a fag. I am dressed as a nun with large, nerdy spectacles, so feel completely at home.

What makes the evening so unique, so utterly Scilly, is the amount of time and effort put into the event. The costumes are nearly all hand-made, allowing full vent to the islanders' frustrated imaginations, the results of weeks, sometimes months, of work, or boredom, or both. I'm standing by the Town Hall, on the Parade, watching Noddy and Big Ears sharing a bottle of vodka, when six Ancient Greek soldiers march past, dressed in full armour and carrying spears, pulling a huge wooden Trojan horse, which they've spent weeks constructing up at Lunnon Farm and have dragged halfway across the island. The horse has a large red flashing neon light on its nose, and I follow it down to the Atlantic, where its escort of soldiers abandon it, so it completely blocks the street, and disappear inside to join a heaving mass of drinkers spanning two millennia and every planet in the universe. The surreal picture is made complete by a very realistic-looking policeman in authentic uniform striding purposefully down the street, who on close inspection is revealed to be a rather bothered-looking PC Tony Kan. I bless him with the sign of the cross as he goes past.

The one family on Scilly not joining in the merry festivities are Father and Mrs Guy Scott and their daughters Alice and Clarrie, who are trapped in the temporary prison that the Chaplaincy has become. I'm sure Father Guy would like nothing better than a few beers and a night on the town, but the convention is that the new priest doesn't enter society until he or she is formally installed in, or inducted into, the parish. That isn't due to happen for another few weeks, so poor Guy is keeping his head down, which must be particularly frustrating, since from his eyrie at the top of Church Street he must be able to hear the sounds of revelry rising up temptingly from below.

The Scotts arrived a few days ago. Some of us were up at St Mary's airport to greet them, although at first we thought they were never going to make it. There had been a southerly gale blowing for days, and with the weather so ghastly not even the old cargo ship *Gri Maritha*—better known as the Grim Reaper because it's such a bad seaboat—has dared put to sea. It's like being on an island under siege; no supplies of any sort are getting through, and most of the shelves in the one food shop on St Mary's are empty.

Father Guy and Kate are on the last helicopter of the day, which we thought would surely be

18

cancelled because of the whipping wind and sudden black bursts of lashing rain that can extinguish all visibility. But no, there's a distant, tiny glow in the gathering, murky twilight, and soon we're treated to a scene straight out of a Vietnam war movie; deafened by the scream of the motors, the twin downlights pierce the gloom and the blades surge as the chopper banks at a crazy angle against the howling wind, forcing a downdraft across the landing area that nearly blows us over.

I wonder what on earth must be going through their minds as they step onto the soaking soil of their new parish. Father Guy comes first, clasping Clarrie in his arms and leaning forward into the wind as he walks, the hooded silhouette of Kate follows, and then comes Alice, pacing quickly to keep up with the others, swinging a large box holding two traumatised guinea pigs. It takes less than half a minute to reach the terminal building, but when they do, they are already wet through.

The ladies of the church have been busy. The lights are glowing in the Chaplaincy when the Scotts arrive, it's warm, dry and spotlessly clean, and the smell of new carpets suggests a welcome fresh start. They are greeted by Fiona, the churchwarden, but are too exhausted or too excited to talk much about the journey. Kate's heard about the lack of food on Scilly and manages to come to life briefly when Fiona opens the fridge, which she's thrilled to see is crammed full of gifts from parishioners. A large jug of Scuppered ale, delivered by the islands' brewer, Mark Praeger, sits enticingly on a shelf in the pantry, so Father Guy is also happy. Fiona asks if there is anything else they need, then diplomatically moves towards the front door. We too now leave them to their fate, a little guiltily perhaps.

* * *

Chaplain to the Isles is an unusual post, there isn't another parish in the whole of England that has no neighbours. He has a responsibility to everyone living on Scilly, so he is seen by many as the spiritual leader of the entire community. The chaplain has more influence than an equivalent on the mainland—everyone knows him, just as he knows everyone. He is a school governor, and his days are busy matching, hatching and dispatching in every corner of every island, armed with an intimate knowledge of nearly every family; he is the subject of endless gossip and intrigue, living every hour of every day in the warm waters of a goldfish bowl, where he is on permanent display and under a three-dimensional, 360-degree scrutiny. There will be no escape for Guy and Kate, no days off when they can hide from prying eyes, no relief.

There are compensations. The Chaplaincy must be one of the grandest houses on Scilly, a five-bedroom Georgian gem with a great sweeping staircase in the hallway—a place Jane Austen would have been at home in. It was built around 1830 for the Governor to the Isles, who promptly decided it wasn't quite grand enough and moved out, probably to Hugh House, which is now the Duchy headquarters, up beneath the Garrison. The Chaplaincy is hidden away from prying eyes

20

by a high wall of hedging, a spectacular mulberry tree with branches that loop magnificently down in front of the front door like the arms of a ballet dancer, and a defiant parade of Dutch elms (the terrible disease which so ravaged the landscape on the mainland never made it across the water). Downstairs there's a large study, as befits the Chaplain to the Isles, an elegant dining room and a huge kitchen with the obligatory Aga, sixty years old and not *quite* hot enough for baking. The main living room is upstairs, so that the families of generations of incumbents could escape the trail of parishioners trooping in below to discuss baptisms, marriages and funerals. The living room leads on to a concrete balcony with a wonderful view of the garden—a natural miniature amphitheatre where Shakespeare plays are performed by a troop of roving actors in the summer—and the rather gloomy Victorian church of St Mary's beyond.

Like so many ecclesiastical buildings, over the years only a bare minimum has been spent on maintenance to prevent the bricks and mortar from actually falling down, but recently the Chaplaincy has seemed almost to be sporting a smile, as scaffolding went up in order for the exterior walls to be repainted and vans unloaded large rolls of new carpeting, sure signs that, after nearly a year of chilly emptiness, the old walls which over the years have witnessed so much happiness and misery are once again preparing themselves for the echo of human activity.

*　　　*　　　*

On St Mary's, the New Year festivities always end

at the Mermaid, the grand old pub on the corner of Hugh Street and the quay, which, as the clock moves towards midnight, is starting to fill up rapidly. At the bar I recognise one of the fishermen, a shy, taciturn guy who has his own stool as close to the pumps as possible and barely speaks or is spoken to as he quietly downs pints. Hooch is banned from the trawlers, so the guys are dry for the three or four days they are at sea, and they make up for lost time once ashore. I'd seen the guy at the bar earlier in the day, just before lunch, and he tells me he's been there ever since—twelve hours and counting—and has lost track of his pints, hardly daring to slip away for a leak for fear of losing his treasured place by the beer pumps.

Winter the islanders like to keep all to themselves. During the exhausting summer months, when money must be made, most people work long hours, seven days a week, and most social activity is put on hold. Now is the moment to make up for lost time, a time to let your hair down. Spring will be here before you know it.

As the sound of Big Ben rings out, it is hard to tell exactly how many thoughts of the future year are in the minds of the inhabitants of the Mermaid—some of whom are having real trouble remaining vertical. The place is so crammed, there's scarcely room to breathe, with Daleks, surgeons, gypsies and pearly kings and queens standing on every spare inch of table and chair, cheering to the rafters. Dancing in the windows are the reflections of the fireworks up at Star Castle, with the brooding silhouette of the Duchy offices high above thrown into dramatic relief by the fountain of dazzling rockets, like a medieval castle. The fisherman, slumped at the bar, is automatically handed another glass of frothing Scuppered. Squashed in the corner, beside retired island vet Malcolm Martland and his wife Liz, is Dr Heike Dorn, who arrived a week or two ago after an 800-mile trek across Europe and is now safely installed in her Duchy house at Old Town. Heike is dressed as a rakish Dick Turpin, with tricorn hat and bright-yellow dress-coat, and is thoroughly at home downing a pint and happily chatting to a man with a bloody knife stuck through his head. She looks rather dashing.

If this is a time of year for ideas, plans and hopes for the future, it is also a moment to reflect on the extraordinary vulnerability of life and society on Scilly. Prolonged bad weather can ruin the boatmen. Two wet seasons in a row could decimate the hoteliers and guest-house owners. Spiralling house prices could force away an entire generation of young people. A big increase in the price of aviation fuel could slowly strangle the tourist trade and, perversely, a sustained proliferation of low-cost flights between the UK and foreign destinations could do the same. At thirty years old, the *Scillonian* is coming to the end of her working life, yet plans have still not been agreed for the commissioning of a replacement. Funding depends on long-term economic security, and anyway a new boat would need a new, enlarged quay, and so on.

Most islanders talk with some amusement and a twinkle in the eye about the most infamous wreck of recent years, that of The *Cita*, a 300-foot container vessel en route from Southampton to

23

Belfast, which went down in the pitch black and gale-force winds in March 1997. The ship simply sailed straight into Scilly, a collision which awoke the watch master on the bridge, who had fallen asleep some hours before, after mysteriously making sure the watch alarm which would have alerted him to any impending doom was firmly switched off.

All the crew were safely picked off the stricken vessel by the St Mary's lifeboat and, in the early light of dawn, islanders began to gather on the cliffs above the bay to watch the ship and its cargo slowly disintegrate. The *The Cita* was carrying containers which, one by one, as the hours slipped by, mischievously started to float off the wreck and bob out into the main shipping channel to the south of the island. Tugs were summoned from the mainland to lasso them up and the *Scillonian*, already steaming up from Penzance, was immediately instructed to reduce speed to dead-slow and alter course, for fear that a collision with a semi-submerged, thirty-five-ton steel box might prompt a second, slightly more catastrophic disaster.

Although some of the two hundred containers ended up on the southern Irish coast, most were washed ashore on St Mary's and, when they had prised them open, the islanders couldn't believe their luck. Inside was the most eclectic of cargoes—fork-lift trucks, racks of tyres, thousands of yards of plastic sheeting, boxes of Ben Sherman shirts, hundreds of golf bags, trainers, women's underwear, linen bags, socks and T-shirts, boxes of computer equipment, key rings and fridge magnets. Like armies of ants, the islanders simply

24

set about carting the stuff away, round the clock. The islands' two police officers tried in vain to prevent the human wall of traffic moving to and from the bays and coves. Police reinforcements were flown in, to no avail, and surveillance helicopters scoured the skies. The squirrelled-away booty was simply hidden beneath huge sheets of plywood, also stolen from the ship. Soon signs on the beaches declaring REMOVAL OF THESE GOODS IS AN ILLEGAL ACT were replaced by others saying WINDOWS WITH FRAMES THIS WAY, WITHOUT FRAMES OVER THERE. This was the biggest single injection into the local economy since the Parliamentarians had taken over the islands during the Civil War 350 years earlier. Orderly queues formed without any need for marshals. Neighbour helped neighbour pull, carry, lug and shove boxes of gloves, thousands of tins of shoe-polish and glue, mounds of batteries and jewellery into garden sheds, lofts and attics. Family feuds going back generations were buried under a mountain of goodwill and unexpected wealth. The broken ship was renamed the St Cita, the new patron saint of the islands.

However, mostly unspoken but certainly at the back of every islander's mind, was a terrifying alternative scenario: had *The Cita* been carrying a cargo of petroleum, or diesel fuels, or poisonous chemicals, or any number of other noxious substances, the Isles of Scilly as we know them today probably wouldn't exist.

Mercifully, such gloomy thoughts are far from people's minds this New Year's Day. We are back in the Mermaid at noon, nursing headaches with the soothing balm of Scuppered. I'd heard there

25

had been a big fight in the pub after we'd left last night: bottles smashing everywhere, tables and chairs flying through the air. The fisherman is still at the bar, not looking too much the worse for wear; he's been at his stool all night, which means he's now been 'on-station' for twenty-four hours. I work out that he must have drunk at least thirty-five pints of Scuppered. I ask him what the fight was like and he says, 'What fight?' and orders another drink.

Further down Hugh Street, outside the Atlantic, the wooden Trojan horse stands where it was abandoned, still blocking the street, its nose still sadly flashing a dim red, a potent symbol of a thoroughly debauched night. No-one seems bothered about moving it; what few cars there are out and about just drive around it—nobody gives it a second glance.

The weather is still terrible, and there'll be no sign of the Grim Reaper on the horizon until tomorrow at the earliest. This is why I'm in danger of going hungry, unlike the islanders, who have vast deep freezers and cunning methods of keeping them filled.

There is a common misconception among medical staff in the south-west of England that Scillonians care more about their health than almost anyone else on the planet. One of the reasons for this is that almost one hundred per cent of the island women take advantage of the national breast-screening programme, the highest in the country. There is a tiny hospital on the Isles of Scilly, in a spectacular location on Buzza Hill, beside the old windmill tower overlooking St Mary's harbour. It has twelve beds and three very hard-working nurses, but, despite its reputation for dedication and improvisation, it has no breast-screening facilities. Islanders are invited to fly to Penzance Hospital for their regular screenings, an invitation which is accepted with alacrity.

The normal cost of a return ticket on the helicopter service from St Mary's to the mainland is £154. What many staff at Penzance Hospital probably aren't aware of is that patients being offered breast-screening are given a heavily subsidised return ticket, which costs just £5, so of course the take-up is universal, and the women plan a full and fun day in Penzance, meeting friends, dining out, and always making sure they visit that most hallowed of temples, the supermarket, staggering back to the chopper loaded down with goodies and treats to last them through until the next trip. The clever ones know that when asked to hold their breath for the X-ray in the breast-screening unit, the thing to do is to keep breathing, which results in a smudged image and a recall a few weeks later, along with another five-quid ticket.

One of my first discoveries is that islanders have a strange ambivalence toward the mainland. Self-sufficiency from the mother country is simply not an option—they need its succour, protection and, above all, its cash—yet they retain a fierce and haughty disdain for a mainland life they perceive as dominated by greed, crime, noise, pollution and overcrowding. There's also a frequent sense of irritation; for example, island authorities such as the Council or Fire Brigade are criticised for not employing their quota of ethnic minorities by Whitehall departments clearly unaware no such minorities exist on Scilly. So there's a sense of trepidation and sometimes fear when islanders set foot on mainland soil, and a lightness of heart and quickening of pulse when Land's End is safely left behind and a return to the comfort of slow, damp island life beckons.

In the run-up to the Christmas holidays, breast-screening appointments reach a peak, and the natives return home to the Isles with straining bags full of supplies. This is not much help to me in my current dilemma, as sadly no-one has invited me to join them for a meal, and, astonishingly, the pubs have completely run out of food.

The restaurants are all closed at this time of year. There is nothing at all to eat at the Mermaid, not even a plate of beans or a bowl of soup. There is nothing either, it transpires, at the Atlantic. The only food shop, the dreaded Co-op, beside the tourist office, is closed, although when I peer through the windows I can see that most of the shelves are bare anyway. At the Bishop and Wolf, further down Hugh Street, opposite Mumfords the newsagent, it's the same story, and so it is at the Porthcressa Inn, on the southern side of the sandy spit which links the Garrison to the rest of St Mary's—a lovely view, if you're not hungry.

So I celebrate New Year's Day sitting on a windy beach, looking across a grey sea towards the lighthouse at Peninnis Point, munching a salty bag of crisps and a small pile of pork scratchings, trying to imagine how the forthcoming months might unfold for the islanders, and Father Guy in particular, and getting nowhere.

*   *   *

Guy and Kate keep themselves squirrelled away up at the Chaplaincy for a couple more weeks, living a kind of Phoney War, with only the occasional, surreptitious excursion into the outside world—to Carn Gwaval, where Alice and Clarrie have started primary school; to the Co-op, where the shelves gradually start filling up again, although most of the stuff seems to arrive just hours before its sell-by date; and to the offices of the Steamship Company, behind the tourist office, to enquire as to the progress of the two containers holding all their worldly possessions, which are currently making a tortuous journey over from the mainland, delayed, like everything else here, by the whims of the weather and the creaking fragility of the Grim Reaper.

Heike calls round to pay her respects to the new incumbent and his missus, arriving like a whirling dervish in her trademark outfit of jeans, knee-length boots and sheepskin coat. She's very tall, with long legs, broad shoulders and a wild mop of curly blonde hair, rather glamorous in fact, and still retaining the air of the fashion model she once was in America.

Father Guy tells Heike how nervous he is about the forthcoming induction service, which will officially install him as Chaplain to the Isles, after which he will be expected to throw himself into his ministry with enthusiasm, consideration, tact and diplomacy. He hasn't slept well for days.

'Don't worry, Vicar, the weather will still be bad and then no-one will come,' Heike says reassuringly. 'Then it will be just us!'

Heike's quite unable to disguise a wide-eyed,

29

lustful envy of the size and apparent opulence of the Chaplaincy's rooms, and declares, 'I want to become a vicar too!'—an interesting ambition for a Jewish girl.

Since Father Guy and Kate can do little but wait for the big day, I secrete Guy in a dark corner of the Mermaid one evening, where he gulps down his Scuppered like a man who's just walked across the Sahara. He's not wearing his dog collar and glances furtively around, unsure if the men at the bar recognise him. Of course, everyone knows exactly who he is.

'I intend to do my best, but I'm bound to let someone down,' he confides, unexpectedly letting out his distinctive high-pitched laugh. 'Probably sooner rather than later.' His almost child-like vulnerability is endearing; I wonder for a moment if it's really a trick he uses to get you on his side.

'Are you really nervous about the induction service?' I ask him, and he says that he is, very. 'Don't worry about a thing, it'll go like clockwork,' I say chirpily, passing him over another pint of Scuppered, which disappears with alarming speed. He just seems grateful for the company.

The first guests to arrive for the induction are Guy's parents, who are immensely proud of their son's sensational rise from chauffeur to Chaplain to the Isles. Next comes a gaggle of priests from diocesan headquarters in Truro, including Bishop Roy and Archdeacon Clive, who will perform the honours at the service. Then, on the morning of the day itself, dropping like great birds from a crystal-blue sky, come two helicopters bearing a group of parishioners from Father Guy's previous parish of Mullion, Cury and Gunwalloe, on the

Lizard Peninsula of south Cornwall.

Guy was ordained late in life—only five years ago—and Mullion was his first parish. He had been in the vicarage only two and a half years when he announced to an astonished congregation that he was leaving for the Isles of Scilly. Most priests spend a minimum of five years in a parish, although Bill Ind, the Bishop of Truro, maintains that it takes at least ten to really understand what and who make the place tick. The reaction of his Mullion parishioners profoundly shocked Father Guy. Some walked out of the church then and there. Others refused to speak to him. Even his own churchwardens accused him of betrayal.

Father Guy had totally underestimated how his parishioners had taken him in and made him, Kate and the girls their own. They had become part of the family. He was the first young priest they'd had for years, and with their help, encouragement and succour, his confidence had risen exponentially. Their incredulity at his decision was increased by the fact that there seemed to be no logical or intelligent explanation for it.

'I had a calling from God to go to Scilly; there was really nothing I could do about it,' was the best he could offer. 'It was as though I was a fish on the end of a line, being hauled in.'

Even odder was the fact that a few years before, when he was a theological student, Guy had taken up a short placement on Scilly, a kind of clerical work experience, and had come home to Kate and declared that this was a place he could never, ever live or work in.

Months later, when much of the hurt over his decision had subsided, the parishioners threw a big

31

farewell party for their vicar and his family in the Mounts Bay, Father Guy's favourite watering hole, where he frequently sang shanties with the Inn Singers and commiserated with his mate Lively, a well-known and very affable village character, famous for swearing like a trooper and professing to being in a semi-permanent state of inebriation. It was a few days before Christmas, and virtually the entire village turned out to see them off; quite a tribute to a man who is not wildly extrovert, who never throws his arms about or bellows about hellfire. Father Guy's a gentle, self-effacing man who appears to lack confidence and whose natural tendency is to be reactive rather than proactive. He's more at home on the streets and in the pubs than immersed in the politics and diplomacy of the dinner-table. Yet he is clearly able to inspire an extraordinary, albeit quiet, loyalty.

The Inn Singers even composed a special shanty in Father Guy's honour, and there was scarcely a dry eye in the house when they sang:

> He's the vicar of the Scillies,
> Oh my Lord!
> With Kate and children side by side,
> The vicar of the ferry ride.
> We've grown accustomed to his face,
> There's no-one else can take his place,
> But where did he learn to drink like that?
> He's the vicar of the Scillies,
> Oh my Lord!

Father Guy's final service in Mullion, on Christmas Day, was packed; even his drinking pal Lively turned up, astonishingly sober and in a shirt and tie, although he'd scarcely set foot inside the church before. There were buckets of tears, not least from Kate and Alice, and, after what was clearly a Herculean effort of self-restraint, eventually from Father Guy himself, who unashamedly broke down during the blessing. This wasn't just a departing, a moving on; this was a bereavement.

So these are the good people of Mullion, who are touching down now on the tarmac in front of the small St Mary's airport terminal, abandoned, yet forgiving enough to take time off and find the cash to make the journey to wish Father Guy well on his launch into the new parish.

The question I can't get out of my mind now is: will his new parishioners take to Father Guy in quite the same way? It's a very different place and a very different community. Does Father Guy really know what he's taken on? After all, it wasn't even really his decision to come here in the first place.

*   *   *

The storms abate for twenty-four hours for the induction service, as if the Lord is indeed smiling on this remote place. Far from being empty, as everyone had feared, every seat in the church is taken. Boatloads of off-islanders have been arriving at the quay all morning, walking down Hugh Street, up past the Town Hall and the Parade and up the hill to St Mary's Church, chatting and laughing in the sunshine.

The service itself is a curiously medieval affair. 'I, Guy Charles Scott, do swear that I will be

33

faithful and bear true allegiance to Her Majesty Queen Elizabeth the Second,' he solemnly declares, an odd reminder that the man who currently owns Scilly like a personal fiefdom, HRH The Duke of Cornwall, as Prince Charles is referred to here, who is the object of much ire on the islands whenever there's even a suggestion of an increase in rent, will one day be head of the Church of England.

Father Guy is formally greeted by the Duke's representative on Scilly, Colin Sturmer, the land steward to the Duchy of Cornwall, which retains its feudal right to veto his appointment; the chair of the Isles of Scilly council, Christine Savill, who runs the campsite up on St Martin's; Andrew Penman, the willowy head of Five Islands School, of which Father Guy is now automatically a governor; lay representatives of each of the five islands; and a rather awkward-looking police sergeant, Ian Stevens, in gleaming ceremonial uniform complete with big silver buttons and brilliant white stripes. With the polish on Father Guy's shoes gleaming in the multicoloured shafts of sunlight beaming down through the stained-glass windows depicting acts of lifeboat heroism and Christ, the great fisher of men, the new chaplain looks curiously composed and confident bearing his new cloak of office; he looks as if he could conquer the world.

'Expectations are running high at this time,' Father Guy says. 'I pray and hope that, with God's help, I may meet just some of them.'

Surrounded by a sea of gleaming white surplices and followed by his loyal foot soldiers, churchwardens Sue and Fiona, who are holding long staves, Father Guy symbolically tolls the bell and slams the main door to the church, at the west entrance, three times, in a gesture of both possession and celebration.

Later, in the church hall down the street, past the museum, there's lashings of Scuppered from a barrel Mark Praeger has labelled with a picture of Guy and the words 'Chaplain to the Ales'. The welcoming cake is cut, and, inevitably, there are more tears from the new chaplain. It takes some courage to display such raw emotion; it disarms as well as endears. Then the retired priest, Donald Marr, who, with his wife Margaret, has been holding the fort on the islands for most of the last year, hands over the keys of the churches to the new chaplain. 'The keys to the kingdom,' says Father Guy wistfully, and the two men laugh and embrace.

Scilly is an outpost of the Diocese of Truro, which has its spiritual heart in the great Gothic cathedral that reaches up to the sky like a huge granite fountain from its modest site in the centre of the city. The towering building is the official seat of the bishop—currently Bishop William Ind, rather better known throughout Cornwall as Bishop Bill—and the place looks at first glance as though it's medieval. In fact, it's a fantastic recreation of what, six hundred years later, Victorian architects felt a medieval cathedral should look like. The foundation stones were laid by Queen Victoria's heir, the then Duke of Cornwall, later Edward VII, in 1880, and the building was largely completed by 1903, the first English cathedral to be built on a new site since Salisbury in 1220.

At about the same time as Father Guy was arriving on Scilly, his boss and the man largely responsible for his appointment, Bishop Bill, slipped away from his official duties to light a candle for the new priest of his remotest parish.

'He'll make mistakes, but if he's honest about them it won't matter,' the bishop said. 'People like their priest to make mistakes, to be more human—and that's just as true if you believe in God as if you don't.'

He paused and gripped his bishop's crook with one hand and the big brass cross that hangs down across his purple cassock with the other.

'Mind you,' he said, after a time, the hint of a mischievous smile playing on his lips. 'Being the Chaplain to Scilly is not a job for everyone. Like living in a ruddy shop window. And no escape! No thanks.'

The day after his induction, it's straight to work for Father Guy. In his study, which is lined with good-luck cards from his loving Mullion parishioners, he's grappling with a little yellow book he's never seen before and which is certainly not an easy read for someone who is dyslexic, like Guy. It's called *The Tide Tables for the Isles of Scilly*, and consists of page after page of bewildering lists giving precise details of the changing tides for every day of the year, according to the predicted lunar and astronomical movements, right down to the final nought point one metre, with all heights referred to chart datum defined as being 2.91 metres below local ordnance datum, lat. 49.55'N, long. 6.19'W. He must learn how to interpret it, and quickly, since one of his first tasks is to book a boat for a trip across to

Bryher, which dries out at low tide, potentially preventing him from landing, or, even worse, from leaving.

*   *   *

So, it is this beautiful, anachronistic little world, where human emotions that are so often well hidden or disguised—ambition, jealousy, greed, complacency, selfishness—are all too visibly exposed, that Father Guy Scott, former vicar of Mullion on the Lizard Peninsula in southern Cornwall, former farm labourer and chauffeur, experienced campanologist but inexperienced priest, sufferer of vertigo, passionate believer in real ale and the power of orthodox Christian theology, is about to enter.

As Bishop Bill said: 'I wish him well with all my heart.'

2

All The Way From Bavaria

Like the ebb and flood of the tide, there is a constant flow of people arriving on Scilly, eager to start new lives, or desperate to escape from the frustration, sadness or tragedy of old ones.

Heike's new home is just below the airfield, where a Hurricane fighter squadron was based during the Second World War to protect shipping entering and leaving the western approaches to the Channel; it saw little action, and most of the high

37

number of casualties among the pilots occurred because of accidents during take-offs and landings on the dangerously short runway. The house is one of a row of terraced, part timber-clad homes built by the Duchy in the 1970s. They are of curious architectural design; for example, the downstairs lavatory of each house is built not at the back, as you might expect, overlooking a parking area, but right at the front, thus stealing most of the view, save for the incumbents of the throne itself, who enjoy a spectacularly panoramic sweep of one of the islands' most beautiful beaches, at Old Town Bay.

I realise Heike is the first person I've met who knows less about Scilly than I. She's giving me strong coffee and explaining, in a very un-English way, how much she enjoys visitors, especially if they drop by uninvited, and she appears to mean it.

She bounces about her new domain with ceaseless verve and energy, undaunted by the fact that most of her belongings are in a lorry that's broken down just outside Dover. The house has been redecorated by the Duchy, and is completely empty. At the back is the smallest surgery Heike says she has ever seen, just room for a small examination/operating table and a few shelves to store drugs, although not horse aspirins. There are three tiny bedrooms upstairs, and again it's the view that saves the day. She waves a long, slim arm at the bedroom window, overlooking the beautiful, empty beach, and looks at me with those fearless, piercing eyes.

'What could be better than that?' she demands. 'We have nothing like this is in the Bavarian forests! Sun, sea, sand, maybe sex—magnificent!'

'It does rain sometimes.'

'It rains? Here?'

She seems genuinely fascinated by everything and everyone around her, rattling off questions like a Gatling gun, and frequently collapsing with laughter, two fairly reliable indications of a strong and confident personality. I take to her instantly.

She looks as if she's come home, and I begin to understand why Dr Dorn made what at first seems the extraordinary decision to emigrate here. She has a five-year-old son, Sammy, and this must be one of the most perfect places on the planet to bring up a small child. Old Town was the original capital of the island, before the superior defensive position of the Garrison above Hugh Town stole its thunder in the sixteenth century. Right next to Heike's house is the remains of the old medieval quay, from where islanders would barter dried fish and seabirds with Arab seamen from North Africa, and where now local kids play each evening, like children from another era. Beyond is the magnificent beach, which swings around to the little church, sheltered from the prevailing winds by the rocky outcrop of Peninnis Point, deserted most of the year. The Post Office stores and the pub are three minutes' walk one way, Sammy's school three minutes' walk the other. There's the riding school up the road, and in time Heike will no doubt get a boat, moored in the bay, for sailing and diving.

Beyond the beach is St Mary's older, tiny church, which dates back to 1120. Candlelight is the only source of light after dusk because there's no electricity. Here, among the graves of shipwrecked seamen and those accident-prone wartime RAF pilots, lies the body of the former Prime Minister James Harold Wilson (1916-1995), buried beneath a massive and very plain granite stone. The Great Socialist loved Scilly with a passion, spending much of his life in a suitably modest little bungalow up on the hill on the road to Hugh Town (where Lady Wilson can still often be seen pottering about) with a garden which, during his premiership, was denuded of all vegetation because Wilson became obsessed with the thought that they might hide bugs planted by Soviet secret agents, or MI5, or both.

Harold Wilson described Scilly as the most egalitarian society he had ever seen, and, thinking about it, he may have had a point. There's no private education or private health here, most housing is owned by the 'state' (i.e. the Duchy), there's no crime, nobody even owns a flash car. In fact, since there is nothing really to spend your money on, there's not much point in even being rich.

The much bigger church up the road in Hugh Town was built only in 1837, but has no churchyard; the convention is that services for bigger funerals are held in Hugh Town, and the coffin is then carried by friends and colleagues over the hill for interment in the beautiful churchyard overlooking the sea down at Old Town. On Lord Wilson's death, Whitehall chose to ignore the local tradition and insisted on sending down a Rolls-Royce hearse from London to transport the body, but the dockers on the quay at St Mary's refused to unload it from the *Scillonian*, so the coffin was carried by hand after all.

Heike tells me about her former life as a model—thanks to her feet. After her upbringing near Munich, she desperately wanted to be a vet, but reluctantly went along with her parents' ardent insistence that she train as a stage and theatrical designer. After two years in Israel, where she was conscripted into the army and, as an Uzi-toting second lieutenant, saw action in Jerusalem and Gaza, she worked in various theatres and opera houses across Europe. One very hot summer, she was working barefoot on the stage when a designer remarked on the beauty of her feet. This led to Heike becoming a foot model and foot double in advertising photography. Later, the rest of her body was allowed to get in on the act, and she became a top sports model in New York. Her photographs portray an attractive combination of wild, uncontrolled confidence and carelessness. Heike fell in love with a charismatic Native American called Vijrah from South Dakota, who was stabbed to death by a white racist after an argument in a bar in the Deep South.

She asks me if I'd like to see some of her sketches of Vijrah, and she clatters upstairs to fetch them. Again, I am startled by her direct, open approach to even intimate subjects. She draws with simple, powerful strokes. I hold the two large, much-loved pieces of parchment in my hands in the strangely sterile and echoing front-room and look down at a beautiful, mesmerising face, its chiselled features, framed by shoulder-length hair, shining out from the paper. 'I really, really loved him,' says Heike, and for a brief moment her Teutonic lack of emotion looks on the point of wavering. Vijrah's killer was jailed for a mere two years, but the elder brother of Heike's dead lover was waiting for the redneck to emerge from prison and killed him in retribution, a 'slow death in the traditional Red Indian way', although I didn't dare ask precisely what this involved.

And now, having survived the near-death experience prompted by the astronomically powerful horse aspirin, here she is, and of one thing I'm sure: the presence of a single, blonde, Nordic beauty like Heike Dorn is likely to cause a tremor among a certain section of the male population, who will be racking their brains for a plausible reason to take the cat or guinea pig to the vet for a check-up.

*   *   *

By mid March, Heike is beginning to wonder whether her original unbridled enthusiasm for Scilly may have been a little misplaced. True, her furniture is all now here; most of it is dark, old oak and valuable, stuff she acquired during her years in Berkshire, and that, coupled with her own brooding, slightly gloomy paintings of horses, badgers and foxes that line the walls, along with a huge brass toad that props open the living-room door, gives the place the air of a small, not particularly profitable antiques shop.

No, for Heike the difficulty is more one of status. She doesn't seem to fit any of the standard island stereotypes. Scilly is still, in some respects, a misogynistic society, so the presence of a carefree, headstrong, attractive, single lady in her forties is confounding enough. Then there are her origins; many off-islanders refer to St Mary's as 'the mainland', and all islanders categorise the true mainland as 'foreign', but how on earth do you pigeonhole someone from Bavaria? Also, as the vet, Heike should, in theory, fall into the same class as the doctors and the dentist, but a further complication is that, right now, there's not much veterinary work for Heike to do, so for much of the time she is technically unemployed. All very confusing.

It is true that in the last few years, there has been a burgeoning animal population on Scilly. As well as the Hicks's Hereford and Jersey crossers, there are an award-winning Limousin herd on Tresco, Shetland ponies and 'landscape cattle' on Bryher, a young beef herd and the new riding stables up by Lunnon Farm on St Mary's and an eclectic range of domestic pets. Even with a house and rent subsidised by the Duchy, though, there simply doesn't seem to be sufficient work for a full-time vet. The previous island vet had left for a more lucrative practice on the mainland, where his starting salary was three times what he'd earned on Scilly. Apart from removing a tick from the ear of an old ginger cat, a service for which, even under the present dire circumstances, she couldn't bring herself to charge, Heike hasn't had any work for five consecutive days.

What kind of social life can she expect? Already I've heard wild gossip about secret assignations and late-night liaisons, which I'm fairly sure are nonsense. Surrounded by wary, eagle-eyed wives, Heike will never be the toast of the dinner-party circuit. The days are drawing out, but even though Sammy (who conversely has settled into island life as though he'd been born in the place) is getting

43

home from his jaunts later and later, Heike must still be there for him every evening, and there's no chance at all of affording a regular sitter. Yet she seems stoical about the prospect of living life largely alone.

'I have never thought of myself as someone interested in r-r-r-romance,' Heike tells me, rolling the word around in her mouth as if she is tasting some particularly sharp wine, an oddly endearing habit. 'Men say of me that it is like biting into granite,' she adds, pausing for a moment.

'Granite?'

'You know, the rock.' We look at each other for a moment. 'How is my English, incidentally?'

'Good.'

Her last relationship hit the skids a couple of years ago, after her boyfriend had prepared the ultimate romantic dinner: champagne, smoked salmon and perfectly grilled sea bass, served on a highly polished dining table surrounded by a sea of candles.

'I demanded he turn the lights on; I couldn't see what the hell I was eating,' she says. 'This did not go down well. No, not well at all.'

'No, I can see it might not.'

'I'm not falling in love so easily.' Heike sighs. 'Maybe someone, somewhere will come along and rip me off my feet.'

'Whisk.'

'Whisk. Quite. Rip me off my whisk.'

So Heike, a little bored and lonely, is looking forward to driving up to the airfield on the hill beside the house to collect a new houseguest, who, with a bit of luck, will also become a new friend. He's called Leo and he is now on his way from his

44

previous home in Cardiff to the heliport at Penzance, obviously classified as a VIP passenger, because the staff there say they will hold the helicopter for him if he's late, a privilege not accorded, the retired vet Malcolm Martland tells me, to any other passenger he's ever known.

I bid Heike goodbye and walk across the beach, up the steep climb to Buzza Hill, past the new health centre and the little hospital, with its splendid views through the palm trees to Porthcressa, then down past the Chaplaincy and the church into Hugh Town. This is a small place in every respect. By the end of the day, I have bumped into Heike on seven further occasions. This happens all the time on Scilly. I'm still unsure of the etiquette here; should one stop at each meeting and continue the conversation where it left off, in which case, nothing will ever get done? Or ignore, or at least pretend not to notice, the acquaintance, which might well be interpreted as 'stuck up' or rude? I still have much to learn.

*   *   *

As the days go by, work picks up a little for Heike. With Malcolm helping with the anaesthetics, she's done a hysterectomy on a nine-month-old Labrador bitch, a far more complicated operation on a dog than a human, and she's made several visits up to Clare Morley's horses at the riding school above Lunnon Farm. On the last visit, she was there to tranquillise the horses so that a large, muscular equine dentist, flown in specially from the mainland, could get to grips with their overgrown molars with a large, industrial file.

45

She also tells me of a terrible case she was called to on St Agnes. A much-loved family horse that had been ill for some weeks had broken out of its paddock and ended up on the rocks by Wingletang Down, on a rising tide. It had tripped and fallen several times on the rocks and soon, covered in blood from its falls and its eyes so swollen it could barely see, the horse was stumbling around helplessly in growing panic and despair. When Heike arrived the distressed owner and a small group of friends and neighbours were trying to shoo away a few holidaymakers who had gathered on the coastal path, transfixed by the appalling scene. With the horse terrified of human contact and now often collapsing through exhaustion, Heike and the others tried to tempt it with a bucket of bran and honey, in a desperate attempt to give it some energy, but it refused to let them come near. Eventually, with the waters rising, the horse unable to summon the strength to clamber back on dry land and the owner pleading for it not to be shot, Heike had no choice but to put it down by injection. She had nursed the horse through its recent bout of ill-health, and was clearly deflated by the sudden and unexpected loss.

The sad incident compounds these less than happy times for the new island vet.

Even the arrival of her new companion hasn't been quite the success Heike had hoped for. Leo, a bull terrier, had been groomed for the show ring by his breeder in Cardiff, but had injured a knee joint in one of his back legs and had, overnight, been rendered worthless and in urgent need of a new home. The breeder's vet is an old

46

acquaintance of Heike's from her Berkshire days, so now Leo has been driven down to Penzance and put on the helicopter, in a roomy, well-ventilated cage bolted to the floor, from which he has a mouth-watering view of the ankles of his fellow passengers.

Heike's first problem is that Leo refuses to get off the aircraft when it arrives at St Mary's, understandable perhaps, since once the cabin door is opened the chopper fills with the smell of aviation fuel, an unexpected downdraft of warm air and the deafening roar of the rotor blades. Eventually, a small army of terminal staff and helicopter crew manage to get Leo out; it's the first time anyone can remember a passenger having to be dragged from the aircraft.

In the terminus, Leo nearly knocks over Malcolm, and on the mercifully short journey down the hill to Old Town, he frantically licks the windows so that it looks as if one of those famous Scilly fogs has suddenly descended. When Heike manages to manhandle him into his new home, Leo demolishes an apparently indestructible plastic bone she has bought for him, tears down the masts of Sammy's model pirate ship, so that it looks as though it has been raked by a cataclysmically powerful broadside, and sets about brutally shagging every cushion he can find.

Heike giggles indulgently, like a schoolgirl on a first date, but behind the hesitant smile, the eyes scream, 'Oh my God, what have I done?'

There are no new messages on Heike's answerphone; the last one she had was two days ago. She knew, of course, that in such a small community veterinary work must inevitably come

47

in fits and starts, but now she's being forced to dig into her savings to cover her outgoings—an unsustainable situation.

One aspect of Scilly life, though, does already seem to have rubbed off on her. To make a living on this rough and remote place, you need an ability to think laterally. So Heike's come up with an intriguing new idea which might just help tilt things in her favour.

3

The Long Journey North

The gigs were built for speed through the water, and are quite beautiful to the eye. Thirty-two feet long, powered by six oars, they are a legacy from the days of sail, when they raced pilots out to ships on the horizon, the winner securing the lucrative business of guiding their charges through shoals, submerged reefs and unexpected currents to the safety of harbour. Today, gig-racing has become the fastest growing sport in the West Country, and the handful of shipwrights who have retained the skills needed to handcraft Cornish narrow-leaf elm into these superb, sleek and enduring symbols of design excellence have never been busier. From Saltash to Sennen Cove, meticulously maintained gigs can now be found in virtually every harbour on the Devon and Cornwall coastline.

In a community imprisoned by water, gigs were an inherent part of life on Scilly for generations, their speed often allowing them to double up as lifeboats or be used for smuggling—gigmen thought nothing of whipping over to France for a few barrels of rum or Burgundy to feed the islanders' voracious appetite for lethally strong alcohol. There are five pubs on St Mary's now, but in the early 1800s there were twenty-three, almost all supplied with illegal contraband by the smugglers. With sometimes as many as two hundred passing ships at anchor in Scilly, gigs would slip out under cover of darkness and collect tea, sugar, cognac and tobacco from the seamen in exchange for potatoes or fresh fish. Even one of Father Guy's predecessors, the legendary Reverend Troutbeck, was found to have been involved in a smuggling ring. Smuggling was the single most important element of the islands' economy, and they were a key staging post for smuggling in the West Country until the early nineteenth century, when the Revenue sited a permanent boat on St Mary's. Indeed, so hard did the Revenue cutters find it to keep up with the traditional eight-oared gigs that parliamentary legislation had to be introduced to restrict the number of oars on all new gigs to six.

It may only be March, but already one or two gigs are beginning to appear in the harbour at St Mary's, in early preparation for the World Pilot Gig Championships, held every year on Scilly on the first May Bank Holiday. More than a thousand oarsmen and women, along with the same number of family and friends, flood in from every corner of the West Country, doubling the islands' population. It's become by far the biggest event in the Scilly calendar, and a fairly reliable indication as to the success or failure of the season ahead.

49

Every available aircraft seat, every bed and campsite pitch is requisitioned months in advance, and the pubs and hotels order in gallons of extra stock. The crews are often coming to the end of a gruelling training schedule and they start knocking back the traditional tipple of port at the end of each race, with bottles often slyly produced from beneath the gunwales even before the boats have touched sand, and spend the rest of the weekend making up for lost time.

Today, I can see two newly painted boats from the quay, one circling gently in the safety of the harbour, the other, a dark, spidery silhouette, braving the chilly evening breeze and thrashing off across the Road to the starting point for most of the races, Nut Rock, just in front of the shadowy outline of the twin peaks of Samson, whose population was evacuated two hundred years ago in the face of imminent starvation, so it's now uninhabited. The St Mary's crews usually assemble at the gig sheds at Porthmellon, glad of the chance to stretch their limbs in the salt air and savour the companionship of the shared rhythm of the rowing and the long hours in the Mermaid after. In a place where there is precious little else to do, there's never any shortage of volunteers to man the gigs.

It's low tide, and on Town Beach I find Fraser Hicks, clad in oily blue overalls, working into the dusk to get his ferryboat *Sea King* ready for the arrival of the first holidaymakers in the run-up to Easter. The small, high-speed launches will fly you through the water and drop you on a beach, whatever the weather or tide, at any time of the year, but they'll knock you back thirty quid a go. In the summer months, nearly everyone travels on the fleet of big, old, wooden tripper boats, for just a few pounds. For the ill, moving backwards and forwards to the little hospital on St Mary's, there's the old doctor's boat or the new, dazzlingly fluorescent ambulance boat, if it's not broken down; and for the drowning, there's the fifty-five-foot, gleaming-orange Severn-class lifeboat. You take your choice.

Fraser inherited *Sea King*, a sleek, oak-framed and pine-decked, red-and-white open launch that can take a hundred passengers, from his father, Mike Hicks, who bought it from a company running passenger trips from the south Devon coast. It was built in Plymouth in 1947, and Fraser is planning a big sixtieth birthday bash for the old girl. 'Treat 'em well and they'll treat you well back, just like a good woman,' says Fraser, slapping the planking of *Sea King*'s topsides as he might the haunch of a buxom wench. 'She's good for another thirty years.'

Fraser's not alone. Sitting on the wet sand, watching the painstaking work, hour after hour, is Sally, a long-suffering spaniel belonging to one of Fraser's neighbours at Old Town. She joins him every morning on his way to work, and spends every hour of the long working day never further than a few feet away from Fraser, her nose often straining over the prow of the boat, her ears flapping in the wind, like some demented figurehead. Sally says goodbye each evening only when she's hungry, and heads home for supper and a good night's sleep.

Earlier in the day, Fraser's wife Julie, the secretary up at the secondary school overlooking

51

Town Beach, had called by to help give *Sea King* its annual lick of paint. It's essential for good luck and plain sailing that the women in the family use the paintbrush on the hull, and Julie had brought down their daughter Rebecca, even when she was a baby, and squeezed the big, red brush between her tiny fingers. They don't have a son, and recently Fraser's been pondering the future of the family boat when he retires.

Unlike some of the other boatmen, Fraser's usually happy to chat to passers-by, especially when there's work to be done, and today he's reminiscing about past boating disasters, which include him scraping virtually every rock on the chart. He once forgot to pick up two German visitors after a trip to Samson; they were eventually rescued after writing S.O.S. in the sand. Then there was the pretty young mother who handed her baby to Fraser to hold as she stepped aboard *Sea King*, saying nervously, 'Don't drop him!'

'Don't you worry if I do,' he replied reassuringly. 'We'll soon fix you up with another one.'

It's a warm, balmy spring day; it's a delight to be here. I wander further up the quay, where Martin Bond is unloading large yellow boxes of monkfish, squid, mullet, salmon, sole and John Dory from his trawler, *Marauder*, a modern miracle. Martin was born and brought up at Appletree Cottage at Lower Town on St Martin's, and like his father and grandfather before him, he went to sea when he left school, working as a crab and lobster man at first, later joining the Merchant Navy and roaming the world on tankers, tropical cargo boats, fruit ships and even ammunition carriers.

Years later, he and his son Joel—back from a stint in the British Army and, like most other young people, desperate to find a way to stay on the islands—took on what was regarded as a real gamble. Convinced that the scientists' dire warnings of ever-diminishing fish stocks was plain wrong, at least in this part of the Atlantic Ocean, they borrowed every penny they could and four years ago commissioned *Marauder* from a boatyard in Hull—and this at a time when ship-owners all over Britain and Europe were de-commissioning thousands of vessels. Much of the fitting-out work they did themselves or with the help of skilled friends on the islands. They ended up with a boat which if built from scratch today would cost the best part of £200,000.

The timing wasn't an accident. Cornwall is the poorest county in England, and one of its best-kept secrets is that it benefits handsomely from EU grants and subsidies. The Isles of Scilly Fishermen's Association had been given money to build a small ice-store at the back of the quay, behind the Steamship Company offices, to keep the fish fresh, a relatively modest investment which revolutionised the ailing industry's potential. It also tipped the balance for the Bonds; if put to use with skill, following the shoals in local waters rather than the longer, fuel-thirsty voyages to deep-sea grounds, *Marauder* might just about earn them both a decent living.

The boat's short enough in length to avoid the dreaded European quotas, and since there's now only one other trawler on Scilly, there could be fish in abundance to be had around the islands.

53

There's no fishmonger here, so while Joel's out chasing the Dory, Martin loads up his old, blue, air-conditioned van from the ice-store and cruises the St Mary's pubs and hotels, selling what he can. If the weather's good and the net holds, they can't get enough of the valuable catches like squid and John Dory; if the weather turns or the net breaks, often snagged by the myriad wrecks that litter the seabed around Scilly, then Martin and Joel have no choice but to spend long hours killing time in 'the office', aka the bar of the Mermaid. They got off to a promising start their first summer, but a long winter of terrible storms, during which they were confined to 'the office' for weeks at a time, has put them back on a financial knife-edge.

When he's finished unloading, Martin brews up a cup of tea and invites me aboard. There's precious little room on the deck to swing a cat, let alone exist for three or four days at a time, often with the boat rolling like a pig in the swell, pivoting either side of the net, which drags like a dead weight twenty metres behind. One man sleeps in a grubby bag in the tiny fore cabin, the other fights off boredom in the wheelhouse, brewing up hundreds of cups of tea on the little gimballed cooker, checking the GPS and depth-sounder, scanning the computer screen above the wheel, where a mass of red lines endlessly zigzag around and between the islands, tracking the route of the vessel as it stalks the shoals of squid and Dory.

I ask Martin why the fish is called John Dory, and he picks a big one up, its pale, flat body like a slippery plate, its eyes bulging blankly, and points to what looks like a dark-grey thumbprint just below the stiff, extended gill.

'Mark of St Peter, guarding the gates of heaven, so they say,' says Martin gruffly, pausing slightly for effect; this is clearly a story he's told before. He rolls a cigarette and lights up. 'The Italians call him "Janitori"—the gatekeeper. Janitori . . . John Dory. That's what we need,' he says, puffing up a good head of smoke and waving the poor creature almost in my face, its gentle, tangy scent an indication that it hasn't been dead long. 'Give us a few more Janitori like this and I'll be a happy man. Happy as a piper, and they don't come happier than that.'

At the deep-water end of the quay, where the *Scillonian* docks in the summer season, I wait for Father Guy in the late-winter warmth, soaking in the low rays of the watery sun like an indolent basking shark. The distant throb of a small outboard motor echoes around the tranquil harbour; silhouetted in the distance, a little dinghy, weighed down with lobster pots that have spent the winter months stored on the Strand, is being press-ganged back into service. Watching these gentle scenes of island life unfold all around, it is easy to understand how people come to fall in love with the place, and already I am feeling myself succumb to its easy charms, its bizarre history and traditions, the quirks of its eclectic range of characters, each striving to establish their own individual styles and roles, yet inextricably bound together by weather and geography. Whether I could ever actually live here—or even how I would feel at the end of my stay—might be a rather different matter.

Eventually, a dim figure clad in black and

topped by an incongruous flat cap appears striding purposefully along the cobbles towards me. Father Guy and I clamber down the wet stone steps, which are dripping with seaweed, and step gingerly aboard the *Lightning*, the high-speed launch based on St Martin's, its powerful jet engine rumbling just beneath the crystal-clear water, straining to whisk us away. With a flick of the wrist, Terry the boatman releases the rope from the rusting iron ring on the quay, and *Lightning* is away, slipping effortlessly past the lifeboat at the end of the quay, carefully circling around the dipping oars of the returning pilot gig, and out into the Road, where Terry thrusts down the throttle and the little boat leaps forward, leaving behind it the first froth of a churning, creamy wake, its dancing mass of bubbles refracting the low sun's orange rays.

Even out here, I can pick up the scent of the bobbing, white, wild garlic that in early spring carpets every bit of grassland on the islands. Because there are few trees and hills, and certainly no high buildings, nearly every aspect, in every direction, of the low-lying islands is dominated by vast, often mesmeric views of the sea and the sky, which is why the place feels like heaven when the weather's good and purgatory when low cloud, fog or drizzle moves in and takes over. In the distance lies the hazy silhouette of St Martin's, with its extraordinary bleached beaches seeming to shimmer and hover just above the water line in the residual heat of the day. It's an exhilarating moment, and I realise this is probably the only place I've ever been to where you can see the sun rise over the sea, follow its progress across the firmament throughout the entire day, and then watch it dip back into the ocean, all from the same point.

This morning, Father Guy has an appointment at the little school on St Martin's, where he'll be taking his first assembly and discussing the forthcoming wedding of the teacher, Lois Briard, who is getting married to a local lad on Easter Monday, which will undoubtedly be the biggest social event of the year on the island. It will be Father Guy's first wedding on Scilly and the largest on St Martin's for years, so he needs to get it right.

St Martin's is the most northerly of the five islands, and it takes longer to get there than the others; it's fifteen minutes in a special or thirty-five by tripper boat. It is also probably the most beautiful of the islands, with its vast, empty, white beaches and astonishing views. We walk up the promontory towards the little settlement on the hill above, past the piles of lobster pots, the grass tennis court and the vineyard beyond, stopping now and then to admire the soft curve of Higher Town Bay round to Brandy Point on one side, and on the other the huge, majestic sweep of Lawrence Bay, leading the eye down to Lower Town at the western tip of the island. We pass a field which has a wooden box attached to its fence bearing the legend 'The blind would love this view, please give generously.' Then we walk up past the tiny Methodist chapel and the Post Office stores and take a left down a track towards the small, pale-yellow school, which looks back across Crow Bar to St Mary's. I would have given anything to have been brought up in a place like this.

There are nine pupils at the school. Father Guy seems happier answering questions than preaching. He's more comfortable with younger children than teenagers, but is slightly taken aback by their curiosity about his unconventional past. He left school with just one O-level, he tells them, branded a dimwit. He was an agricultural worker, a quality-control inspector in a plastics factory, verger at Peterborough Cathedral, chauffeur to the bishop. It's quite a curriculum vitae. Then God intervened. Plain Guy must become Father Guy, ordained priest; once again, a decision taken out of his hands. It was during his theological training that it was revealed that Guy was dyslexic, a fact that explained much of his low self-esteem and prompted a huge wave of relief.

Later, we walk back up the track, past sheep which wander free—there is nowhere to escape to, after all—and stop off at the church where Lois will be married. It's a tiny building, built in 1683, with seating for only about sixty. The original slate roof has long since been replaced with artificial slates, in the face of consistent batterings from the south-westerly storms—it must be one of the most exposed buildings on Scilly. There is no undertaker on St Martin's, no sexton, so all the graves are dug by the island men, friends who are nominated in writing by the deceased. The dead are blessed with breathtaking views over the Sound to Tresco. This is a good place to die, as well as be born.

Soon, we're heading back down towards the quay, veering off left past the Post Office, towards the bakery.

With a name like his, I had imagined that Toby Tobin-Duigan must be some Eton-educated toff with a shooting estate somewhere in the Home

Counties and useful chums in the City. In fact, he's quite the opposite, a practical, down-to-earth guy with cropped, grey hair, little steel earrings and the kind of cheeky smile that must have got him into endless trouble at school. He also smells strongly of dough. I ask him about his odd surname and he explains that while his Irish grandmother was a Catholic, one of a large family called Tobin from the rebel country of Tipperary, his grandfather was a Protestant from the same area of southern Ireland, a Duigan. When their first child was born, Toby's father, they decided on a brilliantly simple plan to end years of strife by amalgamating their names and forging the two families forever as one.

Toby had spent half a lifetime commuting from Brighton to his job as a photographic printer in Soho in central London, and had fallen in love with St Martin's (population: 110) after holidaying there. When his marriage collapsed fifteen years ago, he turned his back forever on the horrors of mainland life and fulfilled a dream he'd harboured for years.

Island life, where daily routine is dependent not on the clock but on the weather and the tides, clearly suits him. He cuts a small but lean and fit figure, and his talk is relaxed and expansive, as he leans laconically against the glass counter of the bakery, despite a patient queue of customers snaking out of the door and down the green towards the old telephone box.

Leaving his ex-wife Liz and young children Sean and Darcy behind in Brighton, Toby took a year's idyllic sabbatical on the most northerly and remote island in the parish, living the gentle, nomadic life he had dreamed of for so long on those relentless journeys to and from work. Living in a tent, he helped out on the lobster boats and worked as a gardener and on the occasional maintenance job at St Martin's Hotel, running every day on the endless, empty beaches, becoming a creditable oarsmen on the two island gigs and taking endless photographs of sunrises over the Eastern Isles. There was no bakery on the islands then and the imported processed bread from the mainland was often mouldy by the time it reached St Martin's, so Toby taught himself to bake. One summer morning he had a surplus of loaves, so he left five in a box on Christine Savill's campsite accompanied by a jar with a pound coin it. When he returned in the evening the bread had gone and there were six pound coins in the jar. Now living in a little Duchy cottage called Ganilly, named after two of the uninhabited Eastern Islands that it overlooked, at Moo Green in Higher Town, Toby was soon baking thirty loaves a day, unable to keep up with demand from neighbours and passing holidaymakers.

On the other side of Moo Green was an old Duchy barn, built in the 1920s for the making and storage of willow lobster pots, and eventually a sceptical Duchy land steward gave permission to convert it into a bakery. Today Toby and his mate Barney bake night and day, producing a vast range of breads, tarts and pies, one favourite being his Lawrence loaf, flavoured with seaweed gathered in Lawrence Bay, just in front of his burgeoning smallholding. They also make pizzas, topped with home-smoked chicken, and at low tide they collect grey mullet they've netted on the beach to produce smoked fillets and taramasalata made with the roe.

His twenty-one-year-old daughter, Darcy, came over from Brighton for a month to help out in the bakery a year ago and has stayed ever since. For many people desperate to escape the nightmare of modern mainland existence, living out their time on a carefree island paradise would be enough. Toby, though, has an itch, another gamble in mind. He has that quality which is often quite incompatible with island life: ambition.

Toby is an affable man and he soon puts Father Guy at ease. This is a relationship that has a future—Toby is a great talker, Father Guy a great listener. They also share an interest: beer. So before we know it, Father Guy's on the back of a quad bike, with his arms around Toby's shoulders, and I'm bouncing around in the little tin trailer, hanging on for dear life. We're en route to the other end of the island and a pub with probably the finest view of any in Britain.

The Seven Stones is named after the treacherous reef seven miles east of Scilly, still marked by an old-fashioned Trinity House lightship, that forty years ago was the scene of the first of the big super-tanker disasters, when the *Torrey Canyon* hit the submerged Pollard's Rock and plastered thirty-one million gallons of oil across the beaches of southern England and Normandy, killing most of the marine life it touched. The captain of the ship, travelling to the oil terminal at Milford Haven in Wales and already behind schedule, misjudged his position south of Scilly. Instead of going around the islands safely to the west, which would have added forty miles and an extra two hours to his journey, he cut through the deep-water channel to the east, leaving the solitary Wolf Rock lighthouse well to his starboard, but was unable to turn the vast vessel in time when eventually he realised he was heading straight for the Seven Stones. The ensuing catastrophe made headlines around the world. The Prime Minister, from his plain little holiday home on St Mary's, ordered the Royal Navy to bomb the stricken ship in the hope of burning off the oil, a strategy that failed, partly because many of the bombs didn't go off. The remaining batch of duff ordnance was later sold by the Ministry of Defence to Argentina, where it was used fifteen years later, to similar abject failure, against ships of the Royal Navy in the Falklands conflict. The abiding memory of that day in the minds of many islanders was the prayers said in the desperate hope of preventing the wind veering from the west to the east, which would have had catastrophic consequences for the future of the Isles of Scilly—prayers that appeared to be answered.

Despite its privileged monopoly as the only pub on the island, in recent years the Seven Stones has failed to thrive. It should be the hub of community life, but many of the locals seem to have turned their backs on the place, and now the Duchy are offering the sixty-year lease for the little low-roofed building, a scattering of outbuildings and two lovely cottages, set in three and a half acres, for £700,000. Owning your own pub in a breathtaking location on a sub-tropical, remote island is the fantasy of many a middle-aged man, but for Toby Tobin-Duigan, Master Baker, it is actually within the realms of reality.

He talks to Father Guy about his plans with passion. High-quality, locally sourced food is the key. Bread and pastries will come from his bakery, fish from his own beach nets and Martin Bond's trawler over on St Mary's, crab and lobster from the St Martin's boats and beef from the award-winning herd across the water on Tresco. He'll be growing his own salads and vegetables, and beer will come from the Scilly brewery on St Mary's. Father Guy picks up on Toby's effervescent enthusiasm, pleased and relieved to be included in the general scheme of things, and soon the Scuppered is flowing and they're at it like old chums. This is Father Guy's natural habitat.

The only real problem with Toby's Master Plan is finding the cash. Here lies the evil genius of his plan. When he reveals to Father Guy that he's intending to go into business with his ex-wife, the new Chaplain to the Isles twitches an eyebrow. In need of an adventure, Liz McPherson, a social worker in Brighton, has agreed to sell up her four-storey, Victorian, terraced house, situated high on the hill above the town's famous Regency Pavilion, and move lock, stock and barrel to begin a new life with her ex-husband on a tiny island in the Atlantic Ocean. Father Guy and I agree, as we head off down towards the quay, that Liz's plan is a bold and brave one, since there really will be no going back and she will no doubt encounter many difficulties. The islanders will be watching their every move with quiet fascination; it will be a soap opera that promises to be much more gripping than anything on television. I suppose the question no-one will dare ask but everyone will be pondering is: will they get back together?

We walk down past the old fishermen's cottages that look across to the seal colonies basking on the

Eastern Islands, past the winsome little cricket pitch which lies just behind Higher Town Bay beside the St Martin's vineyard and reach the quay in time for Father Guy's evening boat back. It occurs to me that the plans, aspirations and dreams of everyone I have talked to today depend utterly on the whims and vagaries of the upcoming holiday season. Sunshine might bring riches; lower air-fares, a change in the value of sterling and rain—financial ruin. It's about as precarious an existence as I can imagine. The exception to this is Father Guy. The success of his year, I suspect, will depend on matters even more unpredictable than the weather.

I wave him off as he climbs down onto *Lightning,* which then spins effortlessly 180 degrees, as if on a sixpence, and scurries out into the ebbing waters of Par Bay and towards the moody silhouette of St Mary's beyond. It has to move swiftly or it'll run out of water.

'Are you around for a pint later?' mouths Father Guy, his words lost in the wind and the growing grumble of the boat's engine.

It's the only question he ever seems to ask me.

Toby may lead an idyllic existence, but it's a tough one which he earns and which he throws himself into with obvious relish. He's up at the little bakery at six every morning, and after four hours of sweating over the dough, he's on his quad bike, roaring back up past his Ganhilly, followed by his three orange Hungarian Vizsla pointers, Jazz, Galty and Shima, who help him with the winter shooting. He drives past the island's only shop, the Post Office stores, and stops on the hill by the church. Stretched out like a glistening white

64

apron is probably the finest beach on Scilly, maybe in England: Lawrence Bay, which at very low spring tides becomes one vast expanse of sand which almost links up with Tresco to the west. Even in high summer, it's usually deserted. To the left is the silhouette of St Mary's and the Napoleonic telegraph tower, rising above the Stone Age village which dates from when human life first came to Scilly four thousand years ago. Free from later human interference, the site has survived remarkably intact, so you can still walk through little streets that are like warrens or sit in a doorway and soak in the view of the islands, just as prehistoric man must have done.

To the right are the legendary sub-tropical gardens of Tresco; the sparkling windows of the Island Hotel; the uninhabited island of St Helen's, sleeping contentedly in the warmth of the sun; and beyond is the lighthouse on Round Island, marking the northerly boundary of Scilly, serene today, but even at forty metres above sea-level still often engulfed by the waves of furious Atlantic storms.

Toby feeds his two improbably named turkeys, Gobble and Swallow, which he keeps by a shed at the top of the hill, then heads off down the track to the bay, the dogs barely able to keep up with him, to collect the morning's eggs from his chickens, which roam down by the beach. Then it's back to the bakery for the lunchtime peak and the cleaning up and other tasks that need doing so that all is ready for Barney to come in for the overnight shift. From now on, that's seven days a week.

Now it's six o'clock in the evening, and Toby's day is far from over. It's almost low tide, so we make our way down through the bracken towards the beach at Lawrence Bay. All I can hear is birdsong and the gentle ripple of the waves on the beach. It's March, but the breeze is balmy, the sea is translucent and the air, tinged with a salty dampness, is a delight to breathe. On the horizon, we see the silhouetted sails of a ketch gently sliding between Samson and St Agnes. Above us, a pair of sheep are grazing among the wild daffodils of an old flower field. Way out on the sand, two tiny figures are dancing in the shimmering sunshine beside a sharp, stark granite outcrop in the middle of the bay. They look like children, but it's hard at this distance to be sure.

Toby is tanned and exuding good health. He used to work in Soho. I still do.

'Far enough away from the Ol' Smoke then, Toby?'

'I can't in a million, million years imagine going back.'

Nor, right now, can I.

'You still single, Toby?'

There's a long pause.

'Yes,' he says slowly, and turns away.

I worry I might step on a snake, but Toby says there aren't any and I should instead worry about stepping on the famous Scilly shrew, a busy little brown creature which originates from the southern Mediterranean and is found on St Martin's, but nowhere else in Britain. No-one knows how it got here; like everything else, it probably stowed away on a ship.

We make our way down past the chickens, who think they are getting a late second breakfast, to the top of the beach, and I feel a growing sense of childlike excitement. At low tide this morning,

Toby had gone through the routine of dragging out his long beach net, securing one end on the landward side with a small anchor and then unfurling the net across the rocks and seaweed towards the sea. There's a row of little plastic buoys which keep the top side of the net afloat, providing it's untangled and untwisted. Then he leaves it, to collect whatever fruits of the sea the high tide may bring.

There's an almost atavistic pleasure in the anticipation as we pad out across the sand, a sense of hunting not for pleasure but to eat, following in the footsteps of hungry men who've been doing exactly the same thing for thousands of years.

It's the luck of the draw. Sometimes Toby's nets are bulging, sometimes not. Even Toby can't disguise his disappointment at today's catch. Only three fish, sea bream, a respectable size all of them, but each with large chunks mysteriously missing.

'I guess there's enough between them for a couple of steaks,' says Toby, carefully extracting them from the netting. 'I'm afraid we're fourth in line.'

'Fourth?'

'The seals had first go.' He's examining them forensically. 'Then it looks like the crabs moved in.'

'That's only two.'

'Then the seagulls. Then us.'

Toby throws the ravaged fish into a canvas bag, then looks at his watch.

'Is that it for today?'

'Just getting going,' he says. 'It's the hard bit now.'

'The pub?'

'Gig-racing, dear boy. Two hours of sheer sweat. Then the pub.'

In the distance, on the grassy hillock overlooking Lower Town, almost at the other end of the island, we can just see the low roof of the Seven Stones.

'Have I got plans for that place,' he says to me wistfully.

How on earth, I think suddenly, in the gentle warmth of the evening sun, could anyone want for anything more than what already seems to o'erflow the cup of Toby Tobin-Duigan, erstwhile photographic printer of Wardour Street, London W1 and now baker to St Martin's, Isles of Scilly ?

*   *   *

Like a waking giant, Scilly is visibly coming to life after six months of slumber. Just as the season for cultivated narcissi is coming to an end, the hedgerows burst with Bermuda buttercups and dancing fumatori, and the fallow flower fields begin to explode with colour and new vigour. There are acres of dazzling wild marigolds, interspersed with red poppies so abundant that visitors think they are a cultivated crop, protected by the extraordinary tall sentries of the pink-tipped Babington's leek, which are unique to Scilly. Great purple and blue sprouts of echium, which are a protected species in their native Canary Islands, grow like weeds on the sides of the tracks and in almost every border, and when the wind drops the scent of wild garlic is overwhelming. Dusk comes to Scilly twenty minutes later than London, so the songbirds up in the woods at Lunnon Farm maintain their deafening crescendo well into the evening. The days are miraculously filled with unbroken sunshine, and the night skies, relieved of the shackles of light pollution and the drone of aircraft, look and sound exactly as they must have for millennia. For the present, at least, it is a joy to be here, and, with the untold tortures of city life slowly being erased from the memory, it feels as though I have already spent half a lifetime on Scilly.

The hotels are opening up their shutters for business after renovations and redecorating, the bed-and-breakfasts have been spring-cleaned, pub signs are being replaced, shop windows polished up, trees pollarded. At the start of next week, the final week of March, the *Scillonian*, all spick and span and gleaming white paint, will begin her summer schedule of daily runs, arriving at noon, departing at 4.30, giving a comfortable rhythm to daily life, except on Sundays, when there are no ferries or flights of any sort in or out of the islands, which is why there's always a long queue of people desperate to get hold of their Sunday newspapers when Mumfords opens on Monday morning. For the first time since the main army of twitchers left in October, there are gangs of visitors roaming the streets of St Mary's, a sea of anoraks and backpacks, most of them congregating on the quay for the ten o'clock boats to the off-islands.

Nearly all the boats of the St Mary's Boatmen's Association, also freshly painted, are back in action after the winter, and now, one by one, they're coming off their moorings and jostling for position on the quay. Alec Hicks is at the helm of the huge, pale-blue open boat *Kingfisher*, with his brother Steve Hicks coming alongside him on the red-and-white *Seahorse*, which he designed and built himself in the boatyard at Porthloo, round the bay. Cousin Paul Hicks is away up by the harbourmaster's office on the deep-blue cabin cruiser *Crusader*, and uncle Alfred Hicks is chalking up the blackboard by the ticket office with sailing times for his glass-bottomed boat *Sea Quest*. Fraser Hicks, though, is still on the sand with his beached longboat *Sea King*. He has problems with his starter-motor, and it's costing him money; while all the other Association boats now have their certificates of seaworthiness and are licensed to operate, Fraser must wait for engine parts to be flown over from the mainland before the official from the Maritime and Coastguard Agency agrees to see the boat. So Fraser tinkers, muttering to himself about what a fool he's been to leave it all so late, while Sally looks on, bored out of her brains, and the other male members of the family start raking in the cash.

Lightning appears round the end of the quay from St Martin's, and I spot a very dapper Toby waving at me, almost unrecognizable in a well-cut blue suit and starched, open grey shirt. We shake hands, and he can't seem to stop beaming. He'll be taking the forty-minute walk up to the airfield and then a chopper will whisk him across the deep-turquoise sea to Penzance, where he'll be meeting Liz, who is flying down to Newquay from Gatwick. Together, they will make their way to the solicitors' office. First Liz will sign the contracts for the sale of her Brighton house and then together they'll sign the contracts for the Seven Stones, and the little pub with the finest view in Britain will formally be theirs. I wave him off, and we agree to meet on his return, to toast the success of his extraordinary adventure.

4

Standing On The Edge Of The World

A century ago, the harbour at St Mary's would have been choked by a mass of schooners, barques and herring boats, many of them built round the bay at the Porthloo shipyard, or often right here on the sand at Town Beach or Porthcressa itself, the growing skeletons of the ships' timbers often dwarfing the little cottages of the men who were building them. It was a relatively massive industry, which one way or another involved nearly everyone on the island. With the sudden decline of the herring trade in the early twentieth century, the islanders were facing a threat that had recurred intermittently through the centuries— starvation—but their ingenuity came to their rescue.

Many of the traditional subsistence farms were turned over to a revolutionary new field system, where land was subdivided into small rectangular sections, each surrounded by fast-growing, wind-breaking, salt-resistant pittosporum hedges, for the production of the island equivalent of pure gold: flowers. Among the palm trees and swaying echium, which thrive in the balmy climate

71

provided by the Gulf Stream, scented narcissi can be produced throughout the winter, along with pinks, anemones and commercial bulbs. Picked and packed in the morning, sent straight to Penzance on the ferry and thence to Paddington via the new overnight railway services, ending up at Covent Garden in time for the dawn chorus, flowers from the Isles of Scilly were adorning the restaurant tables and living rooms of rich London society by lunchtime, leaving Home Counties farmers beyond the suburbs of the capital seething at the frost and the 'foreigners'' lucky, new-found wealth.

Over the years, most of the flower farms have gone under in the face of imports grown by cheap labour and flown into England from places like East Africa every day, and many farmers have simply left the island or ploughed up the little square fields and turned their homes and outhouses into holiday homes or campsites. They still pick wild agapanthus on the sand dunes on Tresco, though, for sale in London the next day, and one or two of the larger daffodil farms have just about managed to stay in business, sometimes selling successfully over the Internet. In the last few days, even though it's nearly the end of the growing season, there has been considerable activity out in the fields, coinciding with preparations for Father Guy's big public debut following his induction.

Most children on the mainland would never connect Mothering Sunday, at the end of the second week of March, with anything to do with the Church, but rather to my surprise, it turns out that on Scilly this is one of the biggest and most popular events in the religious calendar.

Another south-westerly storm has been brewing, and in the early hours of Sunday morning it unleashes its wrath on the islands. Yet in between the billowing clouds scudding across the sky, the sun streams through, creating a slightly mad, melodramatic dawn. You can hear the hammering of the battered Union Flag on the battlements of the Star Castle 100 yards away; vast shadows race across the waters of the Road to Tresco and Bryher beyond, pitted by a thousand white horses; and, down below, the Atlantic waves, forced into a rocky funnel between the Garrison and Rat Island, crash across the granite wall of the quay with such force that spray is sent spinning right across the roof of the Mermaid.

Even on the short walk from the Chaplaincy down to the church for the eight o'clock communion, Father Guy has to lean almost horizontally into the wind. Already his carefully prepared schedule for the day looks like being blown awry. After this first service on St Mary's, he had planned to hurry down to the quay, where the high-speed launch, the *Wizard*, would be waiting to whisk him across the Sound to St Agnes. There he would be picked up in a buggy and whirred across the island for the 9.40 service; then back by buggy and the *Wizard* for the main service of the day, a joint celebration with the Methodists in the chapel in Church Street. After lunch there would be the longer and more hazardous voyage for the fourth service of the day on St Martin's in the north. The Chaplain's is not a job, Fraser Hicks points out helpfully, for a bandy-legged landlubber.

After communion, Father Guy gets a message

from the quay: the boatmen say it's too rough to cross the Sound, so the trip to St Agnes is cancelled and the islanders there must fend for themselves and celebrate Mother's Day in whatever way they can. The eleven o'clock service in the chapel will go ahead as planned, and it's quite a test for Father Guy. Virtually every child on St Mary's will be there, plus parents. Furthermore, this is the first time Father Guy will have preached to the Methodists, some of whom had given him a frosty reception when he first arrived.

He is very nervous, and, abandoning his usual high-minded, grave approach to the Gospels, he takes a gamble with a light-hearted sermon which includes the use of one of Alice's dolls. There's a bit of business with dummies and nappies, and some discussion about the responsibilities of parenting, which he disguises by joshing and joking with several young volunteers he's dragged up front. After some initial hesitation on the part of his audience, the laughter is soon flowing; Father Guy appears to have won them over; helped no doubt by the comic antics of the methodist minister, David Easton, a natural performer and much-loved island figure. Later, the chapel is filled with the scent of hundreds of narcissi, picked at Lunnon Farm up at Poth Hellick only a few hours ago, enriched by the warmth of the sun breaking through the huge windows of the chapel. In scenes generations of their forebears would have recognised and welcomed, the children distribute flowers to every adult in the congregation. It's an utterly charming, timeless ritual.

The wind's still up but it seems to have veered,

so the decision is made to attempt a run across the more sheltered waters between the islands to St Martin's. The *Wizard* is a powerful, modern boat, but still capable of being tossed around by the waves like a cork in a barrel. As we get out into the open sea, the water is cascading right across the cabin roof, and soon the breakers are almost throwing us across Crow Bar. For me, hanging on beside Father Guy inside the little cabin, it's an exhilarating journey. The new chaplain, wide eyes full of wonder, keeps roaring with laughter, although this may have been from sheer terror. What sets the heart racing is the touching of the water by the low, piercing rays of the sun, which transform the tips of the huge waves into iridescent torches, and the spray into dazzling rainbows.

Not everyone's thrilled with the experience. Towards the stern of the boat, a small figure clad in a dripping red anorak is huddled against the wind, determined to be in the fresh air, but lashed time and again by the endless sea spray. This is Father Guy's wife, Kate, who's in the process of discovering, among many other things, that she gets seasick. I hope this won't be an omen.

*　　　*　　　*

As so often on Scilly, the flower farmers find that the best weapons to fight their plight are ingenuity, inventiveness and guile, qualities that Tim and Sue Hicks, beavering away on Troytown Farm, fortunately have in abundance. Overlooked by no-one and nothing, save the huge, empty glass summit of the old lighthouse in the middle of St

75

Agnes and three thousand miles of Atlantic Ocean, there will be more at stake for them in the upcoming summer than most of their fellow islanders.

It's officially a small dairy farm, only fourteen acres, but Troytown is an extraordinary hive of activity, presided over by the inexhaustible and sometimes rather manic figure of Tim, who's up at the crack of dawn distributing milk to key points around the island on his quad with its tin trailer.

'I've got five minutes,' he says this morning, chucking me some Wellington boots, and together we set off at a brisk pace on a tour of the place— and a little modern miracle it turns out to be.

On first sight, parts of the farm appear to be utterly shambolic, a Cornish hillbilly outpost, with rusting old tractors and broken pieces of agricultural machinery scattered everywhere, alongside pallets, bags, urns, buckets, hoses and all kinds of other farming debris. Tim, noticing my reaction, explains with a wry smile that everything is kept in the hope that it can be recycled or re-used, and that disposing of rubbish on Scilly is either prohibitively expensive or downright impossible.

I'd already seen the famous campsite, on the field which runs down to the rocky shoreline, but the weather is better today, and it's easy to see why so many visitors return year after year to the edge of the Earth. The Bishop Rock lighthouse stands immutable, like a great concrete sentry, guarding the Western Rocks, and in front of it, to our right across Smith Sound, is the rocky outcrop of Annet, a famous bird reserve and home to the dancing thrift, or sea-pink, plant, which in summer turns the island into one of the great maritime heaths of Europe. Tim points out the black-and-white guillemots and razorbills, which dive straight into the water and swim around like fish, looking for food. At nightfall you can hear the noisy arrival of the rare manx shearwaters, looking for their mates, which have often been roaming the oceans for days, arriving on Annet after wintering south of the equator.

Over the last few years, Tim Hicks has transformed the place from a traditional, ailing Scillonian flower farm into an enterprise that draws surprise and admiration from larger, mainland farmers. There's a Hereford bull called Ding-Dong who sires the calves that provide the steaks, burgers and mince so beloved by the campers down by the beach; there are also Tamworth pigs for bacon and sausages. The old flower fields, a haven for rare birdlife and butterflies, provide fodder like turnips and swedes for the cattle, which Tim collects every day after the milk deliveries; and potatoes, tomatoes, courgettes and other vegetables are grown in a polytunnel. Since there's no mains water or natural springs on St Agnes, the Hicks provide their own water supply, using rainwater and two deep boreholes. This seems to me to be multi-functional farming at its most imaginative. And that's not all.

Tim and Sue spent hours in the long winter evenings around the oak table in the farm kitchen developing a plan: to borrow all they could, clear out the bats and cobwebs from one of the old dairy barns at the back of the farmhouse and convert it into a small production line to manufacture a product that could transform their fortunes and utilise the excess cream and curds from the herd—ice cream. The rewards could be more than just financial.

Rents on the islands are maintained at market value, so are among the highest in the country, in contrast to wages, which are among the lowest. The cost of living is bewilderingly high. Young people consequently find it almost impossible to find places to live. Some squat in friends' houses or live in garages or garden sheds, or even, in summer, camp out on porches.

Like most of his former schoolfriends, Tim and Sue Hicks's son, Sam, had long since been exiled to the mainland, where he ended up in a dreary job in retailing. For years he assumed that there would never be any chance of returning to St Agnes, even when he married and had a daughter, Isla, named after his place of birth. Then, almost overnight, everything changed. If Troytown Ice Cream went on to be a success, the farm—in one of the most beautiful, unpolluted and tranquil locations in Britain—might just be able to sustain enough of a living to support a second, small, family. This is the argument Tim and Sue put to the council's planning committee, and, after a struggle, they were finally given permission to construct the first new building on St Agnes for over twenty years.

Now, at the end of March, Sam and Laura's house is taking shape, a triumph of determination and logistics, although it still looks slightly as though a bomb has just gone off; ladders, pipes, cement-mixers, bricks, helmets, planks and pieces of scaffolding are scattered all over the windswept site. Since they moved over from the grey suburbs of Southampton at the beginning of the winter, Sam and Laura Hicks and their little dark-curled beauty Isla have been living in the farm's holiday chalet, but this is booked from Easter, so the pressure is now on to get the house finished.

The construction of the new cottage is of consuming interest to the other islanders, and many have been lending a hand. The foundations are dug in less than a week and, once the site has been scanned by an archaeologist from St Mary's and declared free of any artifacts of note, they mix all the cement themselves onsite, and the flooring bricks are laid by a mate Sam met on holiday in the Canaries. Everything they need for the building work—every pipe, brick and nail—must be brought over from the mainland. The materials are driven from the depot down to Penzance, loaded onto the ferry, unloaded on the quay at St Mary's, and then reloaded on to the *Lyonesse Lady*, the busy blue workhorse with its built-in crane which constantly plies between the islands delivering bulky or heavy goods. From the quay down below the Turks Head, everything must then be shifted by trailer or tractor the mile across St Agnes to Troytown. The act of transporting all their building materials to the remotest location in England will add almost a third to the total construction costs.

The arrival of the huge timber-framed sections inevitably coincided with sudden winter storms, and hauling them up on the tortuous journey through the dry-stone walls of the tight track across the island to Troytown proved a nightmare, but there were plenty of willing hands to help, and with the arrival of the specialist team from

Somerset, whom Sue put up in the holiday cottage, the bulk of the house was erected in three days flat. Everything else—the plumbing, electricity, flooring and plastering—they are doing themselves.

So now Sam and Laura are able to clamber up ladders to what will be their bedroom and marvel at the breathtaking views across the bay, over the top of the hallowed pittosporum hedge—the bird haven of Annet; the little church where they were married, by the old lifeboat station, to one side; the watery grave of so many shipwrecks, the Western Rocks, to the other; and the Bishop Rock lighthouse beyond, the most south-westerly point in the British Isles, whose beam will sweep through their house, probably every night for the rest of their lives.

In the meantime, Sam has thrown away his business suit, rolled up his sleeves and is learning the mucky business of becoming a jobbing dairy farmer. He's already getting to grips with the milking, and even his father grudgingly admits he's got off to a good start.

'We still have the odd moment when the cows take charge,' says Tim, tight-lipped. 'But the boy's learning fast. Who knows, he might one day be good enough to let me and Sue get away and have a holiday,' he adds, and then, as always, hurries off before anyone has a chance to reply. I wanted to ask Tim when he last had a holiday, or if indeed he'd ever had one.

Twice a day, Sam herds the four Jerseys and three Ayrshires into a pen outside the milking parlour and then leads them in, two at a time. I'm impressed by his confidence, although he explains how taken aback he was one evening when he tried to attach the pumps of the milking machine to an old girl with a sunburned teat, who released a deafening holler and nearly hit the ceiling. He's not even fazed when the cows spontaneously evacuate their bowels—in one unbroken movement, as if he were a magician, a bucket miraculously appears in Sam's hand, and he holds it horizontally about two feet from the rear of the poor beast, without even a pause in the conversation.

The Troytown model, though, stands on just two pillars. The first is hard work, and, wow, I don't think I've ever seen anyone work quite as hard as this family. It's not that the effort they put in gives them some kind of perverse pleasure, or that they are blindly focused or somehow inadequate, or that they use work to hide some deep failure in the family machine (all explanations I've heard for workaholics I've known in London). No, it's nothing as complicated as that; it is merely a question of survival. If they don't maintain the pace, or they fall ill, they must leave St Agnes, and that is not an option. So it's up at dawn, and it's sheer sweat 'til dusk, seven days a week, every week of the year, with the occasional luxury of an hour or two's practice on the fire-tractor or a thrash at the oars of the island's gig.

The second, fragile, pillar upon which Troytown sits, like almost everyone and everything else, is the vagrant winds of the holiday season, and with this in mind, when all his other duties are done, Sam lends his mother a hand in the dairy. It is going well. Sue is now getting orders from every corner of each of the five islands, even including a provisional one from Toby over on St Martin's, for the Seven Stones. She's even getting interest from the mainland. Today, Sam and Sue are packing tubs of ice cream into boxes and the boxes into special crates for the trip across the Sound, in the *Spirit of St Agnes*, to St Mary's, and something which may, in its own modest way, provide the key to all their futures.

*   *   *

The morning light is beautiful today. The rays of the sun, rising over the old windmill on the hill at Buzza, are already touching the white walls of the harbourmaster's office at the end of St Mary's quay, and are rapidly chasing the long shadows away across the still waters of the harbour. There is a sense that it may be early, but summer is here. After her winter being repainted and refitted in dock at Penzance, the *Scillonian* is hoving into sight between Halangy and Tobaccoman's Point, the first run of her summer schedule. Since it's noon, we stand around a bit and watch the ferry dock, a ritual which will now take place every day except Sundays until October, and it's a beautiful sight in an oddly old-fashioned way. The scene should be tinted with sepia. Her cargo is unloaded by well-oiled teams of swarthy quaymen, who use winches and cranes like the dockers of London and Liverpool in the 1940s.

Police Sergeant Ian Stevens and Police Constable Tony Kan, who together make up England's smallest police force, stand watching benignly as the passengers stream ashore, also looking strangely like they have escaped from a

82

newsreel from a different era. The police put in an appearance every day when the *Scillonian* docks, partly to remind potential ne'er-do-wells among the arrivals that there is indeed a police presence on Scilly, and partly because there isn't usually much else for them to do. Every single item on Scilly has to come over by boat, which is the reason for Scilly's best-kept secret: many islanders don't bother to buy television licences. Not a lot of point, really, until word arrives on the grapevine that a television detector van has been booked a passage over.

On Town Beach, Fraser Hicks, under the gaze of a sceptical Sally, is already hard at work on *Sea King*; unbelievably he's still tinkering with the engine problem that could jeopardise his annual certificate of seaworthiness, without which he'll miss the start of the season.

On the quay itself, the first of the off-island boats are arriving. The twin hulls of the *Spirit of St Agnes* gently slip in behind the *Firethorn* from Bryher and Tresco. Sam Hicks and his mother Sue hurry up the stone steps and into a waiting truck, which will get the ice cream up to the Town Hall and into the freezer before the rays of the sun really start to warm up.

On a good year, Scilly can cope with 140,000 visitors, and since this utilises almost every bed on the islands and there's little room to expand, new sources of revenue need to be created. Once on Scilly, the holidaymakers are trapped, eager to spend their hard-saved cash—on what? Well, the ferrymen running their boats endlessly to and fro between the five islands will be the last to go out of business. People come to explore the islands; to walk; to birdwatch; to photograph the puffins, herons and sandpipers and the sea creatures which travel hundreds of miles to feast on Scilly's rich coastline—the dolphins, basking sharks and Atlantic seals; to paint; to recuperate; to seek solace after personal disasters or to celebrate triumphs. None of this yields large amounts of money in itself for the locals. But recently a new idea has emerged: to capitalise on the new British love affair with high-quality food, and follow the blueprint Toby the baker is already mapping out in miniature on St Martin's, by transforming Scilly from an old-fashioned restaurant graveyard into the gastronomic capital of the West Country.

The key to the plan is a dynamic market in high-quality, locally produced food. Planning permission has been granted for an abattoir on the little industrial estate behind Porthmellon Beach, to spare Scilly's cattle from suffering a journey to the mainland on the *Scillonian* for slaughter and Scilly's farmers from the huge costs involved. Now the islands' first local produce market has been tentatively launched in the old theatre at the back of the Town Hall to encourage visitors, and more importantly the local shops, pubs and hotels, to buy more food direct from island producers and reduce the crippling dependency on imports.

Sue and Tim have bagged the best pitch in the entire place, right by the door, so everyone notices the tubs of ice cream on the way in, and, even though the weather is far from hot, most buy on their way out. There's already a huge queue for the fish on Martin Bond's table beneath the stage where, in the evenings, the Scilly Entertainers are already rehearsing their summer show, and within

84

half an hour of the market opening up, he'll have sold out completely. Father Guy's wife, Kate, who has been tipped off to get in early, is in luck, however, and lands three of his last John Dory. This is proof enough that if the weather's kind and Joel can hit the right shoals, there's a strong demand, and no middleman to interfere. After gambling on new nets, Martin's now working on another new scheme to enlarge his burgeoning business franchise, although no-one knows it yet, which is already taking shape in an old barn hidden away on Longstone Farm up in the middle of St Mary's.

Since they arrived, Father Guy and Kate have been keeping a relatively low profile, heeding the advice of Bishop Bill: bide your time, keep your head down, and wait for the islanders to come to you. This market, though, provides an ideal opportunity to see and be seen, to catch up without seeming intrusive. Father Guy is at heart a gregarious soul and he must have felt increasingly lonely and remote locked away in the Chaplaincy; even the welcome trips to the pub have been curtailed. I watch him now as he and Kate spin around the hall, like a couple of ballroom dancers, much more relaxed than I have seen them before. Father Guy moves from person to person with ease, laughing and slapping backs. There's one of his newest parishioners, Sam Hicks, who updates him on the race to get the cottage ready for Easter and deftly flogs him a couple of tubs of Troytown Ice Cream in the process. There's Mark Pender, selling lobster and crab from St Martin's, and the island chiropodist, Kris Taylor, who looks after Father Guy's little church down by the beach on

Bryher and has taken to producing tons of home-made fudge.

Everyone is selling well, and for an hour or two there's a sense of celebration in the air, along with the unspoken, universal regret that no-one had had the idea of a local produce market years ago. A gentle revolution might just have got underway.

Apart from the Seven Stones, there's one restaurant on St Martin's, in the hotel which overlooks the spectacularly beautiful Sound to Tean and Crump Island. Similarly, on Tresco and Bryher there's one hotel and one pub, and on little St Agnes just the Turk's Head, a legacy of the excursions of the North African traders in the Middle Ages, which probably explains why so many of the islanders are dark-haired and swarthy-skinned. On St Mary's, there are five pubs and half a dozen hotels and restaurants, which are now beginning to open up for the season. Some of the restaurants have a reputation for being expensive and complacent. I'm told that even at the height of the summer, with the island bursting with hungry holidaymakers aching to relieve the pressure on their bulging wallets, you'll be hard-pressed to find a place serving after 8.30 p.m. Sadly, this poor reputation is underpinned by one of my first experiences eating out in a restaurant on the islands.

I arrive slightly early for my booking and am greeted by a visibly hostile, very young waitress.

'What time did you book?' she demands.

'Eight thirty.'

She pauses for a moment, looking me up and down as though I had just spat on the floor. Then, slowly, she checks her watch.

'It's only eight twenty.'

We stand staring at each other.

'Perhaps I could have a drink?' I suggest, to break the impasse.

'Your table isn't ready.'

'Perhaps I could just sit over there while you prepare it?'

With an earth-shaking sigh, the girl looks me up and down again and walks away. I sit and wait. The place is half-empty. The minutes pass.

'Perhaps I could see a menu?'

'It's only twenty-eight minutes past,' she explains helpfully. 'Your booking isn't until eight thirty.'

'I know that. Could I see a menu?'

'We don't have a spare one.'

If there was anywhere else on the island to eat, I would have left the moment I arrived, but I was hungry. The girl, her eyes filled with liquid hate, gives me the worst service I have ever had. What she's saying to me, but doesn't articulate, is: if you don't like it, get the next helicopter back to the mainland.

I have a feeling this is a sentiment I might well bump into again in the months ahead. I've discovered there's a stubborn streak to many islanders which may stand them in good stead in the difficult times but could also be a real obstacle to progress.

*   *   *

Toby's back from seeing the solicitors in Penzance, and it's instantly clear from the look on his face that he is no mood for celebrations of any kind.

87

Liz had arrived, as planned, at Newquay after her flight from Gatwick, and former husband and wife had met up at Penzance station, whereupon Liz announced that less than an hour before she was due to exchange contracts on the sale of her Brighton house, the purchasers' solicitor had called with a demand that Liz drop the agreed price by £8,000. This they simply cannot afford to do; every penny of the sale is required for the purchase and equipping of the Seven Stones.

With their joint finances already dangerously overstretched, Toby and Liz are now at a loss, and the consequences could be dire. This is so much more than just buying a business; it will have a dramatic effect on the lives of a number of people. Liz can't move across from the mainland to her new life on St Martin's; the present landlord of the pub is desperate to leave and return to his family in Yorkshire; Toby's hired a young chef, Pauly Websdale, who has already been waiting a month in Scotland for the go-ahead to move across; Pauly, in turn, has hired a Polish couple, Krzys and Lidia, to help him in the kitchen, and they are also waiting for the call.

Toby is burning with rage at the behaviour of the purchasers of Liz's house; I can almost hear him grinding his teeth. He says it was all a calculated move on the part of the purchasers' solicitor.

'I'm just completely appalled by the whole thing. I'm very, very angry,' he mutters bitterly. 'When I heard about the call, I didn't think I was hearing reality; it sounded like a joke. I was in a complete state of shock, and I think I still am.'

There's sadness in his demeanour, as well as

fury. I wave him off from the quay as *Lightning* takes him back to St Martin's and a future life which might, after all, be confined to the walls of the bakery on Moo Green.

5

Chocolate Eggs And Wedding Bells

The first Duke of Cornwall was the Black Prince, who was given the Isles of Scilly as a birthday present by his father, Edward III, in 1347. Today the islands represent everything the present Duke seems to hold dear: a rugged, primitive landscape, a fierce pride and self-sufficiency among its people, a powerful sense of community and common purpose, a rich sense of humour.

Quite what the islanders think of their landlord is harder to judge. The Duchy is charged by parliament to raise as much cash as it can to reduce the burden of the Prince's costs to the taxpayer, so it argues that rents should be maintained at market value. Many islanders find the inevitable increases in rents inequitable, but are fearful of speaking out. Others are grateful to the Duchy for financial support or grants for setting up businesses; Toby the baker, for example, could never have converted the old lobster-pot barn without Duchy help. The trouble then is that people who are refused grants tend to turn bitter.

The recent conversion of a former gig boatshed on Porthmellon Beach on St Mary's into a restaurant benefited hugely from Duchy funds, much to the delight of the new tenants and, I suspect to the disgust of rival restaurants, who received no such help. In the past, the Duchy has accepted that it has not always been adept at public relations; a couple agreed to move out of their home on Bryher on the grounds that it was urgently required for low-cost accommodation for local islanders, whereupon it was converted at great cost and rented out to rich holidaymakers. I guess the truth is that in a small, navel-gazing community like Scilly, HRH will always be damned if he does and damned if he doesn't. On his brief triannual visits, the Prince is greeted by the obligatory flag-waving crowds standing in front of freshly painted buildings, but much greater numbers stay away, muttering about the injustice of it all, just as I imagine they have done for six centuries. When Charles married Camilla, the fiercely Republican chairman of the Duchy Tenants' Association was sent a slice of the wedding cake, which he promptly auctioned on the Internet for £235.

The population of the islands is about two thousand—the size of a small English village—and most live on St Mary's, where there are cars and one petrol pump, behind Porthcressa Beach, which sells the most expensive fuel in Britain. It's the only island where there are a substantial number of freehold properties. Much of Hugh Town was sold off by a cash-strapped Duchy in the 1940s, and prices there now rival those in Kensington and Chelsea.

The resident population on each of the four off-islands is around a hundred, and there are very few privately owned properties. There are virtually no cars, save the odd Landrover or truck; most transport is by boat, foot, horse, tractor or buggy.

The one island that is quite unlike the others is Tresco, and I'm taken aback by the number of people on the other islands who profess to loathe the place. At first, it's hard to see why. It's beautiful, and immaculately maintained. There's a lovely little school, beside the cricket pitch and the lush fields where the prize-winning beef herd grazes. Each morning, the fifteen children here are joined by a lifebelt-clad crocodile of half a dozen kids who are brought over by open boat from the smaller island of Bryher, which lies just to the west and is overlooked by Tresco's two, small, ruined castles, a legacy of Scilly's significant role in the Civil War. The Bryher children have been coming to Tresco since the 1970s, when the island's population—about one hundred and twenty in the mid-nineteenth century—fell to just fifty and the school there closed.

Up the track from the school stands St Nicholas Church, which, like most places on Scilly, is never locked. It's said that the keys to the church were lost in the war, but no-one can remember which war. The church is really a testament to one family: the Dorrien-Smiths. Although Tresco is owned by the Duchy, the Dorrien-Smith family have taken it over on a very long lease—a fiefdom within a fiefdom. They had the church built at the end of the nineteenth-century, and inside dozens of stained-glass windows and brass plates pay tribute to the role the family has played in the life of the nation as well as the island. On the north wall of the chancel is the family crest and motto, *Preines Haleine Tire Fort* which is old French dating from Richard the Lionheart and means: 'Take a deep breath, and hold it strongly.' Beneath that is a particularly poignant oak panel commemorating almost an entire generation of Dorrien-Smiths who were wiped out in the Second World War: three sons by Arthur and two sons by his brother Edward—two of the cousins, in an appalling coincidence, being killed on the same day and in the same place. Tom survived the death of his five cousins and ran the estate until his sudden death in 1972, when a young and inexperienced Robert Dorrien-Smith found himself taking over what was virtually a bankrupt enterprise and began the long task of turning the monster around, which he appears to have done more successfully than anyone had dreamed possible.

The family still live up in the grand house, the Abbey, beside the ruins of the original twelfth-century Cistercian monastery and the famous gardens, over which the flag bearing the family crest flies when Mr Robert is in residence. He effectively owns and controls every inch of the island: the harbour, the luxurious island hotel, the only pub—the New Inn—and all the estate cottages and houses, most of which have been converted into a rare example of a staggeringly successful timeshare development.

Like HRH, Mr Robert polarises opinion. Many islanders, often, unsurprisingly, those in his employment, claim he is the saviour of the place, and that without his creative genius there would be widespread poverty and unemployment. Others argue that he has ruthlessly torn the heart out of the island, transforming it into little more than a theme park. Indisputably, it's a brilliant economic model. Mr Robert employs everyone on the island, and they, in turn, may have to live in the tied accommodation he owns; if they lose their jobs, they must leave the island. The only places to spend their cash are in the pub, shop and hotel—all owned by the family—so most of the money the staff have been paid is simply recycled back into the estate coffers. The natural demographics are distorted; many leave Tresco when they reach retirement age, thus releasing accommodation for replacements more able to generate income. It is, I guess, feudalism distilled.

On my first visit to Tresco, I instantly sense that it has quite a different feel from the other islands. It is manicured, wholesome, litter-free, almost antiseptic, a surreal corner of a pretty unreal world, populated almost exclusively by rich visitors from the Home Counties. The estate's wealth exudes from every newly whitewashed stone and immaculate replacement window. The only sound piercing the stillness is the gentle whirr of the dozens of buggies most of the staff and visitors use to get around, which gives the place the appearance of an upmarket New Hampshire golf and country club.

I walk up from the idyllic harbour at New Grimsby and stop by the New Inn, where I sit on the terrace and enjoy a beautifully prepared and served sandwich, a pleasure slightly tempered by the accidental discovery that because I'm a visitor I've been surcharged twenty-five per cent.

As so often on Scilly, a verdict on Tresco really depends on whether you are inside looking out or outside looking in. The beer tastes good, the sun is hammering down and the view across Tresco Flats to Merrick Island and Samson Hill beyond is sensational. I can think of worse places.

Tresco is the only island other than St Mary's to have its own heliport, a grass landing-strip right beside the Abbey where the choppers come and go all day during the season.

It is on this modest patch of grass between the dunes on the south-western tip of Tresco that a helicopter has just landed, and among the passengers scurrying out beneath the warm downdraught of the blades is Liz McPherson, the former social worker from Brighton, who carries a hefty bag on her shoulder and clutches a large plastic box containing her cats, Thelma and Wuzzi. Behind Liz is a floppy-haired, ten-year-old boy called Connor, her son and Darcy's half-brother. After collecting the rest of their luggage, which has already been unloaded along with the big, grey Royal Mail sacks, they take a seat on the long, covered green trailer which, hauled by a tractor, is the only form of public transport on the island.

It is one of the curious facts about our world that wars, love and the purchase of property can be turned upside down at a moment's notice, and so it has been with Toby and Liz's acquisition of the Seven Stones pub. Their bank manager has agreed to lend them a further £4,000 against the first three months' bar-takings, the buyers of the Brighton house have, eventually, agreed on a compromise offer and suddenly, after just a few short telephone calls, they are in business again and the former Mrs Tobin-Duigan is en route to the start of her brand-new life on Scilly.

The tractor-bus takes them on the southerly track past Appletree Point and Plumb Island, with views across to the little church by the quay on Bryher, past the shop—well-appointed and very expensive, with shelves weighed down with champagne and foie gras—and on past the old concrete slip and the First World War seaplane base that Mr Robert is now busy developing into new, bijou 'debenture' holiday homes, complete with pools and health spas. They are headed up past the New Inn and St Nicholas Church to the quay at Old Grimsby, on the north of Tresco, from where Terry and *Lightning* will whisk them across to Lower Town on St Martin's. Toby and Darcy are already waiting, waving frantically, to greet Liz and Connor.

With Toby firmly ensconced in his little cottage across from the bakery, Liz is moving into the tiny, picture-postcard house that comes with the pub and which shares the same stunning views over to St Mary's. Next to that is a second house, where Darcy and her boyfriend Steve are setting up home, along with the other newcomer, Pauly Websdale, their bright and bold new chef, who trained under Michael Caines, the famous chef who runs Gidleigh Park in Devon, and Martin Burge, chef at Whatley Manor.

At just twenty-two, Pauly is being given the chance to be in charge of his own kitchen for the first time. He has an uninhibited passion for creative cooking, which strikes me as unusual, to say the least, in someone so young. His idea of a great winter break from the stress of working around the clock during the season is to take a holiday in Thailand, which is where he went last winter, sample as many restaurants as he can and offer to work for two or three days free of charge in the kitchen of the best restaurant he's found, simply to increase his knowledge of international cuisine. He has a brash, dynamic personality, and after chatting to him for just a few minutes, I have little doubt that before long he will be fronting his own TV food programme, to be followed fairly rapidly by the acquisition of a TV station.

But the real drama is to be found in Liz's arrival. She almost dances around her new, empty cottage, her cheeks flushed, like a teenager about to meet her pop idol. She positions all her imaginary furniture room by room (the real stuff is still, of course, on its way to Scilly, due to arrive who knows when). She runs out into the miniature garden and a wall of overwhelming, complementary scents from the abundant wild flowers and garlic springing up on the hill behind her cottage, then shields her eyes from the sun as she gazes across the shimmering waves to the Eastern Isles.

Toby is obviously delighted to see her. I've no idea what has passed between them in the years since they separated, but they are clearly genuinely pleased to be in each other's company again, and no doubt speculation will continue for months to come about the prospect of them getting back together as a couple, rather than merely business partners.

From his study in the Chaplaincy above Hugh Town, Father Guy is monitoring developments on St Martin's with considerable interest. He is moved by what's happening, by two people somehow salvaging something from the wreckage of a marriage.

'I think it's just a wonderful human story,' he

says. 'Their relationship broke down, and it's very heartening to think that they can rebuild it to the point where they can go into business together. They must still share a big part of their lives together, after all, and that must be what brought them together again.'

The honeymoon glow brought about by the start of Liz's new life as an islander doesn't last long. Because of the delays caused by the protracted negotiations over buying the Seven Stones, the new team are now under great pressure to get everything ready in time for the big wedding of Lois, the schoolteacher, in just over a week's time. There is something of a carnival atmosphere in the bar, as the rather gloomy old pictures and flags that adorn the ceiling and walls are torn down. Everyone grabs a paintbrush and, fuelled by lashings of Scuppered, they start splashing around the grey and white paint which will help give the inside of the pub a much-needed facelift.

Toby has scarcely had a moment to celebrate the stunning coup he has pulled off in acquiring the Seven Stones, against all the odds. In fact, right now, as he robotically pushes the roller up and down the wall, spinning spots of paint down his trousers, he looks shell-shocked, almost traumatised.

'Don't tell the others,' he says, glancing over his shoulder, 'But I keep thinking, "What have I done? Is this the worst decision I have ever made?" Sometimes I'm almost paralysed when I suddenly realise what I've taken on.'

I hand the poor man my pint of Scuppered, which he sinks in one.

'You know how I'm getting through this?'

'Alcohol?'

Toby repeats the mantra that so many say has helped them through a crisis. 'I just don't have time to think about it.'

'But you came to St Martin's to escape all that stress and pressure,' I point out, probably, under the circumstances, not very helpfully. 'You're supposed to be enjoying yourself.'

Toby pauses. A trickle of grey paint runs down the side of his pale, dusty face.

'Oh I will, dear chap, I will.'

Toby has taken a series of stunning, wide-angled photos of land, sea and sky from viewpoints around St Martin's, which he is framing and hanging on the walls. Come October and the end of the season, the pub interior will be completely redesigned, but for now, with the hours ticking away, this will have to do.

Lois is marrying local lad Ryan Allsop, who runs the island's boatyard, and after a small ceremony in the church up at Higher Town, conducted by Father Guy, the main evening reception is to be held in the Seven Stones, and a marquee on the terrace is already in the process of being erected. They haven't bothered to draw up a guest list; it goes without saying that everyone on St Martin's is invited. For Toby, Liz, Darcy and Pauly, this is a really key moment in the life of the new endeavour, a very public debut before a critical audience made up of every single one of their future clientele. The place must look great, the food must be exceptional, the service impeccable, the atmosphere special. That's quite a list, but to get it wrong in a place like this could spell professional suicide.

It's 5.45 in the morning, and the lights are blazing in the Chaplaincy. The Scott family is putting on coats, scarves and gloves. Silently they leave the house and walk up Church Road in the early morning chill, turning right up a dark footpath, beneath the dim silhouette of the chimney rising above the emergency power station, and then right again at the hospital and up a track towards the old windmill tower of Buzza, one of the highest points of the island. Other shadowy figures are joining them. There are whispered greetings, quick embraces and handshakes. Just below the tower is an ancient burial chamber, or chambered cairn. A white cross of linen has been laid across a large rock outside it.

The group waits, in a circle. A half-moon hangs in the pale-grey sky to the south, its reflection blinking in the waves down by Pilchard Pool. A distant lug sail of a yacht on a gentle, broad reach to St Agnes inches away beneath the horizon. Slowly, as the minutes tick by, the first orange rays of the sun peek above the black outline of the airfield and Salakee Down to the east. The group begins its dawn service; there are prayers, hymns and much looking around at the extraordinary, multicoloured scenes unfolding around them, as the low, dazzling sun chases away the shadows above Porthloo and Penninis Head, inching across towards Star Castle and the Garrison, soon even kissing the roof of the old lifeboat station down in the harbour.

Easter morning has arrived, and with it the

99

official start of the new season, and the hopes and aspirations of an entire parish.

*   *   *

A few hours later, and even though it is still only the beginning of April, the sun is brilliant in the sky, bringing with it the blanched intensity of a windless, cloudless July day. There's a sense of jubilation in the air. St Mary's is unexpectedly heaving with holidaymakers, who are swarming through Hugh Street, filling the bars, cafés and boats. The islanders buzz about them, relieved to be busy at last, like bees around a honeypot. It's a gratifying scene, with everything clicking away like clockwork—a fabulous springboard into spring.

Easter is the most important event in the Christian calendar, more significant even than Christmas, so after the dawn service on Buzza, Father Guy just has time for a bacon sandwich before the eight o'clock communion in a daffodil-decked St Mary's Church. Then things get complicated.

The morning is young enough for there still to be a chill in the air, so up at the Chaplaincy the girls are putting on their hats and coats, and then together with Father Guy and Kate, they scamper off in a little huddle down the hill to Church Street. High above, from their superior military position on the Garrison, the pair of huge black cannons that guard the haughty Georgian facade of Hugh House and the Duchy offices catch the sunlight. Next door are the upper windows of Tamarisk, the Duke of Cornwall's official residency on Scilly, a favourite when he was still married to Diana and the boys were young. They hurry past the St Mary's Hall hotel, newly modernised and probably the trendiest place in town, much too pricey for the Scotts; past the row of little Victorian bed-and-breakfasts and the big granite Methodist chapel; and then down towards the Parade, where in a few weeks the girls will be joining the other schoolchildren for the traditional May Day dancing. At last, they head down Hugh Street and onto the quay, mercifully slightly ahead of the main phalanx of visitors who are already starting to move towards the harbour to get their tickets for the tripper boats.

Unusually, the *Wizard*, which is still on its mooring, seems to be having engine trouble. A large black cloud is emerging from the boat's engine shafts, but only a few minutes after nine o'clock she comes alongside the quay, and Alice and Clarrie are on board before Fraser's even had a chance to tie her up. The girls are leaping in and out of boats as though they have lived here all their lives. It's dead calm, and the thrash across the Sound, over the sparkling, deep-blue water is thrilling. Even Kate is smiling—not a hint of seasickness this morning.

St Agnes Church stands on the western side of the island, by the harbour at Periglis, two minutes' walk on the coastal path from the Hicks's Troytown Farm. Its big, plain-glass windows look out on the old lifeboat station, built in 1887, which for two decades was the most westerly station in the Isles. The rocky coast is relentlessly exposed to the prevailing south-westerlies, and the St Agnes men would regularly row out in the open gigs in gales, sometimes with a small sail to keep the bow

101

into the wind, to the legendary ships' graveyard of the Western Rocks, a few miles to the south-west, where they were often able to engineer spectacular rescues in conditions hard to imagine. Many of the men were Hickses, of course, and I find it humbling to see the family name on so many graves in the churchyard, and on the RNLI bravery commendations that plaster the walls inside the church. Because it's such a small community, every man was expected to do his duty at any moment, without question, and it's a sobering thought that little seems to have changed today.

The church is nearly full this Easter Sunday, and this seems to put Father Guy in good humour. He's smiling and laughing after the service, as the family climb aboard the buggy which carries them back up by the towering, white seventeenth-century lighthouse, where the Hicks's cattle graze contentedly in the sunlight, and then down past the Turk's Head, just opening up for business, to the quay. They're already behind schedule because there were so many more communicants at church than they'd expected, and when they reach the quay, instead of finding the *Wizard*, with its powerful engine grumbling away, waiting to be unleashed for the roar back to St Mary's, there's one of the old wooden tripper boats instead, the appropriately named *Surprise*, which will probably take three times as long. The *Wizard*, it seems, has broken down. The biggest and most important service of Father Guy's Easter Day is the eleven o'clock in St Mary's Church; they'll be lucky to be there by eleven thirty.

Father Guy is a stickler for detail. His hair is always neatly combed, with side-parting, in an old-fashioned, Baden-Powell kind of way; his highly polished shoes shine like mirrors. If he says he's going to do something, it is done, quietly and promptly. Good manners and, above all, punctuality are indications of an inner health. He is, I'd say, a neat man, with the corners tucked in.

In his last parish, Father Guy would have been mortified to be late for any service, let alone the big one on Easter Sunday.

'You're not only going to be late, Guy,' I point out helpfully, stirring the pot. 'You're going to be *really* late.'

If I'd expected him to be agitated, I couldn't have been more wrong. He gave me a serene smile.

'Well, that's true,' he says. 'So they'll just have to wait for me.'

As we chug slowly back across the Sound, with Father Guy and Kate huddled under the short coach roof at the front of *Surprise*, to shelter from the sun, I chew over his words: 'They'll just have to wait for me.' I take this as something of a watershed, a sign that Father Guy may be beginning to accept the more relaxed, fatalistic island approach to life. If he doesn't, he'll find it very hard going indeed.

Nine hours later, he's still hard at work. Every Sunday from Easter through to October, Father Guy will be holding an 8 p.m. epilogue service in the tiny church at Old Town. Because there is no electricity here, the church is barely used in winter, although tonight it's ablaze with dozens of candles which are hanging on the walls and in chandeliers; it must look almost exactly as it did eight hundred years ago. Among those often present is Harold

103

Wilson's widow, Lady Mary Wilson. Tonight, given the loveliness of the evening and the medieval charms of the church, it's standing room only, and Father Guy again looks well pleased.

There won't be much rest for him tonight. Tomorrow, when many fellow churchmen will be taking the day off after the rigours of the Easter celebrations, Father Guy must be up again at the crack of dawn, to preside over his first wedding on the Isles of Scilly. It'll be a key moment for him, and for Toby, Liz and Darcy, busy preparing for the first big test of the Seven Stones, and even more so for Miss Lois Briard, respected schoolteacher of St Martin's, who by the end of the day, if all goes to plan, will be Mrs Lois Allsop, which will no doubt confuse the nine pupils in her charge for many months to come.

*   *   *

There is really only one track across St Martin's, which links the two quays at Higher and Lower Town and snakes from west to east past Moo Green, the Post Office stores, the church, and then down the long hill to the Reading Room, the telephone box and Ryan Allsop's boatyard at Middle Town, ending just below the Seven Stones, at the hotel and the quay overlooking the beautiful bird sanctuary of Tean and Tresco beyond. The track is going to see more action today than it has in years.

As usual, Toby's been at the bakery since five o'clock in the morning, making pastries and cakes and 150 miniature pasties for the wedding reception. Pauly and the two Polish assistants he's brought with him from their last job together in a hotel in Scotland, Krzys and Lidia, are busy in the pub kitchen, grilling some of Martin Bond's fresh John Dory and baking huge joints of pork stuffed with thyme and basil. Darcy and Liz are sweeping and dusting the bar and marquee. Soon the bunches of lilies and white garlic, grown and cut up the road at Churchstowe Farm, will be arriving. Ian, a local lad who helps out with odd jobs at the Seven Stones, is preparing the vegetables he meticulously cultivates on his plot, just out of range of Snowy, the old, tethered goat, who, like a geriatric, tobacco-chewing sentry, never leaves his post guarding the southern approach to the pub.

Because the church is so small, only family and close friends are invited to the service itself, but one of the biggest crowds seen in years on St Martin's assembles outside to watch the comings and goings, entirely blocking the track. By coincidence, down on Higher Town quay the *Lyonesse Lady* has just unloaded a large blue container with the words 'Liz McPherson, Seven Stones' chalked on its side; this turns out to be the entire contents of Liz's house in Brighton. It's unloaded onto the quay, beside extra casks of Mark Praeger's Scuppered and other assorted jewels from the Ales of Scilly brewery awaiting collection by Ian in the battered old pub lorry, which gets ensnared in the extraordinary melee outside the church and has to back off down the track. The confusion is compounded by the arrival of Toby on his quad on the other side of the heaving crowd, and he is similarly unable to get through with his cargo of steaming pasties.

Watching the event unfold from the end of the

105

lane, bathed in hazy sunshine, I am struck not only by the utter charm of the scene, but also by the realisation that while such an occasion may well have occurred in the England of old, it simply would not occur today. Nothing moves, everything's closed, everybody's here to celebrate the simple union of these two islanders. For St Martin's, at this moment, the world stands still.

Father Guy, despite his nerves at this first wedding in his new parish, has clearly done a good job. The couple are beaming as they emerge into the sunlight, the groom in tails, Lois in a long cream dress, with a small tiara tucked into her short black hair. They then set off down the track at a lively pace, to walk across the island, followed by bridesmaids, family, Father Guy and a long wake of guests and well-wishers, including Lois's little group of waving schoolchildren.

A few bemused sheep pause to look and then scatter as the party slowly moves across the island. There are no cars, of course; in fact, there are no sounds at all, save the distant call of a seagull and the faint murmur of a breeze from the sea to the south, which gently shakes the hedges and the small, square fields left to wild flowers. It is, truly, a beautiful and touching sight, like a scene from a Thomas Hardy novel, and one that the author would not just have recognised, but no doubt relished.

The track eventually takes the party right beneath the Seven Stones. Pauly, Liz and Darcy tumble out, waving and shouting down their congratulations, and Lois and Ryan wave back, soon disappearing out of sight to partake of a small private wedding breakfast for family and close friends at the hotel.

Ian has now returned from the quay in the pub lorry with the first consignment of Liz's belongings, which they had to unpack from the container and load up right then and there on the quay: beds, mattresses, wardrobes, tables, chairs and boxes of clothes, books and pictures. Connor and Steve lend a hand carrying it all up the stone stairs to Liz's cottage. They must hurry—it won't be long before the wedding party moves to the Seven Stones and is joined by the rest of the islanders.

*   *   *

A low sun dips beneath one or two heavy banks of cloud, which are stacked up like huge granite steps on a stairway to the stars, and the vivid, deep-orange rays of sunlight beam down through the gaps between the clouds in great, biblical shafts. It is an awesome sight. Emerging from the dark outline of St Mary's, across the bar, speeds a black dot that gradually, as it gets bigger, takes on the familiar shape of the now-repaired *Wizard*. It slices silently through the still waters, which are white like a mirror reflecting the last light in the sky directly above, then leaving a turbulent kaleidoscope of colour in its wake. Where the dainty little waves lap easily on the beach by the quay, one or two tiny turnstones flitter about, hungrily pecking away beneath the pebbles, looking for sandhoppers; a flock of cormorants rises as one from the rocky outcrop of Cheese Corner on the northern edge of Tean, just opposite, and head off west, their necks reaching out into the purple-streaked night sky. As the *Wizard* moors, the sinister silhouettes of a group of dark-suited men, some wearing trilby hats, jump off and walk slowly up the quay, carrying a variety of black cases. The men stride up the little hill and turn to the left, past the dark outline of Appletree Cottage, and on to the Seven Stones.

Through the windows of the pub there is a scene of joyous, colourful, silent animation: sweaty, laughing faces, invariably hovering above that awkward physical combination of a plate of food in one hand and a full glass of wine and a fork in the other. So nobody eats or drinks much, they just talk a great deal. The tiny pub is packed, and it looks very hot, but it doesn't matter, it only takes one glance to see that the evening is a conspicuous success.

Weaving their way diplomatically through the tight mob, arms raised like ballet dancers, delicately balancing the trays of food, are Pauly, Krzys and Lidia, all starched linen in their chefs' whites, with shiny silver buttons down one side of the jacket, and brand-new, blue-and-white aprons. Up high, the food is picked out by the lights, and it looks good: rows of doubled-over filo pastries, some cheese and powdered with flour, some half-pesto, half-olive; mahogany drumsticks of home-produced chicken, dripping with honey sauce; strips of roast loin of pork (sadly not home-produced, but there is a whisper in the air that this might soon change) stuffed with apple, sage and walnut; and lashings of salad, made up from the contents of the allotments in the old flower fields on the hill below the pub—potatoes, greens, shallots, onions, herbs.

The place looks splendid, all gleaming new paint, polished brass and mirrors, decorated with Toby's eye-catching, wide-angle seascapes of the island and fountains of white flowers. Behind the bar, former social worker Liz, in a smart little black dress, is pulling the pumps like a trooper, happily dispensing advice about what to do with the ancient batty aunt or warring couple next door to anyone who'll listen. There's a lucrative sideline in a bit of social-work moonlighting here for her, if she can stand it. Every now and then she disappears back to her cottage next door where, among the scattered debris of her unpacked furniture, Thelma is about to give birth to kittens. Toby is holding forth about the great issues of the day, washing back the Scuppered like a man just released from prison after a long sentence, leaning at a dangerous angle and, like the famous tower at Pisa, somehow mysteriously managing to avoid collapse.

The men in black have unpacked their jazz instruments in the marquee and now strike up their first number. One or two couples drift out into the semi-darkness and sit, sipping their wine and finally digging into their food. Immediately, groups of sparrows advance, hopping out from the shadows to pick at the crumbs; the birds here are quite fearless, and not only come right up and eat from your plate, but will even take from the hand, something I have never seen before.

The bride and groom, having singled out Pauly to congratulate him on the feast, self-consciously open the dancing, and within minutes the marquee is heaving. Suspended above Great Ganilly, an enormous harvest moon has appeared.

'This is the biggest night that the Seven Stones has seen in the history of the pub,' declares a jubilant Toby, swaying slightly. He pauses and swallows, as if to hiccup. 'We'll have a great time, and the sun will rise tomorrow, and we'll all look very grey and grim, grey and grim indeed!' He looks like a man who should be sharing his moment of celebration with someone. After the divorce from Liz, he married a lovely girl called Louise, who runs the restaurant down at the hotel, but that too didn't last, so Toby now has one ex-wife working behind his bar and another working just down the road. I'm not sure if there are any other suitable single women on St Martin's.

So, Toby and his assorted team have successfully made it over the first hurdle. The real question now is: can they sustain this success? There are a number of livelihoods other than Toby's depending on the little Seven Stones: Liz, Pauly, Darcy and Steve, Krzys and Lidia, and Ian. That's a lot of dominoes that could come crashing down.

I wander up the path just above the pub and lean against a gate. The moon casts a shaking, silver path across towards Tresco. The stars, as always, are clinically clear in their unpolluted skies. Seven miles away, the intermittent white blink of the Bishop Rock lighthouse suddenly transforms itself into a great revolving beam which sweeps the islands. The murmur of the jazz filters up to me, and then, startlingly, stops for a moment. Complete silence descends. Since the entire island is at the party, I can see no other lights at all on St Martin's.

Long after the lights on the other islands have

dimmed, the gentle glow of the marquee, which can be seen from the telegraph tower high up on 'the mainland', will continue to pulse through the night, until the first hints of the new day are detected in the cloudless skies above the Eastern Isles.

6

More Woes For The Vet

During the summer months, there's a reassuring rhythm to daily life on St Mary's that barely changes. At 8.30 in the morning, the boatmen, including Fraser Hicks, Steve Hicks, Alex Hicks, Paul Hicks, Alfred Hicks and sometimes even Mike Hicks, gather on the quay by the Association's ticket office, stand around for a bit, and eventually allocate the day's trips. The working day now satisfactorily underway, they adjourn for coffee while one of the crew chalks up the details on the blackboard at the end of the quay.

At about 9.30, the harbour echoes with the tinny put-put-put of the little outboards of the punts, as the boatmen motor out to the moored tripper boats. After a minute or two, there's the much deeper, throaty throb of the big diesel engines spluttering into life, one by one, with a few coughs of black smoke, and the boats come alongside the quay, often mooring two or three deep. The gentle stream of holidaymakers marching down Hugh Street towards the harbour from their hotels and

111

bed-and-breakfasts soon turns into a flood, and by ten o'clock on a sunny day there can be as many as a thousand people jostling on the quay, most in anoraks and weighed down with waterproof bags, cameras and walking sticks, trying to find the right boat for their trip.

By 10.15, the crews are pulling in the ropes and a convoy of bulging boats is steaming out into the Road. Some head north to Tresco and Bryher, some north-east to St Martin's and the Eastern Isles, and some south-west to St Agnes and the Western Rocks, their wakes gradually spreading out like the points of the compass. Behind them, Hugh Town can take on the air of a ghost town, at least until four o'clock, when the first of the boats start arriving back from the off-islands, and the whole process is reversed.

This morning, Dr Heike Dorn, veterinary bag in hand, has joined the holidaymakers on the tripper boat to St Martin's. The journey takes about twenty minutes and costs around £7 return, and it's this which has prompted her latest course of action. It's expensive and time-consuming for off-islanders to make lots of trips to St Mary's and it's not easy for them to make their way across the island from the quay to Heike's surgery in Old Town, so today, in the first of a series of experiments, Heike has decided to go to them. She has hired the old Reading Room, which serves as a make-do community centre, in the middle of the island, and has let it be widely known that she will be in attendance between 11.45 a.m. and 1.00 p.m. to treat ill animals, of whatever size or shape.

Just below the Seven Stones, at the lovely sand-blown quay by the hotel at Lower Town, which on a sunny morning like today really does look like a millionaire's Caribbean hideaway, a local farmer is waiting to pick Heike up from the quay and give her a lift on the back of his tractor up the hill to examine his sick dog. Then she calls round to the pub to see Liz, whose cat Thelma has produced her litter of eight kittens, just a few inches long, their eyes still squeezed tight shut. Later, she makes her way across to the bakery, where she has a slice of Toby's exquisite smoked-chicken pizza and removes a small, benign growth from the leg of Jazz, his marmalade Hungarian pointer.

The dogs are twitchy. Toby explains that they are missing the shooting, which always stops on the last Friday before Easter, to allow the wild pheasant, partridge and, best of all, the woodcock and snipe to breed in the comfort of knowing that they aren't about to have their heads blown off. Apart from regular sorties against an army of rabbits which can strip Ian's vegetable patch within hours given a free hand, the dogs must now wait until the last day of September for the shooting to resume.

Then, just a few minutes before she's due to start, Heike arrives at the old Reading Room—which doubles up as a home for the toddler's play-group, ladies' keep-fit, library and, on occasion, coroner's court—for the launch of the new experiment which she hopes will help transform her fortunes.

These are frustrating times. In the old days on Scilly, the farmers would slaughter their own livestock and simply sell their meat on to the butcher in town. One reason more farmers don't invest in livestock these days is that slaughter can only legally take place in authorised abattoirs that abide by strict EU regulations, and there is no abattoir on Scilly. Livestock from the off-islands must therefore be carted down to the quays, carried across to St Mary's on the old *Lyonesse*, and then stowed aboard the *Scillonian* or the Grim Reaper for an often traumatic journey across turbulent seas to Penzance, from where they are lorried on to slaughterhouses spread across Cornwall, Devon and Somerset. It's expensive, of course, and the stress inflicted on the animals almost invariably affects the taste and quality of the meat. So, in keeping with the new plans for self-sufficiency and better food across the islands, planning permission for an abattoir on the little industrial estate behind Porthmellon Beach has been given, and of course a vet will be required to oversee things.

Under the rigorous new regulations, one slaughterman at the new abattoir will have to be supervised not just by a vet, but by at least two, and sometimes even three, inspectors, all of whom must come over from the mainland and be paid for, even if there is only one animal to be killed. Now Heike has learned that, after days of negotiation, the plan has been shelved indefinitely. This is a major blow to her long-term prospects on Scilly.

Another potential source of income for the islands' vet is also under threat. With the overall decline in farming, the Isles of Scilly Wildlife Trust has recently invested in a dozen Red Ruby cows, 'landscape cattle', to graze on the now uncultivated ground in order to keep down the bracken and gorse and to add interest to the

114

skyline. Heike has recently been up to Bryher, where six of the cows roam the heathland along with some Shetland ponies, to inject the heifers with hormones to help them into season, and there's lots more work promised.

'Except, of course, that this being Scilly, there have been a number of objections to the scheme,' says Heike, wearily. There's no anger now—she's already been here too long for that—just a reluctant, bemused acceptance of the oddities of island ways.

I can't think of a less controversial scheme. 'People object to lovely cows munching away harmlessly at the bracken?'

'People object to change. They think the cows are a danger . . .' Heike takes a deep breath '. . . to r-ramblers, which is r-ridiculous. There is r-really no r-risk whatsoever, especially from R-r-red R-r-rubies. How is my English doing, incidentally?'

'Wonderful.'

'And they even object to the electric fencing! *Mein Gott*!'

So now the landscape cattle, like the abattoir, may well, literally, face the chop.

As if all this wasn't bad enough, more gloomy news has reached Heike.

A few days ago, Old Town was the scene of An Incident—sadly only partially witnessed by Malcolm Martland, the retired vet—that could have far-reaching, even fatal, consequences for Leo the bull terrier of Launceston Close, Old Town.

According to Malcolm's evidence, the incident involved four principal characters, only one of whom appears to be a suspect:

115

a) An unknown female dog owner.

b) A young black Labrador, owned by the above.

c) Leo. Chief Suspect.

d) A partial witness: Malcolm Martland.

Since he has been on Scilly, Leo has been creating considerable physical and mental damage in his immediate environment, destroying or damaging a number of Heike's treasured antiques and family heirlooms. Recently, his catchment area has dramatically increased, since he learned, with impressive speed, how to leap up and open all the doors in the house, meaning that Heike's home is now the only locked house on Scilly. Yet despite all this, through sheer force of character and personality, Leo has utterly endeared himself to his new owner and companion in life's long journey and, more particularly, to her young son, Sammy.

According to the case for the prosecution, events unfolded as follows.

At about 10.45 a.m., Malcolm was proceeding in a westerly direction when he saw the aforementioned Leo larking about, 'looking for trouble', in front of his home. Heike has done her best to fence in her little garden, but the overweight, very muscular Leo is able to escape by charging like a rugby prop forward through the thick perimeter hedge, or simply by leaning against weaker sections of the front fence and then squeezing through the gap.

According to the account of the principal witness, Leo then spied a nervous-looking Labrador and its hapless owner, who had suddenly appeared walking down the lane, blithely unaware of any impending danger and, in fact, probably rather enjoying the bracing sea air. The accused then immediately gave chase.

Precisely what happened next is unclear, because it took place around a corner in the lane, but Malcolm heard much barking and what could have been a stifled female scream. The very upset owner of the shocked and bruised Labrador then appeared, in a state of some disarray, and ran off. It was later reported that she had been admitted to the hospital at Buzza with a bloody wound to the arm.

So, a defiant Leo, a reluctant defendant unable to explain his side of the story, is most definitely in the doghouse.

When I catch up with Heike, it's plain that she's distressed about what's happened, despite being such a tough-skinned individual. With Leo innocently snoring away in his cage outside the surgery, she explains that it's not great public relations for the islands' vet to have a dog perceived as an ill-disciplined savage who spends his time creating new patients for her. Furthermore, the mother of the attacked woman has called Heike from the mainland, berating her for her gross irresponsibility and demanding that Leo be removed from the islands forthwith, or else she would be contacting the 'relevant authorities', by which Heike assumes she means the local police, not known for their sympathy to dogs who attack innocent holidaymakers and who have plenty of time on their hands to rigorously pursue prosecutions.

'I have phoned the breeder in Cardiff and he has agreed to take Leo back,' Heike explains mournfully. 'What else can I do? This is indeed a sad day.'

Upstairs, Sammy has locked himself in his room and is wailing.

*   *   *

In 1904, Charles John Mumford opened a newsagents on Scilly, and it's still there today, dominating the little square on the corner of Garrison Lane and Hugh Street, still bearing the title 'C.J. Mumford's' proudly beneath a fluttering union jack on the granite stone above the front floor.

Less than five years later, Charles Mumford was dead, drowned whilst trying to salvage the wreck of the SS *Plympton*, which went down on the Lethagus Rocks off St Agnes, bound for Ireland with a cargo of maize and grain from Brazil. Charles was on a gig called the *Dolly Varden* with St Agnes boatman Charles Hicks, but neither body has ever been found, which is why the joint grave of Charles and his widow Susan Mumford in Old Town graveyard contains only one body.

Today their grandson Clive still runs the newsagents. He's also the resident correspondent of the *Cornishman*, and each week, slogging away on his old roll-top desk above the shop, he produces a page of news, buried towards the back of the paper, devoted to the Isles of Scilly. If you were to press the taciturn Clive, he would admit that, just occasionally, he struggles to fill it. For example, there is virtually no reported crime. No-one bothers to lock their front doors and ignition keys are just left in cars. The most common crime appears to be 'bicycle borrowing', committed by late-night drinkers who make use of the nearest available cycle when they can't be bothered to walk home. They are nearly always returned in the morning, sometimes with a note of apology attached.

The most notorious scandal of recent years involved a plumber discovered with over a hundred pairs of women's knickers under his floorboards which had been stolen from neighbours and customers, a haul which also included sex toys. A judge at Truro Crown Court, handing down the kind of draconian sentence hard to imagine elsewhere, exiled the man from Scilly for seven years, later reduced on appeal to two, even though his partner and children live there. 'As well as betraying the trust invested in you, there is a more general trust in St Mary's which you have betrayed, a trust sadly lacking on the mainland, which says we don't have to lock our doors because we know you will behave in an honourable and decent way,' said the judge. 'St Mary's has been shaken.'

Through the winter months there are only the two resident police officers on Scilly, who live in flats above the tiny police station on the corner of Garrison and Jerusalem Road, behind the main street, where the twin cells are sometimes put to good use by stranded holidaymakers unable to find a bed for the night.

In the busier summer months, the force is supplemented by a third officer seconded from mainland units in the Devon and Cornwall Constabulary. Last year there had only been one volunteer for the force's oddest posting, twenty-nine-year-old Nikki Green from Plymouth, single, ambitious, conveniently in between love affairs and sharp enough to spot an opportunity to include the ultimate in 'community policing' on her curriculum vitae. Her last shift in inner-city Plymouth had been a bit of a nightmare, and wearily familiar to her: a warm Bank Holiday evening during which hundreds of youngsters who'd been drinking all day gradually invaded every dockside bar and pub in the Barbican in search of dubious sources of entertainment, ending in a sea of blood, urine and vomit. The next day, by way of some contrast, Nikki flew to St Mary's, where for the first month the only 'major' criminal investigation was into allegations that a group of kids were seen throwing sticks at one of the landscape cows.

There followed a spectacular love affair. It was, indeed, a golden summer, full of beach parties, snorkelling with the seals, barbeques with lots of new friends, the undemanding, gentle police duties interspersed with off-duty days spent sunbathing on a series of empty beaches, followed by endless drinks on the terrace of the Atlantic Inn, overlooking the harbour. Within quite a short time, it became clear to those around her that WPC Nikki Green was hopelessly, irretrievably in love with the Isles of Scilly. At the end of her posting, the tears flowed at the airport as she set off on the journey back to grim old Plymouth, and there were vows to return, come what may. Nikki's friends on Scilly suspected that would be the end of the affair, and that once she was back in the real world, the islands, as for so many visitors, would become a distant memory to WPC Nikki Green.

According to a recent Internet survey published in the press, Scilly has one of the highest number of bachelors in Britain; there are over forty per cent more single men than women. The arrival of a pretty young bobby with a twinkle in her eye and an infectious giggle caused a certain frisson, I've heard, among the boys, and there's been all kinds of speculation—some of it stretching the bounds of credibility and, frankly, even the imagination—about who she may or may not have dated, and who did what with whom, and when and where. The fevered gossip was raised to new levels, because whatever romantic liaisons may have taken place must almost certainly have been conducted in secret or under cover of darkness. Like Father Guy, in a sense the police officers on Scilly can never really be truly off-duty; the idea of the new WPC stepping out in public with a local lad, with all the complications that might provoke, was really out of the question.

So it is with considerable interest that news now reaches the islands that, contrary to expectations, WPC Nikki Green has again applied for the post of summer relief. For an unspecified number of young men, this may—or may not—provoke a tremor in the heart, a fearful sense of anticipation. For the rest of us, and particularly the serried ranks of gossipmongers, it promises to be an intriguing six months.

*   *   *

Across the bay on St Martin's, Heike is beginning to wonder seriously for the first time whether she can sustain a future for her and Sammy on Scilly.

She has been waiting in the Reading Room for nearly two hours, reading old magazines. Whatever way you look at it, the first of the experimental off-island surgeries has not been a success. She had hoped to treat maybe six to eight patients, or, at worst, four; in fact, the sum of her well-publicised visit is a mere two cases. Taking into account the time wasted on the journey and the cost of the return ticket, the result, as Mr Micawber might have put it, is misery.

'It would be a major blow to have to leave this place. Sammy is so happy here,' she says, closing the last of her magazines and sighing deeply. 'But it would also be a major blow to my pride. I'm not sure I could take it.'

The boat trip back to St Mary's seems to take a very long time indeed, even in the sunshine. Heike is not only earning very little, she is steadily eating her way through thousands of pounds of her savings, accumulated throughout her lifetime.

Back home in Old Town, there's a bizarre telephone message for Heike that instantly turns her mind to the idea of a spot of moonlighting, which, after all, is what everyone else does on Scilly in order to survive financially. One of the German nation's favourite authors is, strangely, Rosamunde Pilcher, famous for her sentimental and romantic novels set in Cornwall, many of which have been filmed in well-known Cornish beauty spots for a voracious German television audience. As a result, the number of German tourists visiting the West Country has rocketed in recent years, and many of the more curious move on to explore Scilly. Last year, a German film-maker spent some weeks on Scilly making a stunning documentary about the natural history of the islands, which turned out to be a big ratings success back home, so now there have been bigger parties of Germans than ever turning up on St Mary's almost every week. Another large group is due to arrive on the *Scillonian* in a few days, and an interpreter is required. Would Heike be interested in helping out?

Heike is, above all, a consummate pragmatist who will try anything once, and she will certainly not let the fact that she has only been here a short time and knows little about the history or geography of the place get in the way of being the first veterinary surgeon on Scilly to become a tourist guide. With any luck, the tips will be good.

Despite the days of inactivity and growing worries about paying the bills, the next time I see Dr Heike Dorn she has a large smile on her face. She's had some unexpected news about her doomed houseguest, Leo, whose place is already booked on the helicopter back to Penzance, heading for an unknown future in Cardiff. Further evidence has emerged which puts into doubt the original guilty verdict. There has been a misunderstanding, she explains, handing me the obligatory steaming mug of black coffee. There was indeed a fight between the two dogs, but investigations at the hospital where the victim was treated apparently indicate that there is insufficient proof that it was instigated by Leo; rather, it seems, it could have been the other way round. Reports of the woman's injuries were greatly exaggerated, and may not have been caused by Leo at all; she had, in fact, only a small scratch, requiring no treatment.

123

'Leo has not exactly been exonerated,' says Heike. Leo himself arrives at this moment and leans against my leg, nearly pushing me off the chair. I look at his long, browless, inscrutable face and his thin pink eyes blink back at me. Is there a whisper of a smile there somewhere?

'But he has been reprieved to live another day on Scilly,' continues Heike, triumphantly. 'One wrong step, however . . .'

She takes me through the tiny surgery to the back garden, to show me how Leo has been celebrating. He's digging an enormous hole in a flower bed, already the depth of a grave. Huge chunks of mud and earth have turned the tiny lawn into a scene reminiscent of First World War trench warfare. Heike, though, smiles like an indulgent mother.

'Now he wants to visit New Zealand,' she explains. Leo looks up at me, his white snout now a muddy brown, and gives the merest suggestion of a wink.

*   *   *

I'm told you can never get lost on St Mary's, because there's really only one road which goes around the island, so if you just keep going, in whichever direction, it won't take you long to be back where you started. Although little more than a track, it's classified as an A-road to empower the council to put road markings and signage on it, so legally you are entitled to drive at sixty miles an hour, even, because there are no streets lights, in Hugh Town. This isn't recommended if WPC Nikki Green is on shift, however. Apparently she

124

doesn't take prisoners when it comes to enforcing the spirit as well as the letter of the law.

The road is officially the A3110. Daisy and Katie are the two antique tourist buses that daily ply the A3110 circuit throughout the season. Daisy is a splendid, open-topped, 1957, red double-decker, a London Transport Leyland Titan. Katie is one of only two surviving 1948 Austin K2s—hence the name—with coachwork in immaculate condition. As a backup, there's a rather plain, white executive coach, a mere thirty years old, which presumably must survive another thirty years at least before it becomes remotely interesting to the connoisseur. The vehicles can normally be seen of a morning parked incongruously by Holgates Green, waiting for the *Scillonian* to dock.

What is not quite clear is what exactly there is on St Mary's for the visitor to see. The views over the sea are, in the main, quite magnificent, of course, but you hardly need a coach trip to discover those. Inland, there are no views at all, apart from the odd surviving field of dancing flowers that's not hidden by walls of pittosporum; oh, and the duck pond up by Mark Praeger's brewery.

Even so, there isn't a spare seat when Heike gamely clambers aboard the executive coach in the little square outside Douglas, the chemist's, to face her eager audience, fresh off the ferry, who have presumably spent a lot of time and money travelling from the Fatherland to sample the delights of the A3110. I've no idea what island delights Heike is extolling, because I don't speak a word of German, but they appear absolutely

125

gripped by what she is saying. The undoubted highlight of the trip is when Heike confesses that she isn't a tour guide at all, but actually the Isles of Scilly veterinary surgeon, at which her fellow Germans almost split their sides laughing. Easily pleased, I guess.

Afterwards, I buy Heike a drink at the Mermaid, and she proudly waves the much-needed twenty-pound note she's earned for her afternoon's work.

'But I didn't get much of a tip, to be honest,' she says, looking slightly downcast. 'I had hoped for better.'

'There must have been sixty people on that coach!'

'Well, it wasn't brilliant.'

'How much?'

'Fifty pence.'

'Each?'

'In total.'

There is a long pause.

'Well, they *are* Germans,' she adds.

7

The Return Of The Bobby

The appearance of Holgates Green, the Strand and the promenade above Town Beach, with its quaint windshelter built to celebrate the coronation of Queen Elizabeth in 1953, is changing, almost imperceptibly, day by day. In recent weeks, when the *Scillonian* and its sister cargo boat the Grim Reaper set sail from Penzance, they carry, strapped to the decks along with the myriad other cargo, half a dozen pilot gigs from every corner of the West Country. Since gig-boats originated from Scilly, every spring the boats and their rowers, coxes and supporters make a time-consuming and expensive pilgrimage to the Isles for the World Pilot Gig Championships, held on the May Day Bank Holiday weekend.

Once unloaded, the gigs are stacked on the quay until Justin appears with his tractor after the day's work up at Longstone Farm, in the middle of St Mary's. One by one, he trails them through the town and up to the green by Town Beach, which becomes the headquarters of the event, and when that's so clogged with boats there's scarcely room to walk between them, he trundles the rest up the hill to the farm, where they are parked in a field beside the new herd of beef calves he and Alison Guy bought after shedding many a tear ploughing up the old flower fields. For just one weekend's rowing, it's a huge logistical operation. It'll take at least a month to get about a hundred gigs over, and a month to get them all back, which is why, over the years, there have been numerous attempts by much bigger harbours such as Falmouth to poach the Championships away to the mainland.

This year's event is billed as the biggest ever, promising by far the largest single injection of funds into the islands' economy, so its success is critical. The big fear is fog. The boats were designed to cope with high winds and big seas, but two years ago the Championships had to be abandoned because of dreadful visibility. The fog casts a shrouded curtain around St Mary's and

127

drains away all the colour, so only the closest of the dozens of uninhabited islands that dot the chart like confetti can be seen. At very low tides on dark and gloomy days, these rocky outcrops turn the topology of the place into something akin to a bleak lunar landscape. The tides can drop or rise by as much as five metres, so that up to two billion tons of water can be washing around these rocky outcrops every twelve hours. The prospect of hundreds of crew, unfamiliar with the weird tidal flows and currents, paddling around blind with no form of navigation is too nightmarish even to contemplate.

In fact, fog is the one element that can totally disrupt island life in general and ruin the best-laid plans. Fog means no helicopters or light aircraft from the mainland, and sometimes even no ferry, and that in turn means no newspapers, no food, no washing powder, no lavatory paper, no bricks or mortar or cement, no petrol, no people, no tourists. It's a constant reminder of an isolation that can be both a joy and a horror. Surrounded by the vastness of the Atlantic Ocean, Scilly may be the stuff of dreams, but there are also tales of happy incomers who have been slowly, silently driven mad by the place.

It's mid April, and today there are no worries at all about the weather. The islands have been basking in sunshine for several weeks, and already there are wild predictions of a record-breaking summer, fuelled by an unprecedented number of enquiries at the tourist office, although some rapidly evaporate when the true costs of travel and accommodation become clear.

Through the late afternoon and evening, the

local gig crews are making use of the calm waters and blazing sunshine to get in some training for the big weekend ahead. Over on St Martin's, Toby, Darcy and Steve have left a slightly apprehensive Liz in charge of the Seven Stones and joined the crews of the two island gigs, *Galatea* and *Dolphin*, which are stored in the twin sheds on the sand down at Higher Town Beach, for a thrash over to the Eastern Isles.

Gig-racing is taken extraordinarily seriously, and in a small island like St Martin's nearly every able-bodied young person is expected to participate. Even Pauly, imprisoned in his new kitchen, will have to take his turn sooner or later.

As the sun dips down towards the horizon behind the twin peaks of Samson, Toby and Steve, on the men's gig, and Darcy and the girls, on the other, circle the craggy, uninhabited Eastern Isles, watched by dozens of pairs of eyes. There are about three hundred grey seals on Scilly, and as the gigs beat past, one after another slips and rolls luxuriously down the rocks and into the waves, where they power through the crystal-clear water like rubbery torpedoes, or hang with their snouts just above water level so they can study the rowers at work. They are astonishingly tame, and are unafraid of the sound of engines; it's the human voice that puts the fear of God into them, and sometimes, also living on these islands, I know how they feel.

After a while, the gigs turn south-west and head down towards Hugh Town and the Mermaid, where they'll join the St Mary's teams, who'll have walked or cycled back up from their sheds on the beach at Porthmellon, and together they will set about demolishing several gallons of Scuppered, although this is the arrangement only when they've made sure that Terry and *Lightning* are on hand later to tow them home.

*   *   *

From the moment a tear-stained WPC Nikki Green stepped onto the helicopter after that golden summer on Scilly last year to resume the depressing and seemingly insoluble fight against crime in inner-city Plymouth, she has been plotting a triumphant return to the Isles.

It has not been straightforward. First she had to convince her bosses at the Exeter headquarters of the Devon and Cornwall Constabulary that she was indeed the right person for a second stint as summer relief on their most beautiful and remote beat. After weeks of anticipation, Nikki gets the news that her posting has been approved, whereupon she promptly breaks her leg falling down a gully while out jogging and has to lie up for weeks, bored out of her brains, at her parents' home in a lovely but very quiet village just outside Plymouth, while the Force M.D. pontificates about how long her return will be delayed.

Eventually, after a superhuman and punishing fitness regime, the fractured bone is declared fully healed and she's back, picked up from the heliport by her friend Shirley, the islands' new police community support officer, in Scilly's only squad car, seven years old but only 25,000 miles on the clock. After catching up with a few familiar faces—particularly her chums at the Atlantic: the Scots manageress Lorraine, who rarely stops talking and has the loudest, most piercing laugh on Scilly, and her tall, thin receptionist Neil, the self-confessed 'only gay on the islands' (can this really be true? Hard to be sure in such a fiercely macho place)— Nikki's alone and unpacking in the frugal little flat at the back of the bland, concrete police station. She chats away excitedly. She's thrilled to be back, she says, but I wonder if the obvious impossibility of recapturing the long, glorious days of last summer is already becoming apparent. Nikki had worked so hard to get back, but, rather like an unforgettable childhood holiday, sometimes 'last year' is better confined to the memory.

Sure enough, as the days slowly pass and Nikki relentlessly plods the Scilly beat once more, her uniform loaded down with handcuffs, extendable steel baton and CS gas canister, just in case of sudden, widespread civil disobedience on the islands, I detect a growing feeling of irritation and boredom. To come here once, as an experiment in community policing at its purest, might make sense to an ambitious young police officer, but twice?

It's almost as though there is a vacuum in the young life of the WPC which must be filled, and soon, or who knows what the consequences might be?

*   *   *

By the end of April, there is scarcely a blade of grass to be seen for gigs on Holgates Green and the slip to Town Beach. At the western end of the green, beside the Scillonian Club, where there are huge black-and-white pictures of Harold Wilson cheerfully downing pints with local fishermen in

131

cloth caps, a large wooden stage is being built for the Championship award ceremony, beneath a poster announcing the proud sponsors of the weekend's events: the Isles of Scilly Steamship Company. On either side of the stage are long, white leader boards for the daily lists of results, the winners and losers of this amazingly fiercely fought annual contest, which have now become so tall a long ladder is required to reach the top. With rows of international flags fluttering over the beach, the place has taken on the appearance of a medieval jousting tournament.

Below the stage, a marquee has been erected which will serve as race headquarters for the officials and safety officers, and there's already the strong smell of frying sausages and bacon emanating from the temporary field kitchen, set up by the ladies inside, which will be stepped up to become a dawn-to-dusk production line when racing starts on Saturday, to fuel the carbohydrate-starved bodies of hundreds of exhausted rowers. Heike, who has an eye for the younger man, says she's looking forward to checking out the more muscular of the contestants, although whether she'll be tossing them love tokens of sweetly scented 'kerchiefs with which to wipe their sweaty brows, like the maidens of old, remains to be seen. Myself, I think it's possible.

Mercifully, there's still no sign of fog.

*   *   *

At the end of the nineteenth century, someone at the War Office decided that the Isles of Scilly would be the perfect base for the mighty Home

132

Fleet of the Royal Navy. Surrounded by an almost empty, tranquil archipelago, anchorages were almost guaranteed to be in calm waters, with the bigger warships entering through the deep channel of the Sound between St Mary's and St Agnes and mooring up in the Road or in Crow Sound, to the north-east of St Mary's, in the lee of the prevailing sou'westerlies.

Work began building massive gun emplacements to guard the Sound, and the great concrete ramparts, which cost over a million pounds even then, can still be seen hidden among the trees at the top of the Garrison. This has become a favourite haunt for WPC Nikki Green. The back of one of the ramparts has been turned into a makeshift shooting-range for the Scilly Gun Club, and Nikki spends hours up there, relentlessly practising her aim with the club's rifles. Her two main ambitions in the last year have been curiously at odds: the first to return to work on Scilly, the sleepiest patch in the force; the second to become an expert with a Glock 17 semi-automatic or SMG submachine gun and join an armed-response unit. Whether these twin ambitions are ever likely to coincide, only time will tell.

When, in the early years of the twentieth century, the first section of ramparts was complete, a massive artillery piece was lowered into position, and preparations were made for some trial shots to be fired. When the first experimental shell went screaming across the Sound, without any prior warning to the local people, the shock of the report and the following volcanic vibrations shattered all the windows in Hugh Town. When all the glass had been replaced, it was announced that

133

a second shell would be fired, but this time at a specific time, when all windows in all buildings in the Town must be left open, to reduce the compressive effect of the explosion. At the agreed hour, the gun fired its shell across the Sound, whereupon every window shattered once again.

The coaling stations, munitions depots, new docks and rebuilding programme to house navy personnel would have provided a huge boost to local employment and transformed Scilly into one of the richest corners of the south-west. The Scillonians certainly needed some help. Apart from piloting and smuggling, most islanders in the first half of the nineteenth century eked out a living collecting and burning seaweed in stinking kelp pits, to produce soda ash, which was then shipped to Bristol or Gloucester for use in the manufacture of glass and soap. It was backbreaking work; it took a man, his wife and four children two weeks to make one ton of ash in the foul-smelling pits, which would be worth about a pound, and required the collection of over twenty-five tons of seaweed.

The huge, glass-shattering gun up on the Garrison proved to be an ill omen. Some bastard then invented the submarine, the War Office dropped the plan and the Home Fleet Headquarters was developed instead at Scapa Flow in the North Sea, easily defended by anti-submarine nets.

Today, though, the deep-water channels are being put to good use again. The islands are becoming increasingly popular as stopover points for cruise liners, which drop anchor in the same sheltered points between the islands where once the pride of the Royal Navy could have slung their hooks, and provide the boatmen with the unexpected bounty of ferrying the hundreds of passengers ashore; although, unlike in San Francisco, Honolulu or Sydney, the ships tend not to stay for long, especially if it's raining.

The one part of the islands all the cruise passengers want to visit is the seventeen acres that make up the famous gardens on Tresco, and even though I am no horticulturist, this doesn't surprise me at all. The gardens are a frost-free haven for over 20,000 exotic plants, many from South Africa, Australasia and South America, most of which could never survive on the mainland. Mark Praeger tells me he once had a holiday on Madeira which was a great disappointment because he had already seen all the plants there back home on Scilly. The first time I walked beneath the towering palms of the Bridge Walk, I suddenly realised that there was nothing whatsoever around me that could contradict a hypothesis that I had been sucked up into a time-machine and spat out in some remote corner of Peru or Malaysia. The gardens are fantastic.

This afternoon we are on *Wizard*, speeding past a large, white cruise ship anchored in the Road full of passengers who—although they don't know it yet—will shortly be witnesses to one of the most bizarre ceremonies Father Guy has ever had to conduct.

We are greeted at the harbour at New Grimsby by Mike Nelhams, the curator of the gardens, a big man with a big personality who became a bit of a legend in the horticultural world when he turned down the offer to present the hugely successful television show *Gardeners' World* because he couldn't bear to be parted for long periods from his beloved Tresco. When he shows us his little house at Valhalla, on the southern perimeter of the gardens, you can see his point; his backyard is full of dozens of beautifully restored figureheads from ships wrecked over the centuries on the treacherous shores of the islands, and beyond that, effectively his own back garden, is the tropical paradise that contains some of the most luxuriant and extraordinary plants in Europe.

The latest addition to the gardens is a diminutive and rather uninspiring little tree that I wouldn't have given a second glance to, especially since it seems to be sprouting some discoloured, brown growth among its thick, green leaves. It turns out to be an extremely rare example of the oldest species of tree on the planet, *Wollemi Nobilis*, and is about ninety million years old. The tree, which was thought to be long extinct, was recently found in a ravine in the Blue Mountains of south Australia and is thought to have survived because forest fires would have passed over it. Two hundred cuttings were taken from it and grown at the botanical gardens in Sydney. The Duke of Cornwall has one of them, at Highgrove, and another one, called Hercules, is here on Tresco.

Cruise passengers have been arriving at the gardens by the boatload, and they've been instructed to gather around Hercules for a moment that will be recorded for posterity by the cruise ship's official photographer and will no doubt take a prominent place in the formal history of the famous Tresco Abbey Gardens.

When Father Guy accepted the post of Chaplain

to the Isles, he never for a moment imagined he would be asked to bless a tree, least of all one of a species that is ninety million years old, but he is slowly learning that here you bend with the wind or falter. In short, it is much better to bless a tree with good grace than sit alone in the Chaplaincy wondering why nobody ever asks you to do anything. Anyway, there is nothing he can find in his theological training that even suggests that a priest should turn down a request to bless a tree.

*   *   *

The gently lapping water is a translucent, azure blue. The tide is low, so the *Scillonian* is coming in on the longer but deeper route south of the islands, up through the Sound, and will dock shortly, unloading its cargo of four hundred and forty-seven passengers, two cars, fifty-eight tyres, a thousand bricks, three tons of cement, two bathrooms, a palm tree, sheet glass, and boxes of shoes, medicine, bread, sports magazines and mulligatawny soup—in short, absolutely everything (save fish and water) required to keep the islanders alive and in some basic comfort.

Almost as soon as the ship slips alongside and the gangplank is lowered, the last six gigs for the weekend's racing are already being unloaded from their stowage on the foredeck, and hundreds more rowers and supporters are streaming off down the quay in a bobbing river of red and yellow waterproofs.

Out by the lifeboat, two beautiful, brightly varnished gig-boats, with huge tricolour flags lazily flapping behind their sterns, are slipping out of the calm of the harbour into the open sea, and I can hear the coxswain urging his fellow Dutchmen to pull faster as they head off towards Nut Rock, off Samson, the traditional start of the racing heats, for a final training session.

At the end of the quay there's an upturned mass of faces, like sunflowers, belonging to the family and friends of holidaymakers still coming off the ship. Behind them, casually leaning against the safety rail, I can just see WPC Nikki Green, the peak of her hat shielding her eyes from the glare of the midday sun, her handcuffs catching the light and blazing a sudden silver as she turns for a moment to glance at the Dutch gigs as they inch out to sea. Last year, Nikki had wanted to join a gig crew, for the companionship more than the fitness regime, but, as so often, had hesitated for fear of the complications facing an island police officer seen to be fraternising too much with the locals.

She systematically scans every passenger as they step down onto the quay, and makes it obvious that she is doing so. As her gaze flicks rapidly from one face to the next, she scarcely has time to clock the good-looking, dark-haired, twenty-five-year-old boy from St Ives, who's here with a full wallet, a handful of good mates, and a much-discussed and extremely well-planned mission to spend the weekend having a good time.

However, as I was soon to discover, he obviously had plenty of time to clock her.

*   *   *

Saturday morning. The conditions are perfect. The

138

coxswains have been briefed up on the green, and beneath the rows of flags fluttering in the breezy sunshine, the pageant begins to unfold on Town Beach, which is suddenly teeming with rowers, husbands, wives and lovers, barefoot children running in the wet sand, pasty-faced babies in hugely expensive beach-friendly buggies being covered with lashings of suncream, and grannies sipping from Thermos flasks on tartan picnic rugs. It's low tide, so the gigs are carted, carried or dragged down to the water, while scores of oarsmen and women stand in patient queues to embark, like soldiers calmly waiting to be rescued from the beaches of Dunkirk.

Darcy is launching *Galatea*, the older of the two St Martin's boats, just below race headquarters with the bulk of the other boats on Town Beach, but her father Toby, and boyfriend Steve, are on the other side of the old lifeboat station, on Porthmellon, bringing down the oldest boat in the gig fleet from her shed at the top of the beach. Their usual boat, the *Dolphin*, built in 1969, has developed a crack in the stern of her keel, so has been ignominiously dispatched to Peter Martin's boatshed at Porthloo for repair, and will miss the whole weekend. The legendary old *Bonnet*, built in St Mawes in 1830 for the pilots on St Martin's, has a name that allegedly comes from an old witch who used to wave her bonnet to give the crews extra strength. She is still able to give the newer gigs like *Nornour* and *Men-a-Vaur*, built following the renaissance in the sport in the 1960s, a run for their money, but, designed in an age when the gigs were workboats, she's broader in the beam than the newer boats and a foot shorter, which gives her an immediate disadvantage.

'It's a great leveller, gig-racing,' Toby's muttering, a huge oar slung over each shoulder. 'Whoever you are, however rich you are or wherever you went to school, once you're in that gig, dear boy, with the same spray coming over the bow and the same rhythm to your stroke, it don't matter a fig.'

Heike is there too. She's joined Malcolm and Liz Martland for a drink on the terrace of the Boatshed Restaurant; they give Toby a wave and toast his luck in the racing. The *Bonnet* slips into the water, the rowers raise and then dip their oars, and the boat starts to pick up speed as the men bend their backs and fall into the cox's rhythm, soon becoming just one of the growing flotilla funnelling towards the harbour entrance for the start of the racing.

Then it happens. One moment, an idyllic, almost perfect scene; the next, it has virtually disappeared. One moment, there is the *Scillonian*, her fresh, white paint gleaming in the May sunshine; the next, she has simply vanished.

The speed with which the fog arrives is extraordinary and, when I have a chance to take in what is happening, quite terrifying. I'm standing right on the water's edge on Porthmellon, and gradually, from somewhere within the great, wet, grey wall of silence that has been blown in so suddenly from the Atlantic, I begin to hear voices and muffled shouts; then the two words everyone on Scilly has been dreading begin to echo around the harbour basin, passing like a baton from boat to boat: 'It's cancelled! Hello there . . . it's cancelled!' Then, emerging like a ghost ship, the silhouette of *Bonnet* gradually takes shape, the men rowing, with long, slow, despondent strokes, back to the shore.

The implications of fog ruining a weekend in which over 2,000 people and 100 gigs have been transported at huge cost across to Scilly could be catastrophic. It's much more than just a spoilt holiday weekend, a waste of months of preparation and a depressing launch to the new season. The big mainland harbours, like Falmouth, which have been plotting to pinch the lucrative Championships away from Scilly, will rejoice to hear this news.

I walk with Toby back up to the boatshed, and we stand around glumly for a bit with Heike. They are both naturally sanguine people, yet even so there is an inescapable feeling of gloom and doom in the air. There is no sound overhead of helicopters and planes arriving and leaving, as could be expected on a sunny spring Saturday; at a stroke, the Isles of Scilly are cut off from the outside world.

8

The Biggest Weekend Of The Year

It's hard to predict the arrival of fog, and almost impossible to gauge how long it may stay. It can last for days, paralysing island life. It can also be extraordinarily localised. From her unique viewing platform over on St Martin's, the terrace of the Seven Stones pub, Liz will be able to see the fog as it rolls in like a thick, dark carpet from the west, first unfolding over St Agnes, then moving across the Sound and engulfing St Mary's.

Liz won't dally to stare at a rapidly diminishing view. With the others away at the rowing, this is the first time she's been in charge behind the bar, and the thought will be making her slightly uncomfortable. After the initial exhilaration of the wedding reception, Liz is finding the work more daunting than she expected. After years as a social worker, often handling difficult or traumatic family crises, I sense she finds the casual informality of pub life awkward.

She's also in charge of the books and finances, which again is less straightforward than she had ever imagined, and although the money's coming in, in these early months it's also draining away fast. Sometimes, I guess, she must feel out of control. Then there's her son, Connor, back with his father in Brighton, instead of being just around the corner now separated from her by a large expanse of the Atlantic, most of which, even more depressingly, is now firmly fog-bound.

Below the bar, in the kitchen, blissfully unaware of anything beyond the walls of his self-imposed prison, Pauly toils away and, unlike Liz, relishes his new responsibilities. The end of the gig weekend is traditionally celebrated by a huge bonfire and barbeque on the beach at Porthmellon on St Mary's, but now Toby and Pauly have cheekily decided to defy convention and organise a rival barbeque on St Martin's. It is, in its own modest way, an audacious plan; Pauly's bought in large supplies of tuna, beef ribs, chicken and lamb specially for the occasion, but success depends on luring over many of the rowers and their supporters from 'the mainland', and if the weather is bad, the experiment is doomed.

Evenings are usually quieter at the Seven Stones, because the big tripper boats have stopped sailing and visitors would have trouble getting back to the other islands. On a good spring evening, pub records reveal that they might shift forty or fifty meals. For Sunday's party, Fraser Hicks has agreed to run a special trip over on *Sea King*, so Pauly is hoping he might pull off about fifty covers, which would seriously dent the opposition and earn him the public condemnation, and probably the sneaking admiration, of the other islands.

Pauly is a classic example of that rare phenomenon, a man who is totally happy in his work, and he is content to labour for long hours to achieve his goals. There is, however, one significant downside to this rigorous approach to his career, which, on this of all weekends, is irking him.

Finding a girlfriend on Scilly, populated by so many single men, is tough enough; finding a girl when your work confines you to a small kitchen and extremely unsociable hours, on the remotest of all the islands, seems impossible.

To make things worse, Toby has been taunting him relentlessly about the high standard of the girls who have been pouring into St Mary's for the rowing, often beautiful girls in the peak of health, who after a hard day's sweat slogging away in the gigs, hit the town showered, smelling like daisies, looking a million dollars and eager for nothing more complicated than a good time.

The fog disappears almost as quickly as it arrived, and suddenly, weirdly, it's a stunning May afternoon. As though a curtain is being delicately drawn across the harbour, first the rocky tip of Newford Island comes into view; then the lifeboat, still reassuringly bobbing at anchor; then the silhouette of the *Scillonian* on the quay. The damp has now instantly evaporated, and the sun is beating down. Relieved race officials declare that the gig-racing can now resume. You sense the whole island is breathing a huge, collective sigh of relief. Toby and Steve help launch the *Bonnet* and, as though nothing untoward had ever happened, set off happily to join the rest of the fleet heading out into the Road.

The races start at St Agnes, or Nut Rock, beside Samson, and all end across a line from the end of St Mary's quay to Newford Island, by the boatyard at Porthloo. Having waved the boys away, I walk around the bay, down the almost deserted Strand and up past the Scillonian Club towards the Town Hall.

There in front of me, on the little Parade which is effectively the village green, an extraordinary scene is being re-enacted, and it's a startling sight.

A couple of days ago, I had picked up a book of photographs taken over generations by the famous Scilly family of Gibson, who have been recording island life in pictures almost since the invention of the camera. One picture has stuck in my mind. It portrays a group of schoolchildren on St Mary's celebrating May Day in 1876. All dressed in white and bedecked in flowers, they are dancing around a maypole under the proud gaze of teachers and parents alike. They are on the Parade, which is surrounded by dilapidated houses, and the clothes of the onlookers reflect the relative poverty of the islands in the latter half of the nineteenth century. Yet there is something defiantly optimistic about the image; everyone is smiling. This is, after all, a celebration, despite the circumstances.

As I enter the Parade from the Lower Strand, I find myself standing in exactly the same position as that photographer 130 years ago, witnessing almost exactly the same scene. There's the maypole, with little children all dressed in white holding the coloured ribbons hanging down from it, dancing and singing traditional island May Day songs. There are Rosebud, Buttercup and Violet. Butterfly, loaded down with garlands of flowers, is masquerading as the May Queen, attended by the strewers who scatter petals in her path. This is not just a Victorian scene, it is medieval, and for a moment I wonder if I'm hallucinating. Later, when I relate this to Fraser Hicks, he scratches his head, bemused by my reaction.

'Well, we all done that, every child on the island,' he says. I'm trying to imagine the young Fraser Hicks dressed all in white, scattering petals around Butterfly's feet. 'It was my dad's job to sit on the base of the maypole to stop it falling over!' I walk on down Hugh Street, also unusually quiet, and find Father Guy among the huge crowd thronging the end of the quay for the end of the first race. He is clearly taken aback by what really is a dramatic spectacle.

'When the sun's out, I can't help but think how lucky I am to be here,' he says. Then, after a

145

pause, he repeats, slightly ominously, 'When the sun's out.'

For such a small community, the sheer number of people involved is extraordinary. As well as the crowd on the quay, there are people crammed onto the grassy ramparts of the sixteenth-century breastwork and battery walls of the Garrison beneath Star Castle, some astride the old cannons that guard the southern approaches to the harbour, and the lines of spectators continue to snake all the way around the Garrison parapets to Woolpack Point, overlooking St Agnes. There are even groups, silhouetted by the dropping sun, standing right out in the water, on rocky outcrops like the Barrel of Butter and Doctor's Keys, like rows of soldiers standing by to repel an invading fleet.

The gigs themselves are an awesome sight, a long flotilla of thirty-foot boats, each black, backlit rower using his entire body in long, slow, deep strokes, for all the world like a flotilla of marauding Viking raiders, skimming across the waves in a synchronised unity that sailors through the centuries would have recognised, understood and admired. Following at a respectful distance are every available tripper and fishing boat, press-ganged into service and packed to the gunwales.

The Royal Navy are also here today, as part of the Championships festival, always keen to keep up relations with England's most south-westerly outpost, guardian of the Western Approaches to the Channel. HMS *Quorn*, a minesweeper made of fibreglass so it can handle magnetic mines, is anchored in the Road, looking splendid. It's equipped with two remote-controlled yellow submarines with cameras, like something out of a Bond film, which hunt for mines on the seabed. Amazingly, the *Quorn* has located and destroyed two Second World War German mines in the last year alone.

On the quay, one of the Association boats is filling up with the great and good of Scilly for a reception on board the *Quorn*, to watch the last of the day's racing over a pink gin or two. There are councillors, representatives of the Duchy, tourist board and school, a doctor from the health centre, farmers from each of the five islands, boatmen, the harbourmaster and Father Guy and Kate.

I haven't seen such a formal gathering on Scilly before, the men startled and self-conscious in jackets and ties, the women in a colourful assortment of dresses which look as though they haven't been out of their wardrobes for quite a while. It has the air of a 1960s cocktail party at the Chelsea Flower Show. I sense that these are the people Father Guy, standing out in his dog collar, finds the most difficult: the decision-makers, the policy-formers, the confident movers and shakers, around whom ebb and flow the intricacies of island politics. As the boat leaves the quay and heads out into the Road, Father Guy has the look of a man who'd much rather be down at the Mermaid.

Over on the Green, a dishevelled, patient queue has been in place outside the marquee for most of the day, and now the colours of their textbook uniforms of anoraks, denim shorts and deck shoes are melting together in the dying rays of the sun. Inside, Alison Guy has taken precious time off from her new herd of Belgian Blue calves up at Longstone Farm, and with her merry band of

147

helpers is sweating it out over a vast, aluminium, industrial-sized cooker, their damp, ruddy faces occasionally disappearing in great clouds of steam which waft up from the bubbling frying pans of eggs, bacon, sausages and burgers—anything that will fill the cholesterol-starved bellies of the exhausted crews, soon to be staggering up the beach.

Outside, a crowd is gathering beneath a man with a large clipboard and a bright-red felt-tip clamped between his teeth who is balancing precariously at the top of a large stepladder so he can write up the long list of placings on the results' board.

By the time the elegant elm hulls of the last gigs slide gracefully onto the sand on Town Beach, there is a sharp chill in the air. It's low water, approaching springs, so the full curve of the huge beach is exposed, dissected into thin slices by the scores of mooring ropes which run down to the tenders and smaller boats that ring the landward side of the harbour. All along the shore is the sight of the abandoned, beached gigs, oars akimbo, and the hundreds of crew, laughing with exhilaration, arms over shoulders or hand-in-hand, smiling in congratulation, everyone light-headed with the sheer camaraderie of it all. Already many are indulging in the vitally important gig tradition of uncorking bottles of port; men and women, young and old, down the contents as though they've had nothing to drink for a week. It's a true celebration of effort, of will, of achievement and—above all— of companionship, a coming-together eagerly anticipated all year, to be remembered and relived long after summer is gone.

*   *   *

Unusually for these recent sun-blessed weeks, the closing evening of the gig weekend brings a freshening breeze and a high flotilla of ominous, dark clouds that are scurrying in from the north-west along with a smattering of rain. At first sight, this bodes ill for Toby's plans for a barbeque to rival St Mary's, but, rather to my surprise, *Sea King*, as it heads off to St Martin's, is almost full of people who have turned their backs on the traditional celebrations in favour of a spin at the Seven Stones. I've noticed before that on the Isles poor weather brings out a strange camaraderie, almost a party atmosphere, that you rarely see when it's warm and sunny. I'm looking out for a particular familiar face, but I can't see her.

At the pub, the visitors have been joined by a large group of islanders, and such is the crowd that it takes a moment to check out who's there. Liz is smiling with relief at having successfully held the fort throughout the weekend. Toby and Steve, who, despite the shortcomings of the *Bonnet*, managed to come in a respectable forty-ninth in the fleet of one hundred boats and therefore are in the top half of the list—just—are already getting started on some serious assaults on a barrel of Scuppered.

Pauly, for once released from his prison in the kitchen, labours like a Trojan at a fiery barbeque at the far end of the marquee. This is a perfect opportunity to eye up the talent, but Pauly is too much the professional; he's just too busy. I had assumed he would have pre- or at least par-cooked

149

most of the meat in the face of so many people, but no, each order is meticulously discussed and painstakingly cooked, precisely to each individual's requirement. I still can't believe this guy is only twenty-two years old. After three hours sweating at the stove, Pauly proudly reveals to a delighted and slightly unsteady Toby that he's cooked one hundred and fifty meals, far exceeding the fifty they had hoped for, a new pub record. But by this time, sadly, the place has emptied, and there's not a girl in sight.

At midnight, back on Porthmellon Beach, there's a huge bonfire, and later there will be dancing. The long lines reflected from the yellow lights on the quay lurch crazily in the choppy water of the harbour. The rain clouds have blown through and a half-moon hangs over Buzza. I again scan the faces, glowing orange from the flames.

In a place where it's not easy to hide, WPC Nikki Green, single lady, famous, at least among some, for her off-duty partying, hasn't been seen all day.

* * *

In the north-east corner of St Mary's, the little A3110 breaks off and snakes up towards Higher Trenoweth. There's a pond close by, but, due to the almost total lack of traffic, the ducks and their ducklings spend most of the day on the road, basking in the sunshine. Just behind this, hidden away out of sight, stands a small and rather beautiful Duchy farmhouse. You would never know by looking at it, but the low barn at the back

150

of the house contains the legendary Ales of Scilly brewery, which in its short existence has earned itself a much-loved role in island life. Unsurprisingly, this was one of the first places Father Guy visited on his arrival.

On this Bank Holiday Monday morning, following the revelries and excesses of 2,000 gig-rowers and supporters who knew they'd not have the chance to do this again for a whole twelve months, not much is moving on the island. The exception is at the Ales of Scilly brewery, proprietor M. Praeger Esq., former teacher.

For sixteen years, Mark Praeger was deputy head at the primary school at Carn Gwaval, but at the height, or rather the depth, of the school's problems, he decided to quit in order to pursue a dream he'd had ever since being praised by his chemistry teacher for brewing a fine pint of beer, aged thirteen. He had some second-hand vats and brewing equipment shipped over on the ferry and set about creating a new, stress-free business, producing a fine range of beers—Natural Beauty, Maiden Voyage and Old Bustard, as well as Scuppered—which, literally, went down extremely well with the locals and inevitably led to endless questions about why on earth he'd not made the move before.

Mark's now supplying the island pubs with up to forty casks of beer each week, and this weekend has been the best he's ever had on Scilly. Outside the barn at the back of his farmhouse, he's heaving four casks with the words 'Seven Stones, St Martin's' chalked on them up onto the back of his rusty blue pick-up truck, and soon he's off up to Higher Newford and the Telegraph, then down to

Porthmellon, along Town Beach, the Strand and the deserted streets of town and out onto the cobbled quay. He's delighted with the news that Toby and Liz have got the pub and that he has another secure outlet for his beer. In a sense, he sees Toby as a kindred spirit; they are a similar age and share similar aspirations.

At the end of the empty quay, he carefully unloads each cask, ever-conscious of their weight and his age, and rolls them across to the collection point for the *Lyonesse Lady*, which later will ship them over to the Higher Town quay on St Martin's for Toby or Ian to collect in the old pub lorry.

Mark pauses and looks out across the still, early-morning light of the harbour. The lifeboat bobs reassuringly in the eddy from the falling tide. Behind lie the big, open tripper boats, empty and looking strangely incongruous, the day's work not yet started. Catching the morning sun in the distance, heading home from three days at sea, is Martin Bond's bright-red trawler, *Marauder*, followed by a growing flock of hungry seagulls. A tractor suddenly arrives on the quay and growls slowly up towards him; Mark smiles and waves. Justin is pulling the first of the gigs back up for the *Scillonian* to take home. It'll take him another four weeks to clear them all.

Outside the Mermaid, empty Ales of Scilly casks are scattered in a group by the side door to the kitchen, and Mark, relieved that there are so many, loads them up carefully, one by one, anxious about his back. He came to Scilly when he was nineteen years old and still never takes the place for granted. He intends, he says with pride, to spend every day of the rest of his life here. That,

152

though, depends on the success of a plan Mark has spent years working on to secure the long-term future of the brewery, a plan he is about to put into action.

*   *   *

Later, I track down a bashful and very giggly WPC Nikki Green. With the incisive clarity of Hercule Poirot, I am able to piece together the key moments of her weekend, quite a feat when she is obviously so deliriously happy as to be rendered almost inarticulate. It's actually an attractive trait, that inability or even desire to hide or disguise her excitement, which just tumbles out of her unchecked, like water from a fountain.

The sequence of events I have established so far is as follows:

1) Friday. WPC Nikki Green greets the arrival of the *Scillonian III*, on which is a twenty-five-year-old, single Cornishman called Andrew, over with some mates for the gig-racing. He notices her, but, inexplicably for a keen young bobby with an eye for a handsome lad, she fails to notice him. She later admits to 'thinking about something else', but can't remember what.

2) Saturday. Nikki, off-duty, spends all day in the pubs and gets completely pie-eyed. She ends up in the Mermaid with PCSO Shirley, spots Andrew at the bar talking to a rower she knows, tells Shirley she thinks he's 'eeashy on th' igh', seizes this unique opportunity and totters over to join in the conversation.

3) Andrew offers to buy Nikki a drink. Nikki, strictly off-duty and swaying slightly, says she's had

153

so much cider and vodka she can't drink any more. Despite this, Andrew continues to talk to her. They agree to meet the following morning.

4) Sunday. Andrew and Nikki spend all day together in the sunshine, watching the gig-racing from the boats. She discovers he's a council gardener working in St Ives. He discovers she looks as good out of uniform as in it—so to speak.

5) Monday. A tearful Nikki waves Andrew off home on the *Scillonian*.

6) Tuesday. After persistent questioning, WPC Nikki Green is eventually forced to confess that she is in love.

Quite how a relationship between two working people separated by such a large slice of the Atlantic Ocean can be sustained isn't yet clear. Word is, though, that after working so hard to get back to Scilly, WPC Nikki Green is now starting to count off the days until she can return to the mainland.

*   *   *

Because there were so many terrible shipwrecks on the tangled mass of treacherous reefs and rocks between St Agnes and Bishop Rock, many of them merchant vessels bound for London or Liverpool from America, in 1890 it was decided to build a lifeboat station beside the little church at Periglis, just down the track from the Hicks's farm at Troytown on St Agnes. It's still there today, almost entirely blocking the spectacular view from the church over the lovely harbour and Burnt Island to the wild, windswept bird sanctuary of Annet beyond.

The island crew available to man the new lifeboat had predictable surnames, and included Abraham James Hicks, his son James Thomas Hicks, William Thomas Hicks, Freddie Cook Hicks, Obadiah Hicks, William Francis Hicks, Albert Hicks, Stephen Lewis Hicks and Fred Hicks—along with some poor sod called Walter Long. The boat, still powered only by oar and sail and launched into the harbour on a complicated set of iron rail tracks, was heavy and cumbersome on the water. Despite the huge expense of the project, it soon became clear that the seaworthy little pilot gigs, which often had small lug sails which could be rapidly hoisted and lowered as required, were far more agile and able to manoeuvre between the jagged rocks, and were therefore a much better bet.

With a hint of pride in his voice, and for once deadly serious, Fraser Hicks tells the story of a seven-masted American schooner called the *T.W. Lawson*, the largest commercial ship in the world, which struck Annet in a storm in 1907 and was rapidly smashed to pieces. At daybreak the next morning, with the gale still blowing, the island men went to Periglis, in a gig called the *Slippen* rather than the lifeboat, to see if they could find any survivors. Most of the twenty-seven crew of the *Lawson* had drowned, but the captain and engineer were alive, clinging to rocks on Hellweathers, a small island just south of Annet. It was impossible for *Slippen* to get in to rescue the men in the huge seas, so Freddie Cook Hicks went over the side with a rope and swam to the men, who were hauled back to *Slippen*. The gig's crew were decorated with a gold medal by the American

Government, which also gave Freddie Hicks an inscribed, gold hunter watch for his courage.

On this, the final morning of the gig weekend, a handful of gigs still equipped with sails takes to the harbour, a silent tribute to those gigmen of old, for the traditional sailing race which marks the end of the Championships. The strangely shaped red sails look ungainly compared to modern rigs, almost primitive, but the boats whip across the water, quickly picking up speed, and it's suddenly obvious why they were so useful in an emergency.

While the gigs are beating out into the Road, up behind the Star Castle on the summit of the Garrison a large crowd is gathering by the football pitch. Scilly is home to the world's smallest football league, made up of only two teams—the Garrison Gunners and Woolpack Wanderers— each team thereby standing a fifty per cent chance of triumphantly taking home the trophy at the end of the season. Today, though, Father Guy, Kate, Heike and Sammy have joined the others to watch an unusual game of rugby, much talked about in the days leading up to the weekend: the Isles of Scilly versus the Rest Of The World, a scratch team made up of gig-rowers over for the Championships who are not too hungover to struggle into a pair of shorts.

A player who stands out on the home team is one of the best-known young characters on Scilly: Nathan Woodcock, a huge, blond bear of a man, a real athlete, who hurls himself into the game and any opponents in his way with a characteristic, boundless energy. Nathan is the engineer on the St Mary's lifeboat, at just twenty-three the only island man to be a full-time, salaried member of the

RNLI crew. He is also a prized gig-rower and had been training rigorously, twice a day, in the run-up to the Championships, so he is at the peak of fitness. A few months ago, after a reckless, heavy evening in the Mermaid, he and Martin Bond's son Joel, along with two friends, announced that they intended to row across the Atlantic, in a race scheduled to start in New York next July and end here on Scilly, at Bishop Rock. Some thought the boys would retract their pledge in the cold light of day, but no, not a bit of it, and recently the specially designed yellow rowboat, complete with two rowing seats, a tiny, watertight cabin and solar panels, has arrived on the *Scillonian*. I noticed that Nathan, proudly holding his new baby, Megan, was pictured with the others by the boat on Town Beach in a recent article by Clive Mumford in The *Cornishman*.

After the rugby game, we all troop back down the hill, past the moated entrance to the Star Castle, to the Mermaid, where the fiercely fought contest in the field is re-enacted, this time in a beer-drinking competition. The players line up in two rows, each armed with a pint of Mark Praeger's Scuppered; at the given signal, the first man in each team downs the beer as fast as he can and places the dripping glass on his head the moment he has finished, which is the cue for the next man to do the same. The pubs have been really busy this weekend for the first time this year; today the Mermaid is so full of young people I have to stand on a table by the door which leads down the stairs to the Gents', through which a succession of competitors rush after doing their duty, most returning after a few minutes looking

157

rheumy-eyed and a ghastly shade of pale.

It's hard to imagine, looking around at so many faces brimming over with fun, laughter and spilt beer, that many of the island youngsters here would be technically classified on the mainland as homeless; the pubs, the only places many of them can meet and talk, are effectively their living rooms. The likes of Sam Hicks over at Troytown, whose house was the first to get planning permission on St Agnes for over twenty years, is much the exception. Sam also had the advantage of being able to bring equity over from the sale of his house in Southampton, but even so, he is still a homeowner with one arm tied behind his back. He paid for the house to be built, but the Duchy own the land, for which Sam must pay a monthly rent, and the house reverts to Duchy ownership on his death; he can never sell it, or even leave it to his daughter, Isla. Given the paucity of work on Scilly, it is little wonder that most youngsters never even consider a future on the islands of their birth. After the drinking games, the singing gets underway, and soon everyone is beating out the sea shanties. It's clear that this closing scene of an exhilarating weekend, an unashamed, boisterous celebration of island life, is developing into quite a session. One of the perennial favourites in the Mermaid is a shanty called 'Cornwall, My Home'.

I've stood on Cape Cornwall in the sun's evening glow,
On Chywoone Hill at Newlyn to watch the fishing fleets go.
Watched the sheave wheels at Geevor as they

158

spun around,
And heard the men singing, as they go underground.

And no-one will ever move me from this land,
Until the Lord calls me to sit at his hand.
For this is my Eden, and I'm not alone.
For this is my Cornwall, and this is my home.

Looking around, I'm struck by the thought that wherever they end up in the world, these young people have one huge advantage over the rest of us. Scilly must be a wonderful place to come home to.

And there, in the midst of them, singing with all his heart, is the towering figure of Nathan Woodcock, a picture of good health and, I have no doubt everyone here would agree, a worthy symbol of hope for the future of the islands.

First thing in the morning, on Chapel Carn Brea,
And gaze at the Scillies in the blue far away.
For this is my Cornwall, and I'll tell you why,
Because I was born here, and here I shall die.

9

The Entrepreneurial Spirit

Lorries are few and far between on St Mary's, but this morning a convoy of no less than three of them, almost the entire island fleet, is rumbling out of Hugh Town, up towards Rocky Hill, then past the Telegraph tower and down east, turning left just before the duck pond and the ducklings basking on the warm tarmac, gingerly edging through the narrow, tight track to Higher Trenoweth and the lovely old farmhouse that is home to Mark Praeger and his Ales of Scilly Brewery.

For the last few days, Mark has been preparing for what, in the Scilly world of micro-business, is an epic move. The core of the brewery is made up of four big timber-clad fermentors, a 'copper' for boiling the wort and a 'mash tun' for mashing the grist, or grain, which Mark actually climbs into when it needs cleaning. Each of the tanks is about six foot high and made of stainless steel. Somehow he and Mollie have managed between them to heave them out of the barn, where they now await a rather special collection.

On the first of the lorries in the convoy, now parked in a row on the other side of the barn, is an extendable crane, which is operated by a guy with a remote-control panel strapped to his chest; it's the largest crane on Scilly. At the press of a button, the arm of the crane stretches out, like the limb of a huge ballet dancer, and slowly edges right over the roof of the barn, dipping down a little on the other side, so that long straps can be dropped down and attached to the first tank. Mollie's taking photographs, and Mark, who's had nightmares about the tanks crashing through the roof of the barn, killing and maiming large numbers of people, has his fist stuffed into his mouth. The tank, swinging gently in the breeze, is slowly airlifted high into the sky, back across the roof and down onto the back of one of the waiting lorries.

Faced with limited opportunities, island people need to be financially imaginative, constantly coming up with new ideas to earn money, brave enough to take risks, if they are to survive. The path back to the mainland is littered with the stories of people, once full of hope, who have fallen victim to complacency, the island disease.

Sales of Mark's range of beers have been steadily growing year by year, so now the brewery is in danger of outgrowing the barn at Higher Trenoweth. But more importantly, Mark is also a Duchy tenant, so although he has a business, it is not one he can ever sell. Because of this, he's taking the biggest gamble since deciding to quit teaching; he's borrowed every penny he can raise and bought, freehold, a unit on the little industrial estate on the edge of Hugh Town, behind Porthmellon Beach. Hidden well away from the eyes of the holidaymakers, there's a wholesalers, garden-equipment shop, car-repair workshop (even though cars on St Mary's don't need an M.O.T. certificate), boat-builders, Fraser's sister-in-law Oriel Hicks's stained-glass gallery, and now a small brewery. It's certainly not as pretty as the

161

farmhouse, but it's a business, and Mark owns it. All he has to do now is sell enough beer to keep up the repayments as well as make a living.

Other modest entrepreneurs in other parts of the islands are also, largely unseen, hard at work. There is a small range of shops on St Mary's; apart from Steve the butcher and Mumfords, there's a chemist in Hugh Town, a Post Office, the Co-op stores, a newly opened delicatessen and four clothes shops, mostly selling designer yachtwear; but, strangely for such a seafaring community, there's no fishmonger.

Just down from Higher Trenoweth, in one of Alison Guy's barns on Longtone Farm in the middle of St Mary's, trawlerman Martin Bond is spending more and more of his time as a dedicated landlubber. It's turning out to be a promising spring for catches, and with Joel regularly hauling in bulging nets on *Marauder*, Martin, too, is making a radical new investment for the future. When eventually he allows me to see his new project, it's not, at first, immediately clear what it is. Martin's not a great help.

'There we are, what do you make of that?' he asks, rolling his Golden Virginia tobacco. Martin is always rolling tobacco.

'What is it?'

'Wreck of the *Hesperus*!' says Martin, which doesn't take us forward much. As well as rolling tobacco, Martin talks in riddles.

On one side of the barn is an open, fibreglass boat, which Martin, a fibreglass expert from one of his numerous previous incarnations, is busy restoring for his grandson. On the other side is a large rectangular box on wheels. This turns out to be a decrepit old mobile fish van Martin bought on the Internet for a pittance and has had shipped over from the mainland.

He pulls up the wooden window which takes up one side of the van and props it open. Inside, it's completely empty. A section of plywood is hanging down from the roof.

'Like a glove on a chicken's lip,' says Martin, lighting up and virtually disappearing in a cloud of smoke.

He'll be doing all the renovation work himself, of course—lashings of fibreglass on the floor and in the corners and all the electrics and plumbing. He's already acquired an old steel sink and row of taps, which used to belong to the Turks Head pub on St Agnes and which now leans against a cobwebbed corner of the barn. With the help of one of the waitresses down at the Dibble and Grub, Imogen, who has an eye for design, says Martin, the van will be painted red and white, like *Marauder*, with a picture of the boat and 'M. and J. Fresh Fish' proudly stencilled on the front.

'Keeping it simple,' says Martin, licking the paper of another cigarette and sticking it in his mouth. 'As well as the hotels and restaurants, there's plenty of self-catering out there, as well as all the locals. And when there's no fish, it stays in the barn. No overheads, no nothing.'

'Lot of work.'

'No problems; fresh out of tears.'

There is, however, one small hurdle to overcome. Even though Martin will tow his mobile fish shop down to the town each evening on the back of his van, it still needs planning permission from the Council to the Isles of Scilly, based in the

163

Old Wesleyan Chapel. This is by no means a foregone conclusion. Planning issues are probably the most controversial on Scilly, and every new application is usually followed by a deluge of objections.

'We travel in hope,' says Martin. 'Ain't no other choice.'

Steaming up to St Martin's on the *Lyonesse Lady*, meanwhile, is a cargo en route to Toby the baker which may, in a similar way to Martin Bond and Mark Praeger, help improve his fortunes too, but which, at first sight, is not at all what it appears to be.

In Toby's ruthless pursuit of achieving total self-sufficiency for the Seven Stones pub, one key element has remained missing. Following the startling success of the pub in its opening few weeks, however, Toby has decided to risk plundering some of the pub's hard-earned income to try to redress the balance and thus complete the final piece of his master plan. In the last few days, Toby, Pauly, Ian and some of the other island lads have been at work in the field hidden away up the hill behind the pub, sweating away with posts, fencing, spades, sheets of timber, sledge-hammers and a chainsaw, constructing what they hope will be a scaled-down version of Colditz, the inescapable Bavarian fortress.

The cargo which is even now crossing a choppy Crow Bar is contained in a small cattle truck which is strapped to the deck of the *Lyonesse*, and a hint as to its nature is revealed by the occasional appearance of a small, pink snout against the bars of the truck and muted grunts from deep within.

The epic journey from the farm in North

164

Devon, down to Penzance and across to St Mary's on the Grim Reaper, and thence to Higher Town Quay has been long and arduous for Toby's newly acquired five Gloucester Old Spots, but the final mile might be the toughest yet. Once on the quay, the pigs must somehow be moved out of the cattle truck, into a pen on the back of Ian's lorry, then up the hill to the pub, where they need to be unloaded and by some method not yet devised transported up the footpath and into the high-security compound of Colditz. Gloucesters are very tasty, but have an uncanny ability to spot any opportunity to make a run for it; as piglets yet to be fattened up, they also have a fearsome reputation for travelling across rough terrain at very high speeds.

*   *   *

There has been an air of tension around the Isles of Scilly's secondary school, overlooking the harbour on St Mary's. Grim-looking teachers have been arriving early and leaving late; Fraser's wife Julie Hicks, the school secretary, has told her husband to cook his own dinners for the foreseeable future; the 250 pupils have been instructed to smarten up or else; and, most ominously, the lights have been burning very late every night in the office of the inscrutable headmaster, Andrew Penman.

Nearly two years ago now, Andrew made the tough decision to give up his job, his beautiful house overlooking Lyme Regis in Dorset and, in fact, his entire life, and wave goodbye to his family, friends and neighbours, some of whom he may not be seeing again for years, move his wife and five children lock, stock and barrel over to Scilly and take over an ailing school that had only recently emerged from special measures.

The standards of teaching on Scilly have always been high. One of the great names that constantly stands out in history books about Scilly is the philanthropist Augustus Smith, who bought the lease of the islands from the Duchy for £20,000 in 1834 and set about improving the lives of his impoverished islanders with an almost religious zeal. It was the phenomenally wealthy Augustus who built Abbey House on Tresco, where his descendants, the Dorrien-Smiths, now live, and it was he who created the famous Abbey Gardens, built new quays and roads and saved Scilly from unimaginable poverty by introducing the revolutionary concept of taking advantage of the balmy climate to grow and export flowers to brighten up the dark, wintry homes of the rest of Britain.

Augustus believed education was the key to the future of the islands, and he made going to school on a daily basis compulsory for the island children more than forty years before the same happened on the mainland. He even bribed the children to attend, charging them one penny if they came to school and two if they didn't, an extraordinary idea in the strictly moral, claustrophobic world of the Victorians. On each island, the schools, in the main, thrived, and where tiny classes would have closed schools on the mainland, here there was no choice but to keep them open, so the islanders enjoyed some of the best pupil/teacher ratios in the world.

The problem in more recent years has, inevitably, revolved around the housing and retaining of teachers in a small, remote community where the cost of accommodation can be equivalent to that of London. Teachers would arrive to check out Scilly, often on a sunny day, fall for the place, take the job and then would frequently watch helplessly as their lives started to fall apart. Often trapped in poorly equipped, hugely expensive flats or small cottages, the spouses of the teachers usually fell victim to chronic boredom and powerful feelings of isolation, often leading to depression. Many were back on the ferry within months.

Old Augustus had been right 150 years ago: make a mess of education on Scilly and you mess with the whole future of the islands.

What was required, above all, was a period of stability. Under emergency measures, funds were made available to ease the accommodation crisis. The main secondary school on St Mary's and the four small primary schools on the off-islands were federated into one unit, Five Islands School, for which a new headteacher was now being sought, who would take overall control of education on Scilly and upon whose shoulders the expectations of the community would rest.

Andrew was a teacher of thirty years' experience who had reached an age when he either found a new challenge or adventure or slipped away gently into the long-term preparation of plans for retirement. What seemed to swing it for him was the provision of an utterly charming, subsidised Duchy cottage, hidden away above Porthloo, with spectacular views over Hugh Town and west across the Road to the twin peaks of Samson and its breathtaking sunsets, and Bryher and Tresco beyond. He and Bryony bought a little sailing boat, which they keep on the beautiful beach at the end of the garden, and set about growing their own vegetables and potatoes. The children swam, sailed, played guitars on the terrace and set up camps, in an idyllic, Enid Blyton way, while Andrew set about tackling one of the most difficult tasks in education.

Now, eighteen months later, Andrew's labours—his long hours, sweat and, yes, sometimes tears—are about to be put to the test. A team of OFSTED officials is on its way to Scilly from the Department of Education for a major inspection of Five Islands School, specifically its progress, or otherwise, since being placed in emergency measures.

*   *   *

In 1917, the Admiralty, in its wisdom, decided to build a seaplane base by the harbour at New Grimsby on Tresco, in the face of the growing threat of U-boat attacks in the Western Approaches. Their timing wasn't good. By the time the base was effectively up and running, the First World War had ended, so it never saw military action. The long concrete slip running down into the water where the seaplanes were loaded and unloaded is still there. Some of the original engineering and administrative buildings were converted into storage depots and the offices of the headquarters of the Tresco estate.

Now, in what the estate promises will be the

final phase of any development on the island, the old seaplane site is being redeveloped into a luxury holiday complex, complete with twelve new timeshare homes, a restaurant, bar, sauna, jacuzzi, tennis courts, a gym, steam room and a swimming pool, which, I guess, has not made Mr Dorrien-Smith the most popular of men with many of the locals, but as it seems to me that most dare not speak their views, we shall probably never know.

Much of the building supplies and equipment for the project came over from the mainland in a single, huge shipment last year, on a carefully selected and particularly high spring tide. All the boats moored in New Grimsby were moved out, and, when there was a suitable break in the weather, a specially chartered, flat-bottomed coaster, loaded down with almost everything required to build an entire community, slipped into the quay on the highest point of the tide. With almost every able-bodied man on the island press-ganged into service, working through the night, the ship, resting on the sand at low tide, was entirely emptied by the time the incoming tide re-floated her twelve hours later. From then on, work progressed rapidly, and already the skeletons of the houses in the first phase, surrounded by a mass of scaffolding and ladders, are changing the familiar outline of the landscape on the approach to Tresco from the south.

Developments on the old seaplane base at New Grimsby are being closely monitored from across the water, by a couple living on the other side of the neighbouring island of Bryher, Richard and Caroline Pearce, who live in the most inspirational location I have ever seen.

169

Richard and Caroline are an interesting example of the 'adapt or die' principle adopted by the most successful Scillonians. They live in a remote, whitewashed Duchy cottage that sometimes looks as though it's come straight from the pages of a Grimm fairytale, just down from the wild and notorious Hell Bay and looking straight out onto the myriad outcrops of Norrard Rocks, where the seals give birth to their pups; beyond is the Atlantic ocean, next stop America.

I can't think of a more desirable place to operate a cottage industry. The small, solid front door sensibly faces away from the sea, and there are cans of fuel for the quad bike stacked by it. Caroline wins me over immediately by offering a jug of Pimms, even though it's only eleven o'clock, and takes me through the small, exotic garden at the back to collect eggs in the chicken run, where the hens have the finest view of any in Britain, but run the risk of being washed away from time to time when a big sou'westerly storm hits nearby Merrick Island, sending spray and sometimes even waves right over the roof of the house. The joy of living in this place, says Caroline, is only interrupted infrequently by rabid dreams of pushing a trolley around a well-stocked supermarket.

At the rear of the garden, beneath the obligatory pittosporum, which shelters the tender plants from the raw Atlantic wind, is a wooden workshop; it turns out that Caroline is a seamstress, and spends hours each week poring over a sewing machine, making curtains and cushions for the Island Hotel and the holiday cottages on the Tresco estate. She's helped by her daughter, Helen, who's recently moved back to Scilly after acquiring a husband in Australia, and has now moved into an estate cottage over the Sound at New Grimsby. Helen has clearly inherited the family flair for flexibility; she's just started lessons teaching English to the growing number of Polish workers employed by the Dorrien-Smiths.

Caroline is awaiting news of the really big prize. The estate is currently considering awarding contracts for the interior decorating of the new development on the seaplane base. Caroline hopes she is high on the list of preferred suppliers of soft furnishings, and if she gets the job, it could underpin her financial security for the next two years. If she doesn't, it'll be a major blow.

After I've downed most of the Pimms, Caroline announces that she has to take some furniture over to Helen on Tresco. I ask which boat she's going on, and she says she's not, she's intending to drive across on the quad.

It turns out that I have visited Richard and Caroline on the highest, and lowest, tide of the year: it's the spring equinox. In the last few days, back on St Mary's, I had noticed sandbags appearing outside the doors and windows of the terraced houses along the top of Town Beach and built into low walls outside the Atlantic and Mermaid. Yesterday evening, I had watched, almost as if hypnotised, the water inching up the quay, until it was only a few feet from coming right over the top of it. The islanders were praying that a northerly didn't suddenly blow up, which would have caused, as so often it had in the past, widespread flooding. The geography of the whole

171

harbour was weirdly reversed: the boats were lifted so high by the sea that they almost blotted out the horizon, dwarfing the harbourmaster's office and the Harbourside Hotel on the quay, buildings which normally dominate the skyline.

Now it is low tide, and as Caroline drives me up past the Hell Bay Hotel and down the hill to Church Quay on the other side of the island, I can see that a strange new landscape has emerged from the depths of the ocean. Where normally there would be half a mile of sea separating Bryher and Tresco, now there is nothing but sand. Steering markers and navigational posts are perched incongruously on the tops of dried-out rocks and outcrops. Huge areas of dark-grey granite that never see the sunshine are suddenly exposed, leaving anemones and shell-creatures cringing in the bright light and sending startled crabs scurrying beneath the seaweed.

Odder still, there are distant figures walking from island to island, on damp sand that in less than six hours will be six metres underwater, meeting friends or relatives midway, hugging or shaking hands, relishing the strange experience, while the boatmen twiddle their thumbs, fuming at the lost revenue. The sun is burning down. I wave goodbye to Caroline as she roars off across the seabed to New Grimsby, a wardrobe strapped to the back of the quad, and she slowly disappears into the shimmering heat of the sand, like a scene from *Lawrence of Arabia*. She has to hurry if she intends to make it back today; the tide has turned and is already starting to slyly creep up from Samson, forming puddles and little rivulets of salt water which bubble through the seaweed like the

172

veins of a river delta.

Later, back at the house, I meet Caroline's husband, Richard. Richard is a true island man, and tells great stories of his ancestors burying booty from shipwrecks in the sand to hide from the Customs men, including, on one occasion, a grand piano, which they later dug up and learnt to play. He once found a computer screen on the beach with a huge fish in it, which must have swum in as a little 'un and just kept growing. He's an utterly charming monster of a man, with wild black hair and beard flecked with grey and a winning, Irish smile. Richard has the real genius of adaptability. He comes from a long line of Scillonian seamen and farmers, including his great-grandfather Moat, who in 1927 was involved in the heroic rescue of twenty-eight Italian sailors from a ship called the *Isabo* that went down on the Scilly Rock in thick fog. A huge fleet of little boats set off to help the stricken ship, but once again it was the gigs that stole the glory. The *Isabo*'s hull was split, filling the water with tons of its cargo of grain, which clogged up the engines of the motorised boats, including the St Mary's lifeboat. The Scilly gigmen who saved the lives of the Italians were each issued with an official letter of thanks from the Italian government. Richard has his great-grandfather's on the wall of his kitchen; it's signed by the junior minister at the Italian Ministry of Marine at the time, one Benito Mussolini.

Richard was a flower farmer and smallholder, but badly injured his back a few years ago when he joined a group of island men pulling up a cargo of pit props that had been washed up on the beach. Caroline, frustrated by his growing boredom and irritation at having to be laid up for months unable to work, bought him a set of children's paints in the hope that they would stop him moaning for a while, whereupon Richard discovered he had a rare and prodigious talent, and was soon turning out paintings of the islands, which sold for respectable prices in a couple of island galleries. Soon his reputation spread beyond the islands, and Richard could, just about, afford to paint full-time, although it's still just as precarious an occupation as any on Scilly. His journey to work each morning is the stuff of commuter fantasy. He walks across the sands of a breathtakingly beautiful, empty bay called Great Par towards Droppy Nose Point, stopping off at the renovated gig shed up on the beach which has become his Golden Eagle studio, where he paints magical Scilly seascapes all day, every day, often moving the easel down onto the sand, the better to contemplate the ever-changing ocean and life in general.

Marketing his pictures, though, is far less straightforward. There are only three ways to come and go on Bryher. The oldest quay is down by the little church, which was built in 1742, and it dries out completely at low tide. Further up the eastern side of the island, overlooking Tresco and the seaplane base, is Anneka's Quay, built in less than a week in the 1980s by Anneka Rice's television production team, which leads visitors up to the tea rooms and the few houses, known as 'The Town', and which is more accessible at low tides. To find Richard's studio, people arriving at either quay must make their way right across the island, keeping the lovely, conical Gweal Hill in their sights until turning left just past the Hell Bay

Hotel and following the path around the bay. When the tide's extremely low, the only way for the tripper boats to get people on to Bryher is to anchor off Rushy Bay, on the southern point of the island, and ferry the passengers in small tenders into the shallow waters, where they are left to wade ashore. From here, the only way to get to 'The Town' is up a footpath which runs right past the Eagle studio. So on very low tides Richard makes a killing, and on other days he's left whistling in the wind, trying to conjure up better and smarter ways of selling and distributing his extraordinary work and fighting off the complacency which has killed off so many other island talents.

*   *   *

Up at the school, Andrew Penman is having a busier, and considerably odder, morning than he'd expected when he woke up in his old fisherman's cottage at Porthloo to see a rainbow streaming right across the Garrison and dropping down into the waters of the harbour. After a snatched breakfast, he says goodbye to Bryony, who now runs the pre-school group down at Carn Gwaval, and his two younger children, Mary and George, who will be joining him later and who have no choice but to have their dad as headteacher, because there's no other school to go to.

Like Richard over on Bryher, Andrew has an idyllic, but marginally more arduous, walk to work, down past the boatyard and the little Isles of Scilly Perfumery, then taking the coast path round past Shark's Pit and the boatsheds on the sweeping beach at Porthmellon.

Now Andrew's locked in his study, broadcasting live to a radio audience across Cornwall. A television crew is sitting sipping coffee outside Julie Hicks's office, waiting their turn for an interview. Julie herself is beaming. She's just taken a call from Clive Mumford, in his office above the newsagent, who wants to speak to Andrew before writing his page for this week's *Cornishman*.

The results of the OFSTED report have been stunning. Andrew had secretly hoped they might be good, but even he is taken aback by the praise lavished on the school by the Department of Education inspectors. Overall effectiveness: outstanding. Efficiency of boarding provision: outstanding. Achievements and standards: outstanding. Personal development and well-being: outstanding. Quality of provision: outstanding. Curriculum and other activities: outstanding. Care, guidance and support: outstanding. For once, I notice, Andrew allows himself a rare, wry smile of satisfaction. 'The Five Islands is an outstanding school and the children and young people educated there are a credit to this unique island community,' says the report. 'The headteacher has the vision and determination to bring about change . . . the pupils are confident, motivated, and enjoy all aspects of their learning.' This must make the school on Scilly, if not the best, then certainly one of the best schools in Britain. Harold Wilson was right; why would anyone want to pay for private education with a school like this on your doorstep?

The report acknowledges one aspect of Five Islands School, however, that is deeply

176

unsatisfactory, one over which the new headteacher has no power whatsoever, but which he pledges all his energy, enterprise and deviousness to overcome.

Andrew takes time out to show me around his shambling, unappealing and echoing cavern of a school building. When it was opened by Wilson in the 1960s, it was regarded as a showcase for the architecture of the future: a glittering cathedral of gleaming oak-cladding, shiny blue panels and acres of glass. I don't know what the islanders thought of it then, but it's hideous now, a crude and inefficient monster that is completely out of character with anything around it. God knows what the Duke of Cornwall makes of it; they probably steer HRH well away from this part of the island. The vast windows turn the classrooms into ovens or refrigerators, depending on the season, the roof leaks and the annual maintenance costs top £100,000. I sense Andrew would like to blow it up.

Up by the netball court, which is hidden away at the top of the hill above the school, Andrew shows me the wonderful, unappreciated view over the harbour and across the Road to Bryher and Tresco, and explains that the site alone is worth millions. He has a dream of a new school on an inland site, just to the north of Old Town, which would incorporate a centre of excellence, maybe for the study of marine life, which would host international conferences through the seasons and attract experts and students to Scilly from all over the world, thereby, at a stroke, revitalising the island economy.

I have a feeling that many of the more spirited

177

islanders I've so far met and admire—Richard and Caroline Pearce, Toby the baker, trawlerman Martin Bond, Mark at the brewery—must like the cut of Andrew Penman's jib. One way or another, I sense, he's going to get his new school, and with it secure a bright new future for the islands.

10

Storm Clouds Gather

After an astonishing spring of almost unbroken sunshine, and just as confident predictions of a summer of heatwaves are being made, it has started to rain on Scilly. The rain keeps coming, day after day, often interspersed with dramatic storms, which at least shake up the atmosphere and can sometimes be exciting, but always returning to the default position of a mere steady drizzle, a thick curtain of saturated grey, with only the occasional torrential downpour or thick fog to relieve the monotony.

Unlike in the city, there is no escape from the unremitting bad weather here, no high buildings or even hills to obscure the colourless wall of rain. The gloom of the sea meets the gloom of the sky without even the hint of a horizon.

This morning, in the absence of anything else to do, I wrap up well in oilies and walk down to the quay on St Mary's. It's just after ten o'clock, and in good weather there can be a thousand visitors jostling to get on the boats to the off-islands at this time. Today there is not a soul outside the little

Association ticket office, and only one boat, Fraser's brother Steve Hicks's *Seahorse*, is moored right at the end of the windswept, rain-drenched quay. I walk slowly down towards the harbourmaster's office. The cobbles on the quay retain little puddles of water, like rock pools, and soon my canvas shoes are sodden. I wave to Steve in the high cabin of *Seahorse*, a boat he designed himself and built seven years ago across the bay in the boatyard at Porthloo, just beneath the Penmans' house. It can carry a hundred passengers, but now I see just eight. This is another day's income lost forever for the boatmen, as well as the off-island cafés and pubs that totally rely on this trade.

I walk back up Hugh Street, towards the beleaguered tourist office. The streets are almost deserted, save for the occasional figure bent into the wind, scurrying from one shop to another. A group of visitors waiting for the airport shuttle, surrounded by suitcases, are gloomily huddled on the porch of the Atlantic Hotel. Outside the offices of the Steamship Company, which are shared by the tourist department, the words chalked on the 'What's On Today' blackboard are illegible, reduced to long streaks of grey.

What do people do when it's raining on Scilly? A long line of damp, mournful holidaymakers queue patiently in the rain outside Mumfords; the scene looks like a black-and-white photo of the grim dole queues of the 1930s Depression. That's what you do when it rains on Scilly; you read the newspapers. There seems to be only one happy face on the entire island. I pass a beaming WPC Nikki Green, on her way to pick up the new

179

boyfriend from the airport. He must be keen; this is his second visit since the gig weekend. Last time, Andrew came on the *Scillonian* and was violently sick.

I have a coffee in the deli opposite Mumfords, which is packed to the gunwales with wet, dejected faces. The smell of the hot coffee is almost overwhelmed by the dank, steamy odour of damp clothes. One family who managed to get a table are busy arguing. They have been here for a week of terrible weather, and the parents can't decide on whether to make a third trip to the museum in Church Street. The children start to cry. Then the mother cries. I want to cry. Someone from another table leans over and helpfully points out that there will be a tea dance beginning at three o'clock this afternoon at the Star Castle, with the Carlton Ritz Tea Dance band in attendance, but this merely prompts another flood of tears.

The forecast does not bode well for the celebrations of the sixtieth birthday party Fraser Hicks has planned for his beloved *Sea King*, which was built two years after the end of the Second World War and, says Fraser, will still be around to see the start of the third. Much to his delight, Fraser's daughter Rebecca has arrived home from working in Australia for nearly a year. She'd flown in on the little eight-seater Skybus aircraft, from the grass landing strip at Land's End that still looks like a temporary wartime fighter base, and announced to Fraser and Julie that she would only be staying a few weeks before returning to a boyfriend in Oz; but that plan, in the face of the surfeit of spring sunshine and Rebecca's obvious delight at meeting up with old friends, seems to have been rapidly abandoned. Last year, Rebecca became the first girl on Scilly to work full-time as a qualified crew on the boats, so now she's back helping out her pa on *Sea King*, reviving Fraser's hopes that one day his only child may take over his beloved boat, and so keep it in the family.

We join *Sea King* on the quay during a rare break in the clouds and a blast of unfamiliar, prickly-hot sunshine. Julie and Rebecca are swabbing down the decks and Fraser, who has 'borrowed' a large pole he's found at the back of the quay by Martin Bond's ice-store, is busy putting up a line of flags from bow to stern.

The plan is that Fraser will take a boatload of friends round to the quay at Old Grimsby, on the north side of Tresco, where we'll meet up with a jazz band and another group of old friends, who are staying at the Island Hotel, among them two mates Fraser's known for years, who are also celebrating their sixtieth birthdays. The whole party will then embark on *Sea King*, along with large quantities of champagne, for a jolly around the uninhabited islands that form a circle around St Helen's Pool, followed by a beach picnic on Tean and dancing in the sand.

It promises to be a great day out, but just as we are rounding Tobaccoman's Point on Tresco, the sun suddenly disappears, an angry sky rises up like a phantom from the horizon and we are the recipients of a most monumental downpour, which Fraser, clad from his neck to his toes in oilies and quite used to such things, finds hugely amusing. Just as I am wondering whether we will have to turn back, the sun is out again, and Julie and Rebecca are once again swabbing the water off the steaming decks. This is unusually bizarre weather, even for Scilly.

Sea King takes us past Great Cheese Rock and Rushy Point, past the Old Blockhouse, which was built in 1554 to protect the approaches to Old Grimsby and the Pool, on by the row of Trinity House cottages that were homes for the men who manned the huge lighthouse on Round Island, the northern tip of Scilly, and into the old stone quay at last. There we are greeted by a colourfully clad crowd armed with an eclectic range of umbrellas, and the jazz musicians who've been brought over to Scilly specially for the occasion, along with their flamboyant singer, Miss Sheila Fawkes, who starts banging out, 'Every time it rains, it rains pennies from heaven'. Soon everyone is joining in.

Just as the champagne is about to be loaded aboard and the musicians start unpacking their instruments, which include trumpet, banjo and an enormous brass tuba, the heavens once again open and there follows the heaviest downfall of rain I think I have ever experienced, of true monsoon proportions, with stair rods so fierce that they bounce off the surface of the flattened sea like bullets from a machine gun. The storm renders us unable to move, let alone speak. It lasts about five minutes, and then, like its less dramatic predecessor, the massive, pitch-black cloud hovering just above moves off quickly, leaving us shell-shocked, with even Miss Sheila Fawkes dazed and unable to think of an appropriate response.

The party on Tean is abandoned, the jazz musicians announcing that they are not prepared to risk their instruments, and therefore their livelihoods, to the mercy of such extreme

182

meteorological conditions; it will now take place in the Island Hotel instead. Fraser, after tightening the elastic straps on his oilies, says that as the worst of the rain has moved on, he'll do a trip around the Pool anyway, so off we all set again, with Miss Fawkes removing her shoes and climbing up to stand on the seat in the middle of *Sea King*; dressed in a full-length, cream evening gown, the wind sweeping back her hair, she looks for all the world like a figurehead on the prow of a seventy-gun ship o' the line. She bashes out 'Blue Skies' with such fortitude that even the seagulls veer off in amazement.

Blue skies, smiling at me,
Nothing but blue skies, do I see.
Blue birds, singing a song,
Nothing but blue birds, from now on.

Never saw the sun shining so bright,
Never saw things going so right,
Noticing the days hurrying by,
When you're in love, my how they fly!

Never can any song have achieved such dramatic, instant results. By the time Miss Sheila Fawkes has made it to the end of the second verse, the clouds are relegated to a distant horizon and the sun beats down with an almost tropical intensity.

Soon we reach that great rock citadel called Men-a-Vaur, its sheer walls of granite rising out of the foaming sea, indeed just like the hull of a fantastic man o' war battleship, its topsails pitted with the nests of the small kittiwake gull, made of mud and saliva, which cling for dear life to the summits of the upper rocks. Fraser explains that these vulnerable birds, living such a precarious existence, produce only a chick or two, which, if fish stocks are low, may well not survive. Besides the gannets plunging fearlessly into the waves in search of food, we are dive-bombed by a squadron of tiny, fluttering puffins, or Scilly parrots as they are known here. The earliest record of a puffin comes from Scilly seven hundred years ago. Through Fraser's binoculars, I have a brief chance to study these extraordinary creatures, which, with their famous orange bills and oddly mascaraed eyes, look like badly made-up comedians. Fraser says that they are a favourite prey of the larger seagulls, which is why they are constantly on the move and hard to photograph. Miss Sheila Fawkes has now stopped singing, and is looking with wonder at the scene before her.

It's a stunning, slightly surreal moment, which in a way represents all that is best about Scilly: the unique natural beauty of the seascape, the fortitude and essential good-humour of its people. When I point this out to Fraser, he gives a little burp, and says, 'Yes, quite. Let's get back to the Island Hotel and have a few drinks.'

*　　　*　　　*

Now the season is well underway, there's a sense that the pace of life is accelerating, with a relentless tide of hundreds of holidaymakers coming and going each week, and the islanders, after Fraser's big party, putting their social lives on hold until the autumn. The summer will be over before they know it, so this is the time to knuckle down and work around the clock, seven days a week, and squirrel away the cash that, with luck, will allow them to see through the winter.

Father Guy's diary is filling too, which after weeks of being holed up in the Chaplaincy not doing too much, must be something of a relief. With the population of Scilly swelling so dramatically, there are a growing number of pastoral calls to make, weddings and baptisms to preside over and soon all the islands will be holding summer fêtes, flower festivals and parish days, all major events in a small community. Most importantly, Father Guy must start preparing for the visit of his boss, Bishop Bill of Truro, who is due to come over shortly to assess Guy's progress.

There are also many, oddly formal, duties that lie in the domain of the Chaplain to the Isles, which Father Guy is now rapidly having to learn. In such a claustrophobic community, first impressions are critical, and Father Guy is desperate to get things right.

John Wesley, the great evangelist and founder of Methodism, visited Scilly in 1743 after a horrendous seven-hour voyage from St Ives, during which he and his followers sought courage in the face of mountainous seas by singing hymns without interruption. A Wesleyan chapel was built in his memory in Garrison Lane in 1790, but by the early twentieth century it had been replaced by a new chapel in Church Street, and by 1935 the building had become what at the time must have been a revolutionary concept in island entertainment: a cinema. This soon replaced the pubs as the place to take a hot date, which is something you can't do now, since there hasn't been a cinema on Scilly for years.

Later, the Old Wesleyan Chapel was used for dances, concerts and even as a roller-skating rink, until eventually, a few years ago, it was renovated. It is now the official chamber for the Council of the Isles of Scilly, complete with web cameras and microphones, so that the electorate spread across the isles can use their computers to keep a beady eye on the shenanigans of their elected representatives.

Today, the new chaplain is on his way down Church Street towards the Town Hall, where the council officials are based, an unusually impressive building overlooking the Parade in Hugh Town, with 'VR 1887' sculpted into the stone just beneath its roofline, which is topped with a flagpole much-favoured by passing seagulls in need of a breather. From there, Father Guy moves on down to the Old Wesleyan Chapel, where he is about to lead the prayers that formally inaugurate the new spring session of the council.

Father Guy is shown the chamber and its prize possession, a lovely, ornate hardwood chair, probably mahogany, used by the then Prince of Wales, later Charles II, in 1646, when he was on the run from Oliver Cromwell and the dreaded Parliamentarians. Even though he owned the place, like many visitors to Scilly the Prince came and then rapidly went, without much hanging around, beating a hasty exit to the safety of France. The chair he sat upon remained, a permanent reminder of the islands' loyal support of the Royalist cause. It later carried the weight of various other royal bottoms, including those belonging to Edward VII, the ill-fated Edward

186

VIII and our own gracious Queen, whose outdated and faded photograph now hangs in the debating chamber, like a relic of a bygone age.

Because of Scilly's remoteness and isolation, the council here is responsible for almost every aspect of community life: transport, housing, social services, education, even health. This makes it one of the most powerful bodies of its kind in England.

Not that any untoward influence has had an effect on the council's latest decision. After a short debate, they have agreed to give planning permission to one M. Bond Esq. for a mobile fish shop to operate on the streets of Hugh Town.

Martin celebrates with an extra large roll-up and a couple of pints of Scuppered down at the Mermaid.

*   *   *

The old stone quays dotted around Scilly look quaint and rather charming, and it's easy to forget that they provide a vital lifeline to the off-islands and that without them normal life on the islands would grind to a standstill. They are all over a hundred years old and, in the face of a relentless round-the-clock bombardment from the wrath of the sea, are in constant need of repair. I've stood at the top of the tiny main quay at Bryher, just down from the church, and watched in trepidation as forklift trucks rumble up and down at speed, picking up supplies of every size and shape being unloaded from the *Lyonesse Lady* for distribution across the island. Often within inches of being over the edge and toppling into the water, the trucks have to manoeuvre between groups of holidaymakers waiting for the boats and sometimes gangs of children jostling to use the quay as a diving platform. For years, islanders have been grumbling that, with traffic on the quay increasing year by year, sooner or later there will be a spectacular accident.

For the past few months, there has been a large, unfamiliar vessel moored in St Mary's harbour, which occasionally chugs slowly off on trips to the off-islands. It's long and black, and enquiries at the harbourmaster's office reveal that it's an ex-Royal Marine amphibious landing craft. It looks extremely incongruous parked up next to the lifeboat, surrounded by dozens of bobbing yachts.

The boat was bought by the Steamship Company, sailed all the way down from its base at Inverness in Scotland, renamed *Island Lady* and is now being used to transport tons of gravel and huge concrete blocks which are being brought in on every ferry from the mainland. This is the start of a million-pound project to update four off-island quays on Bryher, St Agnes and St Martin's. It's being funded by the Duchy, which as usual prompts instant, polarised opinion: bigger quays are essential and can only be good for the economy of the islands, or bigger quays will encourage a dramatic increase in traffic, contributing to the long-term decline of island life. The man with the most unenviable job on Scilly, the Duchy land steward and the Duke of Cornwall's representative on the islands, is Colin Sturmer, who has developed the wary, slightly hangdog look of someone who's damned if he does and damned if he doesn't. He's no doubt counting off the days until the end of his posting in two years' time, when he can return to a world of sane and sensible decision-making, somewhere he will not be in any danger of being stoned to death by the locals.

The extension and upgrading of the quays is turning out to have some unexpected effects. The new Bryher quay is now almost complete, all pasty-faced, bright-grey concrete that needs a few decades of weathering and seaweed to make it look at home. Father Guy's next duty is to officially open the quay with a blessing service. It'll be quite a party; the entire island is invited.

The sewing machine has been working overtime in the workshop of Richard and Caroline Pearce's house at Great Par, following the news that Caroline has indeed been awarded the contract to supply soft furnishings for all twelve of the new holiday cottages on the seaplane base; already she's fitting out the show house.

Inevitably, every islander has his or her own opinion about what the new cottages look like from the exterior, but I have to say that inside they are seductive and attractive, and they make devilishly clever use of their outstanding location. Caroline's cushions and curtains in simple pale blues and greens echo the changing shades of the seascape beyond the windows. The bedroom of the show house has a small terrace overlooking the water and the seaplane slip, and the huge bed has been specially raised so you can marvel at the panoramic view over Bryher and Samson without even raising your head from the pillow. They don't come cheap; a debenture to take one of them high-season for one week for the next twenty years will set you back between £70,000-£100,000.

Despite the financial bonus of Caroline's new contract, Richard is, as ever, sitting in his studio, stroking his beard and looking out to sea, pondering devious and imaginative new ways to increase his artistic output. As his fame on the mainland has grown, he has become increasingly frustrated by the limits his location imposes on him. He's always been convinced that his art suits really big canvases and that there is a market out there for them. The helicopters, though, will only carry pictures of a maximum size of six foot by two. The Steamship Company have also been reluctant to take anything much bigger because of the severe restrictions on the quay during the loading and unloading of the *Lyonesse Lady*.

Now all this is about to change.

Richard normally hides away in his Golden Eagle studio during big public island events, like the fête or Harvest Festival, which he generally tends to find slightly awkward and embarrassing. For once, however, he might just surprise everyone by accepting his invitation to the opening of the Isles of Scilly's best designed and most modern quay, now awaiting Father Guy's blessing, which, he is reliably informed, can handle canvases of any size whatsoever.

*   *   *

The weather continues to be unrepentingly terrible, with a series of uncharacteristic summer storms and downpours that come and go so quickly that even the seagulls look perplexed. Martin Bond and Joel are having to put in long hours at 'the office'. Yet, oddly, the sun seems to emerge, obligingly dead on cue, for key moments, such as the wedding of Miss Rebecca Picton, spinster of the parish of the Isles of Scilly, and Mr Daniel Burt of Falmouth, in the county of Cornwall, at Old Town Church, St Mary's. This becomes one of the quickest wedding celebrations the islands have ever known.

Father Guy is a stickler for punctuality, so, since there is no electricity in the church, he arrives early to light the candles, and then stands around looking anxious. Katie, the antique island coach, is transporting the families and a few friends and arrives late, and the bride and her father are even later. Father Guy utterly believes in the dignity and solemnity of the wedding sacrament, so when the ceremony at last gets under way and the ringtone of a mobile phone echoes around the whitewashed walls of the tiny nave just as he gets started on the hallowed matrimonial vows, the new chaplain visibly struggles to control himself.

When the sun is shining, Scilly is the most photogenic location in the world, and all is soon forgotten afterwards as the happy wedding party makes its way down through the graves of shipwrecked sailors to the lawn above the beach, for a session under the lens of Frank Gibson, of the legendary Scilly family of photographers. Rarely can the results have been more satisfying. The midday sun gives everything the razor-sharp definition of a fierce, early summer's light, and the mix of colours—the dazzling white of the bride, the scarlet red of the bridesmaids, the deep blue of the sea—makes the scene dizzying in its clarity. Later, there are more pictures over on Town Beach, with the shiny new Mrs Daniel Burt

191

perched sexily on the prow of a gig, with a glittering harbour, complete with the newly arrived *Scillonian*, as a perfect backdrop.

However, because of the size of the church and the huge cost of travelling to and from Scilly, the majority of the wedding guests are not actually on Scilly. So, after a quick lunch at Tregarthen's Hotel, overlooking the quay, the newlyweds and their party, still in wedding gear, hurry up to the airport, where a helicopter is waiting to whisk them over to the mainland and the 120 guests who have been patiently waiting in Falmouth for the big reception to a wedding they have been unable to attend. Watching Father Guy at work, you might be forgiven for thinking his integration into island life is proceeding smoothly and seamlessly. His formal duties at the wedding over, that all-encompassing, winning smile and infectious, explosive laugh are never far away, and, wherever he goes, the chaplain is ready to stop and chat to parishioners, as though with ne'er a care in the world. I am discovering, though, that this impression is far from accurate. Trips to the pub have all but ceased; the laugh has become increasingly hollow. In fact, Father Guy has got off to a terrible start, and, paradoxically, it is a wedding which has led to the first big dissent of his new ministry.

The current controversy centres around the marriage of the daughter of a well-known and influential Scilly farming family to a police officer from the mainland. The couple asked Father Guy if he would perform the marriage ceremony, and he said he'd be delighted and went through the usual formalities and questions, one of which was:

have either of you been married before? The groom said that indeed he had; his previous marriage had unfortunately broken down and he was divorced. Much to the distress of everyone involved, Father Guy explained that his conscience would not allow him to remarry divorcés, in which he is perfectly within his rights, current practice in the Church of England being that this is a matter for individual priests to decide for themselves. The couple asked Father Guy how exactly the concept of forgiveness fitted in to all this, and requested that he pray long and hard about it, which Father Guy readily agreed to do, coming back to them a few days later with the devastating news that after further lengthy consultations with the Almighty, there could be no question of him changing his mind.

Given that Father Guy has only been on Scilly a short time, this is unfortunate timing, to say the least, and now the problem has been further compounded. What often occurs under these circumstances is that the vicar involved agrees to allow another priest, maybe a curate, who has no such problem remarrying divorcés, to come in and take the wedding, but this Father Guy has resolutely refused to contemplate. His position is made worse by the fact that this goes against the established practice of his predecessor, who did allow other priests to conduct such marriages on the islands. Yet Father Guy refuses to budge; there is no way he's going to agree to anyone else, even the bishop, coming into any church in his parish and conducting services of any description against his wishes.

Once news of what has happened leaks out, a

whispering campaign appears to get underway, which in a tiny and inward-looking community like Scilly can be very destructive. Worse still, letters from furious parishioners have started to drop through the letterbox of Father Guy's boss, Bishop Bill, the Bishop of Truro.

Lacking much knowledge of the place or its people and unable to confide in fellow clergy, Father Guy is feeling isolated, and it is clear he's taken the criticism of his stance very personally indeed. Adding fuel to the fire is Father Guy's reluctance, or inability, to explain his decision publicly, preferring instead to lock himself away in the Chaplaincy. Despite the angry, wounding accusations of pigheadedness, however, it is clear that he is quite determined to stand his ground, and for this I can't help but have a sneaking admiration. He might appear hesitant and self-effacing, but beneath all that is a strength of conviction and courage that takes you slightly by surprise. Some would argue that these qualities are exactly what are missing from today's sometimes wishy-washy Church of England, which many believe to have few convictions about anything. After all, it would have been so simple for him to have given way under all the pressure. Nonetheless, the damage is done, and instead of nipping the criticism in the bud, and moving on, Guy has allowed it to snowball out of control.

There have been other issues too, exacerbated by the disparate nature of the five islands and Father Guy's instinct to avoid confronting his critics. Inevitably, this has been misconstrued as autocratic and haughty. Because he's in his mid forties, it is easy to forget that Father Guy has only been a priest for a few years and is inexperienced. Many islanders dislike his High Church approach to services and fierce allegiance to traditional values, along with the Catholic tendency of the term 'Father'. A request that he conduct some Sunday family services without communion on St Agnes has been turned down. He's been accused of mishandling the funeral of a much-loved old Scillonian, of misunderstanding the nature of island ways. His churchwardens, Sue and Fiona, are defensive, but argue that any new chaplain to such a sensitive and conservative community will be in trouble whatever he does, or doesn't, do.

It is just at this point, then, when there's an air of general despondency around the Chaplaincy and, despite the strangely unpredictable weather, a general wellbeing and optimism amongst the islanders at what is seen as a successful start to the vital holiday season, that a series of disasters occurs which threatens to throw Father Guy completely off course, and engulf the islands in despair.

11

A Tragedy Engulfs The Islands

Nathan Woodcock collapsed over his oar after the gig *Galatea* crossed the line in second place as it entered St Mary's harbour during a regular Friday-night race. The boat was beached on the little piece of sand just beneath the Mermaid, where they had planned to have the usual drinks after the race, and for an hour frantic efforts were made by doctors and paramedics to revive him. The air-ambulance helicopter on the mainland was scrambled, but by the time they got Nathan's body up to the airport it was clear that he was dead.

For people living dissipated, unconnected city lives on the mainland, it may be hard to imagine what an impact the sudden and totally unexpected death of the much-loved, twenty-three-year-old lifeboat mechanic had on such a close-knit, inward-looking island community. Flags everywhere are at half-mast. Scilly is in trauma.

I had known Nathan a little; everyone knew Nathan. He and Andy the coxswain had invited us out on the lifeboat on one of its regular Tuesday evening training sessions. The voyage was a bit odd, because they had blocked out all the windows in the wheelhouse with pieces of cardboard in order to practise navigating, in this case to a point off St Agnes, as if in the middle of a jet-black night. Because of its unusual circumstances, Scilly has the only full-time lifeboat engineer in the RNLI, a job Nathan had dreamed of for years. With it came a lovely little cottage just beneath Buzza, overlooking Porthcressa beach, where Nathan settled in blissful happiness with Vicky and their new baby daughter, Megan.

It was an exquisite sunset on the boat that evening; exhilarating too. The lifeboat sliced sweetly through the gentle waves at forty knots, while Nathan explained that the crew would be simulating the rescue of a man stranded on some rocks just off Troytown. He was eighteen stone, six foot four, an extremely strong guy, clearly in complete charge of what was happening, at the peak of his abilities. He was also instantly likeable; just the kind of man, in fact, you would be relieved and delighted to see hoving into view if you got into trouble on the high seas; just the kind of man you would implicitly trust. He was also part of a lifeboat dynasty: his father Derek, grandfather Wilfred, uncle Peter, nephew Phil and great-uncle Fred were or are St Mary's lifeboatmen.

Most of us find the news of Nathan's inexplicable death, as it rapidly passes, like ripples on a pond, across the islands, hard to believe. How his family or those who knew him well are taking it, I can't imagine; it's a sleepless night for many. After the shock, tears and endless, drunken toasts to his memory in the Mermaid, the next morning dawns bright and blustery. There's a vacuum of emotion. People don't know what to say to each other, yet can't bear to be alone. Nathan's gig team decide to row out to sea and, in a sad little ceremony, toss one of his oars into the water. The other is placed on Old Quay, just opposite the Mermaid, and soon there's a growing mountain of flowers around it.

The sense of utter unreality continues. Some of the tourists look puzzled. The boatmen must work; the tripper boats get off to the off-islands on schedule. Father Guy clears his diary and pays a brief visit to Nathan's grieving family at the guest house on the Strand where his mother lives, saying that he will be free at any time to help if required; he spends the day waiting in the Chaplaincy for a call.

At moments of crisis like this, communities tend to turn to their parish priests, who often become sectarian spokesmen for the people. Father Guy knew Nathan; he had been out on the lifeboat, met all the crew, had even taken the wheel. But for many in the community, the new chaplain is still very much a stranger, an incomer who has only been here a few months and has much to learn about island ways. Some, searching for a scapegoat, are even holding him partially to blame, asking the eternal question: how can your God have allowed this to happen? It's been a baptism by fire, these first few months, for an essentially good and honest man who is doing his best in circumstances beyond his control. It can't be easy for Father Guy, as the hours tick by, waiting alone in the Chaplaincy for a call that never comes.

Nathan's body must go to the mainland for an autopsy, and a huge crowd of friends gathers on the quay to see him off on the *Scillonian*, singing his favourite sea shanties. His gig-rowing prowess was renowned throughout the West Country; steaming towards Penzance through Mount's Bay, the ferry is greeted by the Penlee and Sennen Cove lifeboats, which are acting as escorts of honour, and flares are sent high into the sky.

The odd, squat, bright-yellow rowing boat that Nathan and his mates had planned to race from New York to Bishop Rock next year, now moored in the harbour, is a constant, weird reminder that he was the picture of health. What makes Nathan's death even harder to accept is the news that the post-mortem has revealed that there was apparently nothing wrong with him. There was no evidence of heart disease; his heart just stopped. The medical profession, which needs a name for everything, calls it Sudden Adult Cardiac Death Syndrome. A fit young man pounding the oars of his gig one moment; the next, dead. His fellow lifeboatmen bring his body home, accompanied again by two escort lifeboats from the mainland.

One week to the hour after his death, the gigs, instead of racing the usual route from Nut Rock back to the harbour, row slowly, in rhythm—as if in a Slow March—in Nathan's honour. As the boats glide across the finishing line, oars are held aloft in silent tribute. In *Serica*, another of Nathan's favourite gigs, one berth remains empty.

As the days pass, painfully slowly, the disbelief seems, strangely, to increase.

WPC Nikki Green knew Nathan from her secondment on Scilly last summer, and is close to tears. 'He was a legend; you'd never meet anyone else like Nathan. Always full of fun, full of jokes. Nobody had a bad word to say about him. It makes you realise that you've got to live life to the full. He was part of the soul of the islands.'

'Lovely, charming guy, just so full of life—and pranks,' says the ever understated Fraser Hicks, whose daughter Rebecca was at school with Nathan. If the words don't quite do it, his face says it all. 'Just a nice bloke to meet. If you met him only once, you'd remember Nathan.'

Nathan's best friend was Tom Jackman, a merchant seaman, who, like many of the young men, talks as though Nathan is still with us. 'Whenever I come home from sea, the first thing I do after dropping my bags off is go down to the boathouse and see Nathan. Talk about what's been going on, what I've been missing while I've been away. I know I'm home then.'

Included in the growing mountain of flowers on Old Quay are poems from young friends of

Nathan, some of whom have never attempted poetry before, like these verses from Tom's twenty-year-old younger brother Billy:

When my time comes, I know not when,
I hope it's you at the gates to let me in,
For the rest of them up there mean not much
    to me
It's you, when I go, I'll be going to see
So I say goodbye to you, my friend, but I know
    it's not for good.
I will see you again, boy, when I get there,
    sooner if I could.
The flags are at half-mast, mate, and the grief
    is all for you,
Just look at what you've done, boy; my heart is
    torn in two!

The union flag does indeed fly at half-mast over the Town Hall and the Star Castle up on the Garrison; the RNLI flag too flutters at half-mast by the old lifeboat station in the harbour. For the first time ever, the airport is closed, as a mark of respect, for the funeral. The two o'clock tripper boats are all cancelled. Pubs and shops close. Instead of Father Guy, the family have asked a Methodist minister to conduct the funeral; and so many people turn out for the service in the Methodist chapel in Church Street that latecomers can't even get anywhere near the front door of the building, while Father Guy's Anglican church at the top of the street, which has three times the capacity, lies empty. A note on the Order of Service explains that donations can be made to Megan's Trust, to support Vicky as she struggles to

200

bring up Nathan's daughter alone.

From within the chapel, the words of Nathan's favourite sea shanty, sung by the men he'd sung it with a hundred times, drift across Church Street.

> I've left childish footsteps in the soft Sennen
>   sand,
> I've chased the maids there, all giggly and
>   tanned.
> I've stood on the cliff top in a westerly blow,
> And heard the wave thunder on the rocks far
>   below.
> First thing in the morning, on Chapel Carn
>   Brea,
> And gaze at the Scillies in the blue far away,
> For this is my Cornwall, and I'll tell you why,
> Because I was born here and here I shall die.
> And no-one will ever move me from this land,
> Until the Lord calls me to sit at his hand.
> For this is my Eden, and I'm not alone.
> For this is my Cornwall, and this is my home.

Then, in the dazzling sunshine, according to tradition, the coffin is carried up Church Street by six of Nathan's fellow lifeboatmen, in their distinctive blue RNLI jumpers. There could be a thousand people in the procession, and among them, towards the rear, are Father Guy and Kate. WPC Nikki Green, in ceremonial uniform, stands to attention and removes her hat as the cortege walks by. Then it heads over the hill, to the graveyard at Old Town, where Nathan is laid to rest beneath some red roses, a green strip with the single word BONNET across it and the lifeboat tie he wore with such pride. Clive Mumford tells me that the funeral is bigger even than Harold Wilson's twelve years ago, whose remains now lie a few metres away from Nathan's.

Two days later, just as the islands are beginning the painful process of coming to terms with normal daily life, another tragedy appears to be unfolding. This time it's on St Martin's; or, rather, somewhere in the hundreds of square miles of water that surround it.

It seems that seventeen-year-old Robert Morton, a well-known gig-rower and cricketer, took a kayak out for an evening's paddle and disappeared. His brother woke up next morning in the distinctive red-tiled family house at Little Arthur, where the family runs a small café and which overlooks the beautiful cricket ground where Robert loved to play, to discover his bed empty and kayak and lifebelt gone. There's been a huge search involving Royal Navy helicopters, the St Mary's lifeboat, dozens of local boats and teams of coastguards, police and local volunteers scouring the beaches, and the kayak has now been discovered, afloat some miles off the island, but there's no sign of Robert.

Once again, Scilly is plunged into shock, but this time grieving has, perforce, to be suspended because there is no body. There's another, strange, inertia. Inevitably, rumours abound. Did Robert stage his own disappearance? Was crime involved? Everyone waits for news. Alfie Trenear, the St Mary's undertaker, says that if the boy's still at sea, he'll come ashore in two and a half weeks.

The next Sunday, by an odd coincidence, it's the annual lifeboat service by the beach on Holgates Green, and Father Guy's down to take it. He spends hours under the desk lamp in his study, poring over the sermon. In a sense, this is Guy's moment, a chance to show he is capable of rising to the challenge.

Predictably, the crowd gathering in the blinding evening sunshine is the biggest anyone can remember for the lifeboat service. They sing the lifeboatmen's adopted hymn, and never has it seemed more appropriate or more poignant.

> Eternal Father, strong to save,
> Whose arm hath bound the restless wave,
> Who bidd'st the mighty ocean deep
> Its own appointed limits keep;
> Oh, hear us when we cry to Thee,
> For those in peril on the sea.

Then Guy, dressed in black, makes his way up to the podium, which is draped in the RNLI flag. Behind him, an armada of glittering little boats bob in the dusk light, shepherded, or so it seems, by the glowing, orange silhouette of the lifeboat itself.

Father Guy gathers his thoughts. The congregation blinks expectantly in the low sunshine.

'Very soon after I arrived on the islands, when I was first told about this lifeboat service, it seemed a fairly straightforward matter. A quick something about the awesomeness of the sea, and the selfless bravery of those who risk their lives to save others in peril. Easy. But events have intervened and conspired to make this service as far from straightforward and easy as it's possible to be.'

A sudden breeze has the RNLI flag, at half-mast further around the bay, suddenly flutter and seem to reach out towards the congregation. From a few yards behind Father Guy comes the gentle, hushed rustle of waves lapping on the sand.

'What's happened gives us the opportunity to confront and explore the depths of what it means to be human. Nathan's death has hit this community hard. A tidal wave for his friends and colleagues; for his family it's been a tsunami, destroying hopes and dreams, apparently laying waste to the future . . .'

I start to realise that this is probably the most important sermon, the most important speech that Guy has ever made.

'The ripples of Nathan's death have spread throughout our island community; there'll be anger. Take your anger out to Penninis Point when a storm's blowing and bellow it out to God. We must be ready to respond to the unpredictability of life, and, like the lifeboats, always be ready to go to the aid of those in distress; it will go a long way to building a better world in the here and now, reflecting better the other world, so very close, but beyond our reach.'

It's a difficult service for everyone. Quite how Father Guy's performance has gone down with the islanders is hard to assess; time will no doubt tell. My view is that, under the circumstances, he has done an almost impossible job pretty well.

The next day, Father Guy, Kate and the girls leave for a few long-planned days back in their old parish on the mainland, at Mullion, on the western coast of the Lizard Peninsula. They will be among well-loved friends there, and I'm glad Father Guy has a chance to escape the pressure-cooker that the Chaplaincy has become. I have a feeling, though, that returning to the place and the people where he once enjoyed such happiness might just have the opposite effect.

*   *   *

The oddities of island life continue to confound me. For example, I've discovered that the gardeners at Tresco Abbey Gardens are not only horticultural experts, they are also highly trained firemen. Why? To the multi-tasking islanders, the answer is obvious. The gardens are adjacent to the grass field that classifies itself as the Tresco heliport, and they are simply the nearest band of men to be on hand in an emergency. So when the siren goes, it's down hoes and trowels and a hop over the hedge.

At the main airport on St Mary's, it's the baggage handlers who are also the firemen, and often the fire-engine parked up by the terminal building is surrounded by the arresting sight of half a dozen pairs of boots standing on the tarmac, each pair smothered in dark-purple fireproof trousers and yellow braces. At first glance it looks as though the occupants of each pair have suddenly been sucked up into the sky by a powerful vacuum. In fact, it's almost the opposite; the boots are waiting for their owners to leap into them, and into action. Very efficient.

In the last couple of days, the firemen here have been busy. The pilot of a light aircraft coming in to land appeared to misjudge his height and speed, bounced off the runway, up-ended and, like so many of those Hurricane pilots of sixty years ago, crashed, ending up in the field on the far side of the runway. The plane had been almost full of fuel, and the air traffic controllers, looking on helplessly from their tower, assumed that there would be an explosion and all four people aboard would be killed. In fact, only one man was slightly injured, a doctor who broke his collar-bones. The wrecked plane is still there in the field this morning, left untouched where it landed, awaiting the arrival of the air accident investigators. It is a sobering reminder of the fragility of human life in this exposed and vulnerable outpost.

His visit has been planned for some time, but as it happens, with the islands still reeling from the tragic news of the two young men, Father Guy at a particularly low ebb, despite, or maybe because of, his recent break back in Mullion, and the holiday season threatening to implode as a result of the sudden, terrible rain storms, the arrival of Cornwall's most famous right-arm spin bowler, Bishop Bill, the Bishop of Truro, could not have come at a better time.

As Father Guy's boss, Bishop Bill has been watching events unfold on Scilly with a concerned eye. This is a man who is a fanatical birdwatcher and who likes nothing better than a quick autumnal trip to Scilly to check out the birds blown across from America in the first of the winter gales, so he is only too aware of the islands' remoteness and isolation.

Bishop Bill will be staying at the Chaplaincy for three days, and as Father Guy drives him down from the airport and walks him up through the bowers of the lovely mulberry tree that embraces all visitors to the house, I sense an immediate

206

lightening of spirits. The bishop is a natural communicator with a sharp wit and a phenomenal memory for a good story. Alice and Clarrie find him endlessly amusing, and Kate's smiling. After a coffee and a natter around the big kitchen table, Father Guy guides him down past the school and across Porthmellon Beach to Sue's house, where Fiona joins them for lunch. Sue has two male tortoises called Bigtort and Littletort who, she explains, only ever do four things: eat, sleep, show-off and copulate. Just as the bishop arrives, Bigtort and Littletort begin to combine these last two pastimes and, much to his surprise, have violent sexual intercourse.

Then Father Guy tactfully withdraws, so the bishop has a free rein to quiz his two churchwardens about the true state of play in his remotest parish.

*   *   *

There is a large crowd assembling on Porthcressa Beach, down below the Dibble and Grub. Cameras are being held expectantly aloft and the presence of a serious-looking Clive Mumford, on behalf of The *Cornishman*, suggests something portentous might be about to take place. After the tragic drowning of his grandfather whilst salvaging the wrecks, Clive's father was never allowed anywhere near the water, and nor was Clive, which is why it's unusual to see him on a beach.

After a few more minutes of patient waiting, a tall, thin lady with an elegant ponytail of grey hair emerges from the restaurant, blinking in the sunlight. She is wearing a swimsuit. This, in itself, is an unusual sight; despite its semi-tropical climate and boasts of being warmed by the Gulf Stream, the waters off the beaches of Scilly are much colder than those off the mainland, and its very unusual to see anyone, other than crazy children showing off, taking to the sea. I tried it once and nearly froze to death.

What is even more extraordinary is the sight of a bald, pale little man with a plump tummy, wearing only a pair of spectacles and skimpy, flesh-coloured swimming-shorts, following the woman out on to the sand. Bizarrely, the man is carrying a bishop's crook. To a rapturous round of applause, he crosses the beach and starts to address the crowd. If this vision of semi-nakedness has left anyone puzzled, then the gentle, educated voice must surely reveal that the figure belongs to none other than the Right Revd William Ind, the Bishop of Truro.

'The last time I did this, I wore a wetsuit,' announces the bishop, which may, on sober reflection, have been more appropriate, since the flesh-coloured trunks at first glance make the bishop look naked. 'My photograph appeared next day in *The Times*, after which a friend phoned me to say that not only was he unaware that the paper had a new policy of printing obscene pictures, but that he was amazed it was technically possible to manufacture such oddly shaped wetsuits.'

Amidst the laughter, I notice one person, Father Guy, is looking slightly embarrassed. The contrast between the two priests couldn't be greater. The bishop goes on to give a blessing and, of course, have his photograph taken, beside a revolutionary new wheelchair with large, soft rubber wheels designed to help the disabled get on and off the beach, before plunging into the waves. Churchwarden Sue is already in the sea, monitoring the bishop's reaction to the icy water, lest he exhibits early signs of a heart-attack; but, in fact, with his spectacles slowly edging down his wet nose, Bishop Bill swims around energetically in small, doggy-paddled circles, like a tubby tadpole, and the crowd, snapping away, is delighted. I'm half hoping Father Guy will strip off and do the same, which at a stroke would win the hearts of so many, but the moment is lost.

*   *   *

The Chaplaincy gardens are large, and on one side, because of a raised border, there is a natural amphitheatre. After the unlikely scenes on the beach, we get back there to find rows of wooden seats have been laid out, transforming the garden into a delightful horticultural theatre. Cylindrical, multicoloured, medieval-looking tents have sprung up to house a small team of travelling actors, who are about to perform *A Comedy of Errors* for the islanders. Bishop Bill, now mercifully re-clothed and looking a little like Henry VIII perched on his throne, is guest of honour. Father Guy, sitting beside him, shifts uncomfortably as the play gets underway with the story of a terrible shipwreck.

For what obscured light the heavens did grant,
Did but convey unto our fearful minds
A doubtful warrant of immediate death,

Which though myself would gladly have
    embraced,
Yet the incessant weepings of my wife,
Weeping before what she saw must come,
And piteous plainings of the pretty babes.

The clock in the church tower rising high above
the Chaplaincy gardens dolefully rings out the
hour.

    The sailors sought for safety by our boat,
    And left the ship, then sinking-ripe, to us.

Later, when I'm alone with the bishop for a
moment, I ask him for an honest assessment of
how Father Guy is really getting on and, being
Bishop Bill, he gives me one, although he does
choose his words with care.

'Guy has hit some difficult questions over the
remarriage of divorced people, and he feels—
conscientiously—that he just can't do it, and he
has the perfect right to think so,' says the bishop,
starting off gently.

'That didn't go down well around here; that's no
secret,' I point out, lest Bill was in any doubt. It's
clear from his expression that he doesn't need any
reminder.

'It certainly didn't go down well with some
people, but others thought it was a good thing that
the Church is seen to be standing up for itself.
Something we should be seen to do more often,
perhaps.'

This is a good point, and one I wish Father Guy
had been able to articulate.

Then Bishop Bill says something which really

210

surprises me.

'To be honest with you, I like coming to Scilly, it's a beautiful place and the people are lovely . . .'

The bishop pauses, glancing up into the portentous clouds scudding overhead.

'Yes?'

'But I couldn't be the vicar here. Not in a million years.'

This is quite an admission from the man who runs the Diocese and who appointed Father Guy. I wonder whether he'd said this at Guy's interview, but think it unlikely.

'Why not?'

'The goldfish-bowl effect can be quite awful. I couldn't bear not to be able to escape.'

The clouds are blacker than ever, heavy with moisture.

'Father Guy did know all this when he came.'

'People told him that. I told him that. But you know how it is with kids? You tell kids you'll find this, this and this, and they say no, no, no, and then of course they find it out for themselves. That's exactly what has happened here.'

*   *   *

Next morning, it's raining—great, thick drops that are so heavy they almost splash your knees as they hit the cobbles. The weather, even by Scilly standards, has been extraordinary. Breathtaking, translucent Caribbean days are followed by weeks of rain, drizzle and storms. Martin and Joel Bond are virtually living in 'the office'. People who are already here on their holidays have little option but to make the best of it, but the number of day-trippers on the *Scillonian* has dropped dramatically and the tourist office reluctantly reports that a spiralling number of future bookings are being cancelled.

Fraser and the boatmen shake their heads with disbelief, and sometimes despair; the shopkeepers seem quietly, smugly satisfied, as people take to the stores to escape the weather; the dainty little museum in Church Street, opened by a ridiculously young-looking Queen in the sixties and rather well laid out, is just about the only other place to go when it's wet, and so is enjoying one of its best years on record.

The islands need to find more ways of entertaining the visitors and teasing money from them when the weather is terrible, and not just by feeding them all day. Away from the beaches, and often out of sight of the holidaymakers, you can find burgeoning cottage industries if you know where to look. Making use of the brilliant light on the blue-and-white seascapes, there's a growing colony of artists such as Richard Pearce on Bryher and Jo Probert on St Mary's. There are also some potteries, one or two new arts and crafts workshops and even an Isles of Scilly Perfumery, the smallest shop I've ever entered, where Pete 'The Hat' Hobson distils exotic potions and fragrances from the natural world around him: the narcissi, and the wild agapanthus that spring up on the sand dunes beneath his laboratory, the curious legacy of a ship wrecked across the Road which had been carrying barrels of agapanthus bulbs from the Mediterranean when it went down in 1798.

Down on the ramshackle industrial estate

behind Porthmellon Beach, there's also a stained-glass studio, where you can observe Fraser Hicks's brother Steve's wife, Oriel Hicks, toiling on her latest creation: a new set of stained-glass windows for the beautiful church over on Bryher.

Oriel is also building a new workshop for another eight artisans and craftsfolk, who'll be scouring the islands and beachcombing for wood, stone, sand, shells and even old plastic bottles, to recycle and mould into island art for the tourists to admire, buy and take back home—particularly if it's wet.

*   *   *

Bishop Bill is a sanguine man at heart, who has a rare, confident ability to see the best in people's hearts. It seems that, metaphorically as well as physically, he has brought with him an unusually uplifting few hours of warm, brilliant weather. Next morning, the sun is out and we join a boatload of excited churchgoers going to Bryher and the newly blessed Church Quay, for a service to dedicate Oriel's stained-glass windows to the church.

It doesn't happen very often on Bryher, but today every seat in the church is taken. Bishop Bill talks about the importance of light in life's dark corners, and in the process of spraying holy water on the four windows, sprays half the congregation as well, which provokes much laughter, as he knew it would. How can such a simple act prompt so much hilarity? The answer, I guess, as I study this diminutive, smiling figure going about his business, lies in the character of the bishop himself, blessed,

213

according to the faithful, with a powerful, higher, fearsome authority, yet able to inspire, through a combination of humility and dubious jokes, almost everyone in that room. So simple, so hard to achieve. Father Guy looks on, smiling, in admiration.

After a picnic on the beach, the day moves on with another voyage, pushing further north up past Hangman Island and through the narrow channel out into the open sea. The ruins of two castles stand sentinel above us, guarding the narrow, strategically important channel between Tresco and Bryher. The higher is King Charles's Castle, allegedly abandoned after it was discovered that the guns couldn't tilt down sufficiently to fire their cannonballs anywhere near the water; the second, much more imposing, is Cromwell's Castle, sensibly constructed on the water's edge in 1651, at the end of the Civil War.

*   *   *

The best views in Scilly—and admittedly you are spoilt for choice—are undoubtedly from the summit of the twin-peaked, uninhabited island of Samson, just south of Bryher. It has a strange, compelling allure. Even the heather is lusher here, thriving after the heavy summer rains, the best for at least five years say the boatmen. Samson must look now almost as it has done for years from here; there are no buildings of any description to be seen, and of course there's no quay. We disembark from the big tripper boat *Osprey* onto a rubber dinghy, which beaches us on dazzling, silky sand bleached almost white. I feel like Captain

214

Cook stepping onto the shore of Botany Bay, a timeless moment which is slightly spoiled when I lose my footing clambering out of the dinghy and promptly disappear into the water. This momentary lapse causes much hilarity among my fellow travellers, who whip out their mobile phones and take pictures and videos, which can, if anyone is bored enough to be interested, be instantly transmitted via the internet around the globe. Trying to retain some measure of dignity as I struggle to stand, salt water streaming down me, on a primitive island with no electricity and no phone connections, indeed scarcely touched by human hand, this is a sobering thought.

I climb up North Hill, dripping, and look across to White Island, which was the location of probably the most dramatic rescue in Scilly's history, prompted by the sinking of a three-masted steamer called the *Delaware*, en route from Liverpool to Calcutta with a cargo of silks, cottons, lead and tin, in December 1871. Since even quite young children have mentioned it to me in passing, it's clearly become something of a living legend, because of the famed heroism of the men of Bryher.

The *Delaware* was blown off course by a fearsome December north-westerly gale, which forced it between two rocky outcrops, Seal Rock and Mincarlo, which I can now clearly see to the west, and onto the hidden teeth of Tearing Ledges. An itinerant poet called Robert Maybee, who sold groceries around the islands door to door and who couldn't read or write but had his work written down by a friend, immortalised the story:

215

On the bridge the Captain stood,
He was a valiant man,
Though his leg was broken, foot as well,
He still kept in the van.
Then an awful sea broke on the ship,
And snapped the bridge in two,
The Captain then was swept away,
And near fifty sailors too.

The unfolding drama was being monitored by lookouts on Bryher, who could see five survivors in the water near White Island. After some discussion about the wisdom of the plan, the gig *Albion* was brought out of the boatshed now used by Richard Pearce as a studio at Great Par and, with the boat resting upside down on its oars, which were lashed across the beam for handles, was carried down across Bryher to Rushy Bay and rowed through mountainous seas to Samson, landing at East Par, just beneath where I'm standing. The six oarsmen, already soaked and exhausted, then carried the *Albion* across the island and rowed out to White Island, where the only two survivors of the *Delaware*, half frozen to death, had made a pile of rocks, ready to stone their rescuers because their captain had told them Scillonians were savages. They all made it back to Samson, where the crew of the *Albion* collapsed with fatigue.

Now may God bless those Bryher men,
And all that they have done,
Their deed of daring shall be known,
Wherever shines the sun.

At the other end of Samson, on South Hill, there is evidence of previous human habitation. First you stumble across the ruins of a well, black water still bubbling up through startling, bright-green weeds. Then, further up the hill, there are the crumbling remains of half a dozen tiny cottages, the roofs and most of the walls long since collapsed, the granite stones scattered in random piles around the foundations. Even now, it's easy to imagine how bleak and wild existence here must have been.

Samson was inhabited until 1855. The few families here struggled to survive on dried fish, potatoes and donations from passing boats. My Lord Proprietor of the Isles, the 'philanthropist' Augustus Smith, declared they faced imminent starvation and had them forcibly removed, whereupon he converted the island into a deer park. Much, I imagine, to the delight of those he'd evicted, this spectacularly failed.

Across the water, on another uninhabited island, St Helen's, there's more intriguing evidence of previous, harsher eras, when life was something you wasted no time getting down to, lest at any moment it be snatched away. Most prominent from the southern approach are the eerie ruins of what's known as the Pest House, built in 1764, after an Act of Parliament decreed that any plague-ridden ship sailing north of Finisterre and heading for England should anchor at Scilly until declared free of disease. Ill seamen would be lugged ashore and left to die in the Pest House.

I can imagine worse places to live out your last days. St Helen's, too, is covered in rich, purple heather, which here smells sweet, like honey, and

217

the view across the rocky outcrops of the Pool to Tresco and Tobaccoman's Point is sublime. The sun is dropping now, and the still sea, devoid here of plankton and the pollution of rivers, is a sub-aquamarine turquoise.

St Helen's is the final destination on Bishop Bill's visit to Scilly, and in some ways his most significant.

Every year in mid August, the islanders make a pilgrimage to St Helen's, where Christianity first arrived on Scilly at the end of the eighth century, and where this evening the bishop is leading them in a last act of worship.

As on Samson, there's no quay here, so everyone clambers off *Osprey* and into the dinghy, which drops us on the shallow beach. We wade ashore, with Bishop Bill rolling up his trousers like the rest of us, holding aloft a suitcase containing his stoles and surplices in one hand and his bishop's crook in the other. Beside him is Guy's daughter Alice, holding high the tall crucifix and leading the others forward, their dark figures silhouetted against the low sun, like those early Christians arriving over a thousand years ago.

Just down from the Pest House are the foundations of the ancient chapel built by St Elidius, where it's said the Viking King of Norway Olgar Tryggvason was converted to Christianity. It is around these ruins that the large group of pilgrims solemnly gathers. After all the emotional traumas of the last few weeks, I sense there's a feeling of relief, of rejuvenation, at Christian minds being able to return to Christian roots.

There's a gentle northerly breeze, and the words of the hymns and the solitary flute that accompanies them, drift across the water.

'Muslims go to Mecca, Hindus to the River Ganges; there are ancient holy places like these, dating back centuries, all over England too, from where people went out and colonised the country,' Bishop Bill begins, almost shouting as the wind gains strength. 'They provided comfort and succour for people, often after a tragedy or the death of a loved one, and they still do.'

Just above the horizon, the edges of the billowing dark clouds are ablaze, backlit by the dying sun, with great columns of light slicing between them into the sea.

'These are thoughts we should share together at this moment. Journeying back to a special place like this can be an essential part of our lives, an act of cleansing . . .'

The timing of the bishop's visit could not have been better. He has been a tonic at a rare low moment in the recent history of Scilly. Quite how well Father Guy and the islanders will cope when he's gone, only time will tell.

The bishop will retire in a few months' time. I sense a slight sadness behind his smiles as he opens his eyes and looks around this lovely island, in the knowledge that this is his last official trip to his remotest parish.

Next morning, the visibility is unusually good. From the high ground of the airfield, I can just see the low, slightly ominous outline of the mainland, for the first time since I've been here.

As quickly as he came, Bishop Bill is suddenly gone, in a black helicopter that seems in a hurry to return to civilisation and which rises like a bird into the azure skies.

12

Bounty from the Butcher

Heike is flashing her enormous smile, which, in an odd way, as she hunches her tall frame slightly like a naughty child, seems to take over her entire body.

'I am rich!' she declares, pushing the customary mug of steaming coffee into my hands, then adds, after a short pause, 'At least, I am not poor. Not so much!'

Three discoveries appear to have produced this feeling of light-headed *joie de vivre*. A rare examination of her accounts and comparisons with her diary has revealed that a) Heike has failed to bill a large number of her clients, and b) since she's been on Scilly, she has actually been paying her monthly rent to the Duchy twice.

The third discovery, though, will have a much more far-reaching effect. Heike has got to know the island butcher, Steve Griffin, whose shop in Garrison Lane, just opposite the old Wesleyan chapel where the Council to the Isles now sits, is marked by a parrot called Percy in a cage by the door, and where he keeps scraps for Heike's monster-dog, Leo.

Griff lives with his partner Stella up at Carn Friars Farm on the eastern side of St Mary's, alongside a strange secret of which even many of the islanders seem completely unaware. Over the years, Griff has developed his own, extraordinary, private zoo, hidden away behind the trees. It now consists of over three hundred exotic animals, scattered around in sheds, behind fences or simply running free. Most them, at some stage, will no doubt require the services of a qualified veterinary surgeon: chickens, geese, ducks, rabbits, goats and sheep, to be sure, but also peacocks, parrots, quails, black swans, wallabies, alpacas, ostriches and kangaroos. It is a rare privilege to be invited to this bizarre menagerie. I've seen some odd and unexpected sights during my short time on Scilly, but this beats them all.

As a child, Griff longed to be an animal-keeper in a zoo. His parents insisted he join the family business, so for years he has earned his living slicing up dead animals, the antithesis of his childhood dream. Even now, he can't bear to see carcasses or whole sides of meat, and can only work on them once they've been reduced to smaller, less identifiable cuts.

Heike skips around like a delighted schoolgirl, wiping spit from a bad-tempered alpaca she recently castrated from her coat and enquiring if the wallabies are rock or red-necked. Then it's down to business. One of the baby emus appears to have injured the hock on one of its legs and is waddling around with its foot turned strangely outwards. Heike examines the bird and decides it must be brought down to the surgery, so that she can find out whether the hock is dislocated or deformed. The bird doesn't seem to be in pain and hobbles about comically, and I think that this is hardly a serious problem, which just shows what a lousy vet I'd make.

*   *   *

221

Heike and the hyperactive Leo have recently taken to frequent walks around the bay to the churchyard at Old Town. After the 'incident' with the Labrador, the details of which remain murky, although, judging by the angelic expression on Leo's mug, he's still pleading 'not guilty', Heike castrated him. Far from emasculating Leo, this gross invasion of his physiology seems to have spurred him on to further defiance, so that he tugs and strains on the leash more than ever, dragging Heike behind him quite as badly as before. She maintains that there is still a large amount of testosterone whizzing around his body, which, she says, smiling hopefully, will disappear in time. Leo gives me a look as if to say that he intends to hang on to every last drop for as long as possible.

If Heike and Leo turn left out of their front door, they walk around the rocks of Tolman Point and up the footpath, which leads across the end of the short airfield runway and across to Salakee Down. If aircraft are landing or taking off, there's an odd little traffic light by the footpath which turns red, to let you know to wait a moment or you'll have your hat blown off.

Beyond Salakee, there's the little rocky bay of Porth Hellick and a stone memorial to the oddly-named Sir Cloudsley Shovell, the ill-fated admiral of four ships that went down in a terrible storm on the Western Rocks in October 1707, drowning 1,600 men. The loss of his flagship HMS *Association*, along with *Romney*, *Eagle* and *Firebrand* gives Sir Cloudsley the dubious distinction of having created Britain's worst naval disaster, which can be attributed to his dubious navigation.

Sir Cloudsley's body was washed up on the beach here, and the story goes that a passing fisherwoman saw the glint of a ruby ring on the dead man's hand and tried to steal it, but his flesh was so swollen by its time in the seawater that she ended up cutting off Sir Cloudsley's finger. Racked by guilt for the rest of her life, the woman never dared attempt sell the ring, producing it, along with a full confession, only on her deathbed.

Later, Sir Cloudsley's widow had his body retrieved from the temporary stone grave the islanders had made for it and brought to London, where, apparently forgiven for the appalling navigational errors he had made, he was buried in Westminster Abbey.

If Heike and Leo turn right out of their front door, they walk around Old Town Bay and up into the absurdly picturesque churchyard. Old Town is the only place to be buried on St Mary's. Many of the other bodies from the wrecks of Sir Cloudsley Shovell's fleet were brought here. If you walk up the stone steps that lead up the little hill at the back of the church, from where more and more of the spectacular view across Old Town Bay is tantalisingly revealed, you will find two bleak obelisks, covered in moss. The first is in honour of the Lord Proprietor of the Isles, Augustus Smith, who died in 1872. The second, at the summit of the steps, stands in memory of a young American girl, Miss Louise Holzmaister, who drowned in a major shipwreck in 1875, eight days before her twenty-fourth birthday. The engraved tribute ends simply—'This monument has been erected in her memory as a mark of affection by her husband'—

but behind these few sad words lies an epic story, still raw in the minds of older islanders, some of whose grandparents could recall the awful scenes that ended it.

The SS *Schiller* was one of the largest and fastest steamships of her day, a curious-looking vessel with sails fore and aft and two large funnels amidships. She was on passage from New York to Southampton and thence to her home port of Hamburg, packed full of rich Germans, when she hit thick fog just off Bishop Rock, struck Raterrier Ledge and started to sink rapidly. Often subsequently compared with the *Titanic* disaster, there were reports of chaotic scenes as men pushed aside women and children to clamber onto the boats, only two of which managed to get away successfully. When these arrived on Tresco, there were twenty-seven survivors on board, including only one woman and no children at all. Two other boats, full of passengers, were crushed when a red-hot funnel collapsed. The islanders seemed to have been unaware of the disaster. A gig from St Agnes put to sea much later and discovered people clinging to the mast, still visible in the water above the Ledge, and a further five passengers were saved. The bodies of the remaining 315 crew and passengers were washed up on beaches all over the islands and were buried, after the funeral service in St Mary's Church, in the traditional way—in a mass, unmarked grave at Old Town.

Maybe because the tragedy led to the deaths of so many of her fellow countrymen, Heike is drawn to the *Schiller* story; she likes to linger by the obelisk and the unmarked grave. It's said that the German government's debt of gratitude to the islanders for their heroic rescue attempts and the dignified way in which the funeral was conducted extended right up to the Second World War, when Hitler gave orders that the islands—and the Scillonian ferry, a sitting duck for submarines, aircraft and E-boats—should never be attacked.

There's not much of the *Schiller* left in its watery grave on the seabed out in the Western Rocks, but there are plenty of other wrecks around Scilly to be explored. Heike's made a decision: she will do more to take advantage of her wild and remote new home and start to explore the myriad stories and treasures that lie beneath the waves, as well as those above.

*   *   *

There is, of course, a downside to the work of a vet, which is largely unspoken and which most of us much prefer to avoid witnessing. It's all the more distressing when it comes as a complete surprise.

Sammy's making sandcastles on the beach and Leo is snoring away in the living room, traces of mud on his snout from recent renewed bouts of frantic digging. Heike is at the back of the house in her tiny surgery with Stella, from Griff the butcher's zoo, about to give the baby emu's hock a thorough and detailed examination. The bird itself, only six weeks old, looks healthy, even chirpy, as it peers around the room and out into the little garden, where a growing mound of earth shows that Leo has been making substantial progress on his journey to the centre of the earth.

Heike sedates the emu and starts to establish if

the injury is a dislocation, which she may be able to reset, or a deformity; it begins to look like the latter. She asks Stella to feel the hock with her, explaining the lack of ligaments that would normally prevent the foot from moving too much out of place. Then she makes a call to Griff. Stella, starting to cry, leaves the room. Heike fills a big syringe with a thick, blue liquid, a massive dose of general anaesthetic, and injects the emu. With a final lift of its rather beautiful, long, sleek, brown neck, the bird is dead. Just like that. I'm slightly shocked, not least at the speed at which it has happened. I don't recall ever seeing a real moment of death before, either of an animal or a human.

Even Heike seems sad. She sighs. In the silence that follows, she clearly feels an explanation is necessary. 'It's not a poison. It would have felt no pain.' Another silence. 'It is better for the bird this way.' I stare at the lifeless corpse, not so sure. 'The emus grow quickly and soon become heavy. They only have two legs. If it was a four-legged animal it could manage with an amputation.'

'It's seems a pity though.'

'Yes. Coffee?'

The mourning doesn't last long. The caffeine soon kicks in, and Heike is talking with great animation, fizzing with new plans and ideas. A poster campaign up at the airport offering tranquillisers to pets with a fear of flying has, so to speak, taken off. Her reputation as a skilful and caring veterinary surgeon is spreading rapidly. The artist Jo Probert was so impressed by Heike's treatment of her beloved black Labrador Dizzy's sudden intestinal trauma that she has promised to start organising a vet support group, to raise funds for new equipment, such as an X-ray machine, for Heike's spartan little surgery.

As the islands' holiday trade picks up, so does Heike's, and she has started to ingest the gentle Scilly art of adaptability. Her latest wheeze is looking into the feasibility of importing a pair of Highland Cattle, complete with long orange shag and great, wild horns, to breed in the corner of a field she can borrow at Normandy, a hamlet on the eastern side of St Mary's.

And now there's also a chance to learn to dive, an introduction to an exciting new world.

*   *   *

In June 1967, a Royal Navy minesweeper, HMS *Puttenham*, equipped with twelve divers, slipped out of the Road and dropped anchor off the notorious Gilstone Ledge, just to the south-east of Bishop Rock. Two divers were dispatched to search the seabed. Nothing was found. A couple of hours later, two more divers were sent down; they reported seeing a cannon. On the third dive, silver and gold coins were spotted in the murky sand. The site of Sir Cloudsley Shovell's flagship HMS *Association*, had at last been discovered.

The Ministry of Defence were desperate to suppress news of the discovery of the gold and silver bullion, for fear of provoking a stampede of bounty-hunters, but word that the wreck itself had been located was soon out and excited huge national interest. Pictures of a cannon being lifted to the surface went around the world. Then, in an unguarded moment during a live television interview, one of the minesweeper's lieutenants let

227

slip that coins had been found too, and for years after the wreck was ruthlessly plundered of its most valuable cargo.

Today the site is protected by law, and in a couple of months' time there will be a big ceremony by Gilstone Ledge to honour the 1,600 men who died in the disaster. It's been announced that central to the events being built around the 300th anniversary of the sinking of the *Association*, along with the *Romney*, *Eagle* and *Firebrand*, will be the Chaplain to the Isles, the Revd Guy Scott. He's been asked by the Royal Navy to hold a wreath-laying ceremony with the Chaplain to the Fleet onboard the navy mine countermeasure vessel HMS *Ledbury*. A host of dignitaries have been asked to attend, including the fourteenth Astronomer Royal, Sir Arnold Wolfendale; Bishop Bill; and Dava Sobel, the award-winning author of *Longitude*, which tells the extraordinary story of the Yorkshire clockmaker John Harrison's lifelong attempts to develop a chronometer to determine the longitude of a ship's position to within half a degree or two minutes of time and claim the prize of 20,000 guineas offered by parliament after the *Association* disaster. The school on Scilly is even planning a trip to the National Maritime Museum at Greenwich to see Harrison's famous timepiece. Mark the brewer will be producing another new ale for the occasion, to be called Firebrand (how many more new ales can this man produce?). Father Guy has also been asked to hold a special service of commemoration at Old Town Church on the day before the ceremony.

There are photos of the original diving expedition in the Old Wesleyan Chapel, of the team leader Lt Roy Graham and a navy doctor examining human bones from the wreck, alongside the ship's bell of the *Firebrand* with 1692 engraved on it, cannons, a 1799 celestial globe showing the planets, stars and nebulae and a poster of the 1974 auction held in Penzance, by authorisation of HM Receiver of Wrecks, where over 1,500 coins were sold off, including many rare Spanish and American pieces of eight. The disaster must have been the biggest news story of the day, and I guess it will become so again; the upcoming weekend of celebration and commemoration will receive widespread coverage in the newspapers, radio and television, and could be an important vehicle in helping to establish Father Guy as a cornerstone of island life.

There are more than 3,000 wrecks dotted around the hundreds of razor-sharp outcrops that lie, like dragons' teeth, guarding each of the five islands. In order to pursue her fascination with them, Heike has made friends with Anna Cawthray, who lives in the terraced cottage next to Toby the baker by Moo Green on St Martin's, and who is regular cox on the islands' gigs, and Anna has agreed to teach Heike how to dive.

So today the sun is obligingly beating down, and Fraser is giving us a lift over to Higher Town. Fraser wants to know what we're about, and when I explain that Heike is about to have her first diving lesson, his eyebrows do a little leap.

'Let me know if you want a hand getting her into her wetsuit,' he says with a wink. 'I'm a dab hand with the talcum powder.'

Anna picks us up in the battered old diving-school Land Rover, and after a couple of hours studying theory in the dilapidated Reading Room's classroom, it's off to Great Bay on the north coast of the island, and one of Scilly's most glorious and best-kept secrets.

On the highest point of St Martin's, Chapel Down, on the north-east corner of the island, stands an enormous white- and-orange-striped obelisk that can be seen from many miles out to sea. Built on the site of an old lighthouse in 1683, this incongruous structure is still a Trinity House daymark to assist navigation. Beside it are the ruins of a Napoleonic signal station, both structures marking the most easterly point of Scilly, nearest to the mainland. Falling down around them is some of the most spectacular scenery on Scilly: great, black granite cliffs tumbling out of the heather into the turbulent swell that's in a permanent state of flux around the base of St Martin's Head and Burnt Hill. To the west, the cliffs gradually give way to Turfy Hill Point and the massive sweep of Great Bay, the great blue pool broken only by the crash of waves over Mackerel Rocks and the Satamana Ledges. The huge beach itself is usually completely deserted. There's no track to this part of the island, and no buildings, so it is almost as wild, isolated and slightly scary as any of the uninhabited islands of Scilly.

This afternoon, unusually, there are some signs of activity. Sammy is building a sandcastle, alone on the gigantic stretch of sand, and from the back of the Land Rover parked up on a grassy bank emerges the black, wet-suited figure of Anna, holding the long, hesitant arm of the islands' vet, in full diving gear, complete with mask, large fins and oxygen bottles, who starts to walk awkwardly, like an elongated penguin, down towards the water's edge. She'll be fine, she says, as long as her mascara doesn't smudge.

After a few minutes standing in the water and adjusting the breathing apparatus, and a final, mute rehearsal of the emergency signals, they are gone, dipping silently beneath the surface of the sea like a pair of mating seals, with only the twin, slightly flattened circles of water, like plates, hinting that something alive is down there.

Sammy looks up, blinking in the shimmering light, for a moment startled at the empty seascape before him.

*　　　*　　　*

Halfway up the quay at Hugh Town harbour, there's a white bollard sticking up from the cobbles, about eighteen inches high, that the *Island Lady* and the bigger visiting yachts use for their mooring ropes. Most people don't give it a second glance, but in fact it's the muzzle of an eighteenth-century, thirty-two-pound cannon that is almost certainly a relic from another of the most celebrated wrecks on Scilly, that of HMS *Colossus*, from whose wreck floated those barrels of agapanthus bulbs that now keep Peter 'The Hat' busy in his Isles of Scilly Perfumery.

The *Colossus* was a seventy-four-gun ship of the line that was damaged in the famous British victory against the French in the Battle of Cape St Vincent in 1797. A year later it joined a squadron under the command of one Rear Admiral Lord Nelson in the Mediterranean. In November 1798, she sailed from Lisbon to England with a cargo of sick and injured seamen from Nelson's stunning victory in the Battle of the Nile, and the agapanthus bulbs and crates of vases and pottery that had been collected by Lord Hamilton, whose wife Emma was Nelson's famous mistress. After a terrible journey across the Bay of Biscay, *Colossus* anchored up in St Mary's Road, but with the winds growing to a gale-force storm and lacking a vital spare bow anchor, which had been handed over to Nelson's flagship *Vanguard* in Naples, she was dragged across to Samson, went aground and, with her hull beams splitting, started shipping water. At daybreak, and still in mountainous seas, a small fleet of Scillonian gigs rescued all but one of the six hundred crew. Many of the Greek vases from the wrecked warship were washed up on St Martin's and were returned to Lord Hamilton. In the 1970s and 80s, a further 30,000 pieces of pottery from the collection were brought to the surface, and can now be seen in the British Museum.

The wreck of the *Association*, way out of Gilstone Rock, is too deep for a novice diver like Heike; so instead it has become one of her ambitions to dive to the *Colossus*, which now lies in only fourteen metres of water. The diving lessons with Anna have been progressing quickly, and together they have been swimming with the seals at Menawethan in the Eastern Isles, where Heike was intrigued to see her flippers being nibbled by the unbelievably trusting young pups. Now Anna has decided that Heike is sufficiently experienced to explore the hidden secrets of the *Colossus*, so they are out with local diver Dave McBride, who

232

moors his boat to the buoy which marks the site of the wreck, just off Samson's eastern shore, and films Heike's descent into the still waters below, a delicious pale-blue flecked with thousands of tiny, twisting grains of sand that catch the low afternoon rays of the sun as they move in the gently swirling currents.

The mask and snorkel distort Heike's long, pale face, so although she would be delighted that there is no smudged mascara to be seen, her cheeks are distended and her eyes are weirdly pulled apart and glazed, like a chronic heroin addict's, as she drifts through this slow-motioned, hallucinogenic world. She touches the tips of the long metal rivets that stand out from the sand, maybe three feet long and three inches wide—some still gripped by plate-like washers—that would have held together the numerous layers of wood of the ship's thick hull. Many are so eroded by the movement of the water that they've become as sharp and as dangerous as sabres.

Heike swims through a line of seaweed-clad columns that look half alien, half artificial and that turn out to be five of the *Colossus's* eighteen-pound cannons from the upper gun deck (the bigger thirty-two-pounders were on the main gun deck below). They are at the crazy angle at which the hulk has ended up on the seabed, muzzles through the portholes, stuck in the sand, breeches reaching up like drunken guards in a row of sentry boxes. Heike shines her torch on the brass centre-wheel of a pulley that would have hoisted the great square sails up the masts; some still have the manufacturer's serial numbers visible, along with the broad Admiralty arrows stamped into them to show they had been approved and paid for. There are even muskets lying in the sand, their brass trigger-guards glinting in the shafts of sunlight reaching down from above, untouched since they were last held by Nelson's sailors over two hundred years ago.

Heike seems so much more confident about the future now. Jo Probert has fixed a date for the inaugural meeting of the new vet support group, and she thinks a supplier of veterinary equipment will pledge £2,000 to get the fund rolling. After solidly working her way through eighty per cent of her £10,000 savings from Germany, Heike is near to breaking even financially, and despite a visit by her wealthy but authoritarian parents, who disapprove of the house at Old Town Bay, of Sammy's lack of discipline and of the islands in general (the loyal Leo bit Heike's mother in the hand, drawing a large amount of blood and still more disapprobation), she is determined to stay and forge a future on Scilly.

She's had some German friends to stay and she invited them to join her on a shark-tagging trip with local fisherman Jo Pender. A two-metre blue shark was hauled aboard in a sling, tranquillised and injected with an identity tag in a muscle by the dorsal fin before being returned to the deep. Recently a shark tagged in Scilly turned up over 6,000 miles away, in South America.

Sadly the trip wasn't a complete success, and ended in what Heike graphically describes as the entire party making 'huge sacrifices to Neptune'. Her friends were particularly violently seasick, and so was Heike, for the first time ever, although her reaction to it was unlike any I have known. While the others simply hurled over the side of the boat, Heike lay down on the deck and fought the urge to vomit, until eventually she too capitulated, with a great, heaving and very noisy 'Harrumph!', but instead of throwing up, she retained Neptune's offering in her mouth, breathing heavily through the nostrils and gaining strength until she was able to swallow the lot back down. I can't imagine what this must have been like, especially since she repeated the action over and over again, but I find myself hugely impressed by such a pointless but heroic demonstration of Teutonic self-discipline. Note to self: don't mess with this woman.

13

The Sun Seems to Know
When to Put his Hat On

The summer weather becomes stranger by the day, and it's picked up an almost supernatural tempo— a week of unremitting rain and drizzle is followed by a short burst of dazzling sunshine, which arrives just at the moment when it is most needed. Alongside these brief outbreaks of optimism, and probably aided by the undoubted tonic of Bishop Bill's recent visit, it seems that the tide in Father Guy's fortunes may, just, be on the turn.

Set into the worn, dark nave between the pews of Old Town Church, is the tomb of a young man who died of cholera at the Pest House on St Helen's. It's just possible to make out his name: Lt James Allen Corsse. I assume he was an extremely brave man, since he was a surgeon and therefore must have volunteered to work on that island of death. He was twenty-seven years old.

It is over this tomb that Father Guy, dressed in a long, white linen cassock, is now walking to and fro; aided by Kate and the girls, he is busy lighting dozens of candles on the chandeliers and around the walls. Today there is to be one of his first baptisms on Scilly, a moment of celebration, and I detect a certain spring in his step.

The baby in question is Abigail Pritchard, a flame-haired youngster with a bad cold, whose parents, Julian and Rachel, have travelled over from their home in Dubai specially to have her christened in Old Town Church. Julian was born on Scilly, and, as the large, expensively dressed congregation start to assemble in the sunshine outside the church door, I follow him into the churchyard, past Lord Wilson's grave and down to the end of the adjacent field, where the recent funerals have taken place. There, beside the fresh grave of Nathan Woodcock, he shows me, with a certain pride, three more graves: those of his father, who died two years ago; his grandfather, who died last year; and his grandmother, who died a few weeks ago.

Strangely, this is far from a macabre moment.

'That's why it's important for Abigail to be christened here,' says Julian, the proud grandson, son and now father. 'Nothing's more important than family links, nothing.'

Father Guy takes the baptism solemnly. He believes passionately in the sanctity of the sacrament of the christening service, and looks intently at the godparents as they pledge themselves to renounce evil and the devil.

It is also clear, though, from the sudden outbreak of smiles at the end of the service, that he shares the joy of the occasion. Afterwards, he tells me what a huge relief it has been, after the terrible past few weeks, to celebrate a simple baptism.

A few days of misery and rain later, up at the Chaplaincy the day breaks to reveal a sublime August morning, which is bizarre because Guy's churchwardens Sue and Fiona are actually praying for rain. Or rather, praying for rain until about twenty minutes past ten, when the tripper boats setting off to the off-islands will be away, with any luck empty, leaving St Mary's bulging with holidaymakers with full wallets and nothing much to do. Then, in this perfect arrangement, the sun will blaze down for the rest of the day, and the parish fête on the Chaplaincy lawns will make a fortune for church funds. Or so the theory goes.

At the height of the summer, most islanders simply put their social lives on hold; there is, however, one exception to the rule. In August, each island has its fête, which almost everyone attends. They are planned months ahead, consume huge amounts of energy and ingenuity and are quite simply the best fêtes I've ever been to.

This morning, Father Guy is up early to mow the lawn one last time, and an hour or two later he's joined by the good ladies of the church, who busy themselves putting up miles of bunting, trestle tables and tents. Their prayers have not been answered: the sun blazes down with a ferocity rarely seen in the last few weeks of winds and storms. Both churchwardens are in full flow. Fiona

237

has created her own version of a coconut shy with empty baked bean cans she's collected from the wholesale shop she runs with her husband David next to Oriel Hicks's stained-glass studio down on the industrial estate behind Porthmellon Beach. Sue has her own version of a lucky dip—parcels costing a pound containing delights of varying value wrapped in plain paper and blue ribbon for boys, pink for girls and a kind of murky yellow for those unsure. This is always the most popular stall at the fête, she declares, and will sell out in twenty minutes. When Father Guy innocently starts to examine a parcel to work out what is in it, Sue barks out: 'Put it down! No rattling!'

It is another of those shamelessly charming Scilly scenes, with nothing really to tell you that this is the twenty-first century, save the fact that the result of the 'Guess the Weight of the Cake', baked by Kate, must be in grams. There's a stall selling second-hand buttons, which is apparently always a big hit—there's nowhere to buy buttons on Scilly—and another with a large selection of dog-eared toys, which, since the nearest toy shop is forty miles away over a large slice of the Atlantic Ocean, will be just as popular. There are home-made doughnuts and ice cream and even a Punch and Judy show, run by a bespectacled little chap called Reg Payn, who's constructed a perfect replica of a collapsible Victorian stand-up theatre which he's brought over on the *Scillonian* in a series of suitcases. Reg hasn't missed the St Mary's fête in thirteen years and swears it is, without doubt, the best of the fêtes and beach shows he plays throughout Cornwall. Except Bodmin, that is—he doesn't know what that one's like because

238

Reg and his puppets have been banned by the Town Council for encouraging domestic violence.

'Isn't it all just a bit too twee and old fashioned?' I ungallantly suggest to Sue.

'Of course it is, that's exactly why people come,' she says, slapping me down without a moment's hesitation. 'If you want pinball machines and video games, you can jolly well go to Newquay.'

She's soon proved absolutely right, of course. Fuelled by the recent heavy rain, the rich-green lawns of the Chaplaincy look like something out of a gardening advert, and are soon packed with locals and visitors alike. The sun keeps blazing down. I stand on the top lawn, beside the fiery colours of the flower borders, with great blue-veined echium leaning over the dozens of youthful red-hot pokers exploding with flame-orange and yellow heads, like small fireworks. The wonderful Blue Tango Orchestra (a dickie-bowed Malcolm Martland on clarinet) strikes up that unforgettable 1930s classic 'Pasadena'. If you gave Spielberg a blank cheque and instructions to create the ideal image of a traditional English fête for his next Hollywood blockbuster, he could not possibly do better than this. It's quite perfect.

Down below, Reg gets to work in his overheated tent, and soon Punch, like most men unable to multi-task, panics at what to do with the baby, so decides to flush her down the lavatory and then beats the hell out of Judy when she complains. Amazingly, the kids go crazy for the show, a curious phenomenon which seems to bemuse all the adults present.

One of the most intriguing moments of the afternoon comes courtesy of a cheeky idea

239

designed to wring cash from a large number of Father Guy's irrepressibly nosey parishioners. He and Kate are offering guided tours of the Chaplaincy, for which they are charging £3 a ticket (£1 for children and OAPs), which might be reasonable for Blenheim Palace but I think may be a bit steep for a quick look around a nice but unexceptional Georgian house in Hugh Town. As so often on Scilly, I'm proved quite wrong. Such is the inquisitiveness of his parishioners that Father Guy is soon packing them in, and by the end of the day they've raised no less than £134 for parish funds with this one idea alone.

The off-islanders are even more creative.

*   *   *

With just a few days to go before the fête on St Martin's is due to take place, on the very same cricket ground where young Robert Morton loved to play, and just beneath the family house itself, the organisers have been in two minds about how to proceed in the wake of the boy's disappearance and the mystery that still surrounds his fate. After much debate, it's decided that the fête will go ahead, but that there will be a break with convention. Instead of the money raised going towards the usual project—funding a replacement for the rather shabby Reading Room, where Heike held her first, abortive off-island surgery—it will go to the RNLI and the island coastguard and emergency services, so islanders feel that by gathering for their much-loved annual celebration on the cricket ground, they will at least be doing something appropriate.

Right on time it's fine again, of course, and all morning the tripper boats from the other islands have been ferrying hundreds of people across Crow Sound for the biggest day in the St Martin's calendar. Up at the bakery on Moo Green, surrounded by a sea of glorious sunflowers, Toby and his team have been working through the night preparing for their busiest day of the year; by noon they've already taken over £1,000, a vast amount for such a tiny place.

The fête is a reminder of the greater simplicity, the quaintness of off-island life. Father Guy's eyebrows shoot skywards when we are told there is no beer tent, for example, because of the event's traditional connection with the Reading Room, originally funded by the Methodists and the Temperance Movement; we all drink lashings of lemonade instead.

Like the St Mary's fête, there are lots of bric-a-brac and second-hand stalls, because, apart from the little Post Office stores up by the church, there are no shops on St Martin's at all, nowhere to buy clothes, furniture, kitchen equipment, books or jewellery. The men of the island fire brigade, complete with shining red fire-tractor, are, naturally enough, in charge of the barbeque, and later there's a demonstration to an admiring crowd on how to put out a small fire. This appears to be one of the highlights of the afternoon. Two men dressed in the full brigade fire-resistant uniform light the flames, on a small dish; another steps forward with a fire-extinguisher and instantly puts them out. OK, this is island life, and all that matters is that it greatly impresses the crowd, which breaks out into a spontaneous round of applause.

But there is one difference from the St Mary's fête. St Martin's is the home of the influential parishioner whose daughter Father Guy refused to marry to a divorcé, and throughout the island there was a degree of real hostility towards the Chaplain. The couple in question ended up being married by the Methodist minister up in the tiny chapel above the cricket ground. Is there any residual bad feeling? It's hard to tell.

Conscious of a slightly strained atmosphere, Father Guy seems to be making a renewed effort to win over the parishioners of his most northerly island. Bishop Bill's advice to him had been simple: don't hide away in the Chaplaincy, now is the time to get out there and be with your parishioners. Perhaps fuelled by the diaphanous blue skies and the warmth of the sun on his back, Guy looks at his best, chatting and laughing with everyone about him, moving seamlessly from group to group, appearing, to my eyes, to be much like the Father Guy of old that I met in Mullion for the first time since his arrival.

He has the tricky task of judging the cake-baking competition, which he somehow turns into his own comic sideshow. Then he crosses over the grassy dunes and goes down by the boatsheds to the fabulous beach on Higher Town Bay, a heady, Mediterranean mix of blinding blue sea and endless, bleached-white sand. This is Par Beach, recently voted the second loveliest beach in Britain, missing the top slot only because it failed so badly on the 'car-parking and café facilities' category, apparently essential to secure the number-one slot. I can't imagine anywhere else in this country where so many people would throw themselves wholeheartedly into a sandcastle competition, but here, dotted between the sunbathers, boats and games of beach cricket, there are dozens of castles of every shape and size. I guess this is just what you do on St Martin's on a sunny summer's afternoon.

I watch Father Guy—an unmistakable figure, even from a distance, dressed incongruously in his uniform of black—as he moves down the pearly beach from one extraordinary sandcastle to the next, surrounded by a growing, half-clad crowd of smiling onlookers. This is a new, slightly more assured Chaplain to the Isles, seemingly at ease among his parishioners, and they, in turn, seem to share his mood and feel the better for it.

Then hundreds of coloured balloons are suddenly released from the cricket field behind and, carried in the gentle north-easterly breeze, float away above us towards Crow Sound and the 'mainland' of St Mary's beyond, soon becoming tiny pinpricks in the piercingly blue sky. I'm told they are bio-degradable these days; presumably making it even less likely we'll ever see any of them again. Beyond St Mary's is St Agnes, and beyond that, if the wind is constant, ten thousand miles of sea. This is not the best place, perhaps, from which to launch a balloon race.

It's been a memorable afternoon. I wonder if this is just an unusual, exceptional moment or the start of a new era.

*   *   *

The slightly stooping, white-bearded undertaker

on St Mary's, the only one on Scilly, Alfie Trenear, lives in a small, unidentified terraced house on Church Street. Alfie is the seventh generation of undertaker in his family, but he tells me sadly that his children have decided not to follow in his footsteps and he has no idea what the islands will do when he retires.

Just as the mood on the islands has started to pick up and rally, fate once again intervenes, in a summer that even the boatmen describe, wearily, as weird and unnatural. Which is why Alfie is having a busy few months.

The undertaker had predicted that the body of the lost boy from St Martin's would be washed up two and a half weeks after he went missing, and sure enough, almost exactly two and a half weeks after poor Robert Morton disappeared, a body is found at Gugh, the tiny island with just two houses on it that at low tide is connected by a thin sandbank to the eastern side of St Agnes. The lifeboat is dispatched to pick it up in the early morning sunshine, and the body is indeed identified as that of young Robert. WPC Nikki Green grimly confirms that there is no suggestion of crime.

Then comes word that another young boy from St Mary's, Adam Mallon, has been killed in car crash on the mainland. His body too is brought back to Scilly for Alfie to attend to. At the wake after the funeral, at the Mermaid, a twenty-three-year-old friend of the family, who has been drinking with the best of them, throws himself onto rocks in the sea and severely damages his back. After being airlifted by a Royal Navy helicopter from St Mary's to the hospital at Truro, and later to a specialist unit in Plymouth, he's told he'll never walk again. How much more agonisingly bad news can this tiny community take?

Between bursts of summer sunshine, the terrible rainstorms, sudden winds and surprise sea-fogs have kept on coming, and even the Chaplaincy has been pressed into service as an emergency billet for stranded visitors. Along with the delayed aftershock of the deaths of the three young men, I detect a feeling that the islanders are intent on keeping their heads down and are trying, with grim determination, to make the best of what is left of the season.

Many of them have memories of the terrible havoc wreaked on the 1979 Fastnet Race, one of the toughest ocean races in the world, which was hit by an unpredicted force-eleven hurricane. More than three hundred yachts had set off on the 600-mile voyage which every two years is the traditional end to Cowes Week in the Solent. They were heading west to Fastnet Rock, off south-west Ireland, and were due to return via the Bishop Rock lighthouse on Scilly to the finishing line at Plymouth. The hurricane blew up in minutes; fifteen sailors were lost and twenty-five yachts were sunk or disabled. Many of the damaged boats were brought to safety by the St Mary's lifeboat.

This year, just as the race is about to begin, the Met. Office issues a warning of severe weather in the western approaches to the Channel and, for the first time in its eighty-three-year history, the Fastnet Race is postponed, for twenty-four hours. For Scilly, the timing of this and the publicity it generates, is disastrous. Visiting yachts scurry for the mainland, holidaymakers book early flights home or cancel plans to visit Scilly altogether and posters appear everywhere announcing that even the *Scillonian* is cancelled.

With all hatches firmly battened down, we wait for the storm to arrive. It never does. The Fastnet Race goes ahead, and now the final five yachts are racing past Bishop Rock in near perfect sailing conditions.

Some of the islanders are having trouble suppressing their frustration, yet the weird events of the summer continue unabated.

Martin Bond's new mobile fish van is lying idle up in the barn at Longstone Farm, all wired, plumbed and painted white, although the outline of the bow of *Marauder* and the letters 'M. and J.' are still waiting for Imogen to paint them in red.

Martin may have got his planning permission to use the fish van on the streets of Hugh Town, but the problem is that there is no fish to put in it. Just as Scilly is buzzing with hungry visitors in search of good, local produce, a combination of the endless bad weather and bad luck means that Martin is scarcely able to supply his regular chefs in the island pubs and restaurants. When *Marauder* has been able to put to sea, her nets have either missed the shoals or the shoals have decided to shimmy around elsewhere.

'Got be one or t'other, I reckon, don't you?' asks Martin, rolling up a smoke and sticking it in his mouth, determined not to be obviously perturbed by his current situation.

'Might the fish have gone for good?'

Martin looks at me with a degree of pity.

'If I knew how to predict where fish is and ain't,'

246

he says at length, disappearing behind a pale curtain of smoke, 'I'd be a very rich man.'

Then comes some amazing news from, of all places, the south of France. It's not exactly hugely significant, but, oddly, it seems to cheer everyone up. One of the balloons released from St Martin's appears to have defied the prevailing wind and has turned up in St Precuil Poitiers, a small village near Cognac. This just goes to show that it's easy to know where a wind is coming from, but almost impossible to know where it is going to.

*   *   *

Dead on cue again, the sun breaks out at the start of the last of the off-island summer fêtes, on Bryher. This is by far and away the best fête I've ever been to.

I notice a group of elderly ladies carrying large bags who have been loitering for an hour or two around the huge jumble-sale stall, by far the biggest in the field. Some of them I recognise as Bryher folk, others seem to have arrived early on the boats from other islands. The moment the fête is officially declared open, all becomes clear. The ladies hurl themselves at the jumble stall, arms and bags swirling around like the sails of a windmill, and within just a few minutes the stall has almost sold out of serviceable second-hand clothes.

The fête is a triumph of invention over an almost total lack of resources.

I spot Father Guy and Kate in the queue to be photographed sticking their faces through twin holes in Caroline Pearce's Treasure Island billboard, so he is immortalised as a slightly manic

247

pirate and she a demure mermaid. Meanwhile, a band of spotty-looking teenagers strike up a song; it's surprisingly accomplished. Mercifully, there seems to be no legacy of the Temperance Movement here, so beer is flowing in fountains.

A huge crowd collects around a medieval-looking contraption of ropes, ladders and wooden scaffolding, under which the island boatmen nobly volunteer to sit, waiting for the successful throw at the bull's-eye that will send a teetering bucket of icy water cascading over their heads. I don't know why, but it's fun; we all roar as those hoary, sunbeaten faces, one by one, are drowned in saltwater. Believe me, this is a huge improvement on the St Martin's fire-extinguisher demonstration.

Even more people gather to watch the famous cake-eating competition, which has the voyeuristic fascination of a particularly vindictive gladiatorial contest; a row of increasingly nauseous-looking contestants race to stuff down great wheels of cream-laden pastry. We are hysterical.

Two of the mainstays of the Bryher fête over the years have been the phenomenally energetic sisters, Marian Bennett and Kris Taylor, who live side by side in a pair of idyllic old farm cottages near the fête field. Kris, in Veronica Farm, is Scilly's chirpy chiropodist and a legendary home-made fudge-maker; Marian, in South Hill, is an outspoken councillor whose son Daniel has taken over the island's boatbuilding business from her late husband and whose petite, pretty blonde daughter Charlie is famous for her infatuation with the heart-throb actor Jude Law.

Jude Law has a well documented love-affair with Scilly, recently going on the top-rated David

248

Letterman TV show to tell the USA that the islands are straight out of a 1950s post-card, and the best place in the world for a holiday. Jude and his friend 1980s pop legend Gary Kemp were both married to the same woman, the actress Sadie Frost, and the two men make an annual pilgrimage to Scilly with their gaggle of children who share the same mother, to savour the privacy and miles of empty beaches. Young Charlie, while not technically stalking Mr Law, nonetheless seems to pop up with unfailing regularity whenever the actor is seen out and about, notably at last year's Bryher fête, when he uttered to her, to mesmerising effect, the single word 'hello', a moment to relish and be told to anyone willing to hear. Later, things came to a head when Mr Law and his mate visited the island's only pub, the Fraggle Rock, where Charlie was working behind the bar for the summer.

'What can I get you?' says Charlie, heart shuddering, cheeks delicately flushing, struggling to contain herself.

'Two pints of lager please, love.'

It is all Charlie can do to stop the glass rattling against the pipe as she pours the beer. She can't bring herself to look at the two international stars, who are peering over their shoulders at the pub, as men do, for fear her eyes will give her away.

'And a couple of baked spuds please, love. Cheese and ham.'

Charlie takes a pad of paper and writes down the order, unable now to hide her trembling fingers, but at the same time anxious not to appear too pathetically girly. She then comes up with a line that's been immortalised in modern island legend.

'Sorry, but I'm going to need a name, please?'

No wonder he loves coming here.

Charlie is here at the fête this afternoon, and it is she who walks Father Guy up the track above the field to an old, bleached-timber building with lovely views across Samson Hill and Green Bay. This used to be the old schoolhouse, before the children started to be ferried across each day to the school on Tresco, and since then it's been used as the island's community centre. Listening to Charlie talk as she shows Father Guy around, I realise how fundamental to society here this humble, ramshackle building must be. Apart from the tiny church and pub, there is nowhere else to hold a doctor's surgery, the whist drives and musical evenings, the talks and lectures, the children's shows, the quiz nights and dances, all of which help to keep the islanders sane, especially in the long winter months. They certainly realise it. They need £130,000 in order to start work on a much-needed new building and since fund-raising began five months ago, this island of barely eighty people has raised over £60,000, nearly one thousand pounds per person. An extraordinary achievement.

Down the hill on the fête field, a further £7,000 is rolling in, more than has been raised by any of the other island fêtes, although the fact that there's a beer tent here may well be a significant factor. Guy's impressed.

At four o'clock sharp, just as Father Guy and I are warming up for another pint or two, the fête is all but over, as the first of the boats arrive to ferry away the holidaymakers, and the islanders, conscious of summer passing, hurry off to continue the day's work, reopening the Fraggle Rock and café, hiring out a dinghy or two for a sunny evening's sail or preparing evening meals for their guests. Within a few weeks, the season will be over.

So we leave the beer tent, and wander off up the track to seek out Richard Pearce in his Golden Eagle studio. The walls and beamed roof of the old boatshed hold rows of Richard's distinctive blue-and-white canvases, but I notice there are gaps and there's an unbroken stream of visitors queuing to get in. I ask how many commissions for large canvases Richard's had since the opening of the enlarged quay down by the church, and he grins mischievously and says he's been so busy selling pictures to walkers sheltering from the endless rain that he hasn't had much of a chance to think about it. Father Guy is gripped by Richard's story of his chameleon-like transformation from humble flower farmer to self-supporting artist; it is, after all, a pretty good lesson in the art of survival on Scilly.

Back at the fête field, there's been a drama that shocks us all. Charlie's aunt, Kris Taylor, has been the victim of something I'd assumed never happened here; it appears she's been robbed. Throughout the summer, Kris has a table outside Veronica Farm for selling her deliciously decadent fudge, a huge hit on the islands, and at some stage this afternoon, while Kris was busy at the fête, the cash tin has disappeared.

'It's just not what you expect, it really isn't, not here,' says the usually irrepressibly optimistic Kris, busying about to hide her obvious disappointment. Charlie can't believe what has happened either.

251

'Scilly's ruined, this would never have happened a few years ago. I just can't believe it, I really can't. Not here, not on Bryher.'

Immediately, plans are organised for 'Wanted' style posters to be printed and distributed across the islands in the hope of shaming the culprit into confessing. People are genuinely shocked, shaking their heads with disbelief; this is an ugly invasion of a cherished world.

Just as it seems this might be a welcome bit of business for WPC Nikki Green, the tin turns up. It contains £62.45, and is discovered hidden away just inside the front door of Veronica Farm, where a well-wisher who had bought the last bag of Kris's fudge had carefully placed it for safe-keeping.

It seems that God is indeed back in his heaven, and all is right with the world.

14

An Indian Summer to the Rescue

Just behind the boatsheds on Porthmellon Beach, on the other side of the road that leads up to the Telegraph and just up from Oriel Hicks's studio, there's a tiny estate agency. It's run by Tim Guthrie, who sports a large Mexican moustache and who can be seen hunched over his desk during working hours, trying to sell the few freehold properties that come onto the market on Scilly and renting out holiday cottages and apartments for the islanders. He looks rather like a retired Scotland Yard detective.

Porthmellon is usually a quiet corner, but in the last few days there has been an almost continual banging and crashing in the attic above Tim's normally tranquil office. Today, since all the furniture has now been removed, Keri Jones sits on the floor, poring over a laptop, while around him his energetic, young, blonde sidekick Zoe Parry is sloshing white paint on the walls and ceiling. It's hard to imagine right now, but in just a few weeks' time this will be the studio headquarters of the world's smallest professional radio station.

This is something Keri has been working on for years; it's become a true labour of love. He has sold his house and business interests in south Wales and moved over, boats truly burned, for a new life on Scilly, in charge of a station with a resident target audience of just two thousand. Many of the programmes will be presented by islanders and the operation will be run by him and Zoe alone, a self-financing, non-profitmaking enterprise about which Keri feels so passionately that he has pledged to support it with his own money if necessary.

In principle, Radio Scilly is a brilliant concept, linking five separate but inter-dependent islands, each compelled to share vital information about tides and weather, boat times and routes, delays on the helicopters, planes and ferries, pub and shop opening times, shows, plays and concerts. Most of the listeners will know all the presenters; everyone will already be aware of the advertisers. It's a kind of radio heaven.

Even so, given the constraints of time, personnel and money, this is an ambitious project for Keri and Zoe to pull off. They need about £50,000 to get started and begin paying themselves a small salary, and over the last few months they've been talking to organisations and companies about grants and sponsorship and selling advertising to local businesses, from the comically low starting point of £2 a week. An added pressure is that, far from Radio Scilly being ignored as an eccentric outpost of the radio world, as I had imagined, the broadcasting industry is watching their progress intently, to assess whether such a tiny station really is sustainable and replicable elsewhere.

Keri is a determined and persuasive operator, and already the wheels that could create a raft of local showbiz legends are inexorably turning. Dazzling debuts await people like 'Scots' Lorraine Bruce, who manages the Atlantic Inn and is famous for her outspoken opinions on everything from WPC Nikki Green's love life to the colour of the new assistant harbourmaster's trousers, and who finally agreed to be the Radio Scilly agony aunt after negotiations that involved several bottles of wine. Churchwarden Fiona, behind her book-keeper's desk just yards down the road at the wholesale stores on the Porthmellon estate, would be brilliant presenting 'Thought for the Day'. And the laconic Fraser Hicks is the perfect choice to start the broadcasting morning off with an exposition on the upcoming day's boating movements in and around St Mary's harbour. The council's chief planning officer, Craig Dryden, has been signed up as a late-night, alternative-music DJ, Charlie's mum Marian and aunt Kris will be giving weekly advice on health and well being, with, presumably particular emphasis on feet, and the landlady of the Porthcressa Inn, Rachel Gaulton, is doing a live girly-gossip show called 'Ladies What Lunch'.

It is hoped that the listeners won't just be islanders. Scilly ex-pats and holidaymakers who've become addicted to the station on their visits to the islands can avoid painful withdrawal symptoms by continuing to listen at home, on the Internet. In fact, Keri plans to install webcams around the studio, so people from Papua New Guinea to San Francisco, from Alaska to Tierra del Fuego can observe the goings-on at Radio Scilly, as well as hear all about the big—and, much more intriguing, the not so big—talking points of the inhabitants of the tiny Isles of Scilly, every day, seven days a week.

Radio Scilly goes on air in the first week of September. I can't wait to tune in.

*   *   *

As well as no Chinese or Indian restaurants, no trains, cinemas, motorways, pollution, A-levels or Sunday papers, there's no solicitor's office on Scilly, which is why, a few months ago, Louise Southwell found herself in a helicopter rising up over the old seawater swimming pool at Penzance, across the rows of neatly moored trawlers that still fill the quays at Newlyn and out over the lovely little harbour of Mousehole, towards a horizon broken only by the distant outline of the islands.

Louise, tanned, blonde and with dazzlingly bright teeth, may defy the stereotype of a provincial solicitor, but she is an expert in her field of trusts, tax planning, estates, wills and, particularly, inheritance tax. As such, she has the dubious privilege of a more intimate insight into the lives of her clients than even their nearest and dearest. She tells of a wealthy man in his eighties, who had apparently been happily married for sixty years, who instructed her to draw up a will leaving his wife not a single penny, on the grounds that she'd had a brief affair with an American GI in the Second World War. He died recently, and when Louise revealed the contents of the will to the widow, she was devastated, unaware that her late husband had even known of her brief wartime indiscretion.

A few weeks ago, Louise had left her office in Penzance for an appointment with an elderly lady on the Strand, overlooking St Mary's harbour. In need of a signature for the will, she dashed out into the street and stopped a man wearing a dapper suit who turned out to be Keri Jones, in the process of setting up the world's smallest radio station, which is why Louise Southwell has become Radio Scilly's 'Legal Eagle'. She's already getting nervous about her first broadcast in a few weeks' time.

As the days go by, I have a growing admiration for Keri and Zoe, now burning the midnight oil to get their station up and running in time for its launch. The workload is huge. Keri has made a number of experimental trial broadcasts on Scilly before, so he knows what he's taking on. While he is camping out in the attic above Tim Guthrie's office, wrestling with the technology, Zoe is out and about, spreading the word among the great and the good in a frantic 'awareness campaign' and pressganging reluctant islanders to become DJs and presenters. She met Toby and has persuaded him to do a weekly 'Letter from St Martin's', and little Charlie Bennett has been recruited to do the same from Bryher. The tourism chief, Steve Watt, has been signed up to do a Scilly version of 'Desert Island Discs' called 'Stranded on Samson', Pete 'The Hat' from the perfumery will be offering a 'heady mix' of folk music and island chat, and Tim Guthrie will be recording 'Scilly Memories'. It sounds irresistible. Probably for all the wrong reasons, but does that matter?

Zoe is also trying to top up the revenue needed to keep Radio Scilly on air, and they've come up with an ingenious plan to raise cash: two thousand people are each required to pledge £1 a week towards an island lottery. Every Monday at noon, a winner will be announced on air, who will receive £1,000. The rest will be split between station running costs and local causes. Because the numbers involved are so small, within just a few weeks everyone on Scilly will know someone who has hit the jackpot, which in itself is a brilliant piece of public relations, but the real evil genius of the plan, which I only really appreciate once I've signed on the dotted line, is that you can only pay your weekly £1 by direct debit, which, let's face it, once you have set up you are unlikely ever to bother to cancel. If I live for another forty years, I have just signed up to hand over to Radio Scilly the sum of £2,080; if this is replicated two thousand times, then this stunningly simple stunt has guaranteed the station more than £4,000,000 over the next four decades.

Keri's also been looking into the cheapest way to record his radio station's identity jingles, which he insists must sound as professional as possible.

'Will you have to go all the way back to London to do that?'

'You must be joking,' says Keri, a phrase he likes. 'London's way too expensive. I've found somewhere much cheaper.'

'Penzance?'

'You must be joking. Milan.'

'You must be joking.' (Actually me this time, not Keri.)

'It's about a third of the cost of anywhere in the UK. Professional singers too.'

'But isn't it expensive just to get there?' Am I beginning to sound like someone planning a Grand Tour in the seventeenth century?

'You must be joking. It's about a quarter of the cost of getting from London to Scilly.'

The one worry he has, says Keri, is the Italian singers, who he will have to tutor to sing 'Leeesten to Radeeeo Sceeely' with an English accent. I wish him luck.

Have I said this before? Can't wait to tune in.

*   *   *

The odd weather is continuing well into August, and a sense of quiet bewilderment seems to have settled over the islanders, almost as if they are contemplating giving up on the season. The *Scillonian* has been sailing on Sundays throughout August, the only month of the year in which this happens, and it's an utter delight to be able to read the Sunday newspapers on the intended day; there's an almost carnival mood among the long queues forming outside Mumfords, who open up

258

specially, at one o'clock, in honour of the event. The day-trippers, though, are reluctant to run the risk of suicide-evoking seasickness, and even those who brave it and come over have discovered—to their amazement, and mine too—that, inexplicably, most of the shops stubbornly remain closed all day, and all the restaurants. What are the islanders thinking of? Henry, the harbourmaster at Tresco, tells me that the number of visiting yachts is down by forty per cent, and now an armada of the dreaded Portuguese Man O' War jellyfish has been spotted heading towards Scilly. A thrilled Heike has already seen one of them down in the harbour, as big as a mattress.

There used to be a big carnival on St Mary's to mark the coming of the end of the summer season, and later this was replaced by a water fiesta in the harbour. Now there's a more modest festival to celebrate the islands' music and sports, up in the fields behind the Star Castle at the Garrison, and everyone's making an effort for it. There's six-a-side football, starring the cream of the world's smallest football league, a large range of local bands, of hugely variable quality, and mountains of sausages and burgers washed down with copious quantities of cheap beer and wine. WPC Nikki Green is showing off her athletic skills to Andrew, her new boyfriend, in the netball competition, and taking pride of place at the event is the extraordinary thirty-foot yellow rowboat that Nathan Woodcock and his three friends had planned to race in next year's New York to Scilly challenge, now sponsored by the Tresco estate and named *Scilly Boys*. It's announced that the Atlantic row should go ahead, although it's not yet clear who will replace Nathan.

This will be a major story. *Scillly Boys* will be shipped over to New York in a container in early spring, and the race to Scilly will begin in late May or early June. This is the time of year that the *Titanic* went down in the same waters, so the final go-ahead will only be given once the last of the St Lawrence icebergs are safely out of view.

Zoe is manning the first ever Radio Scilly stall, and the station's new agony aunt, a tipsy 'Scots' Lorraine, is warming up her act by giving out plentiful advice on personal problems to anyone who'll listen. Later, she falls down the stairs at the hotel and tears some ligaments in her leg, so she'll be making her debut on Radio Scilly armed with crutches, no doubt prompting the question: 'What should an agony aunt do when she's in great pain and trying to broadcast a live show?'

Despite the energy and laboured enthusiasm of the organisers, and the blustery sun that obligingly chases away the early-morning blanket of grey cloud, the event is somehow burdened with a leaden atmosphere, doomed to spoil a party that should have everyone throwing their hats into the air to celebrate the joyous final throes of the holiday season. Worse still, there's no-one at all here from St Martin's, and no Father Guy. Today is the funeral of young Robert Morton in the tiny Methodist Chapel over at Higher Town.

The sun holds through the afternoon, just, but there's a stiff northerly breeze, and by four o'clock news is rapidly spreading across the Garrison of another tragedy at sea. An elderly couple and an islander in his eighties who the couple have been visiting each summer for years set off this morning in bright sunshine in a sixteen-foot boat for a day's fishing off St Agnes. They weren't wearing lifejackets and the boat capsized. The two men were rescued and the woman has just been picked up by the *Firethorn*, en route from Bryher. Kris Taylor's husband, Geoff, is aboard; he is one of four 'first respondents' on the island, trained to use a defibrillator and in basic paramedic skills such as cardio-pulmonary resuscitation. He gives the woman mouth-to-mouth on the journey in to Hugh Town, but in vain. She has drowned. For Scilly, a community of only two thousand, to suffer four unexpected deaths in just a few weeks is unparalleled in recent history.

Groups of islanders start drifting away early from the Garrison. There's an unexpected chill in the air. The glint of the Bishop Rock lighthouse, way out in the moody, grey Atlantic, looks bleaker than ever.

I've learned, though, that the mood on Scilly continually oscillates, in a far more vigorous and reactive way than anywhere I've known on the mainland. The determining factor is the powerful concoction of a joint will to survive, to get on with life, and the weather. In the days that follow the Garrison festival, the weird meteorological phenomena of the last few weeks start to calm. The sun appears and decides to stay with us, growing ever hotter, until it feels almost tropical, beating down hour after hour, lifting the gloom like an evaporating sea-mist. It's as though summer proper has arrived at last, just when autumn would normally be preparing to get cracking.

The last week of August is the best since the

glorious spring, and suddenly there's a sense of energy and renewal. The Steamship Company reports an unusual increase in day-trippers and extra flights are scheduled up at the airport. Once again, the quay is busy at ten o'clock every morning, and the boatmen seem more chipper than they have been for months. If there was any hay on Scilly, they'd undoubtedly be making it.

Up in his study at the Chaplaincy, Father Guy has just received some news which will no doubt put a spring in his step too. The two legendary retired priests, Donald and Margaret Marr have called to say they have booked their flights back to Scilly, earlier than he was expecting, after their summer break in Cheshire. Known affectionately as the Revd and Mrs Bogoff—as in 'buy one, get one free'—they will, as usual, be wintering in the parsonage just up from St Nicholas's church on Tresco, and will be available to do whatever they can, in whatever way, to help the new chaplain.

Father Guy is counting off the days until the Bogoffs' arrival.

*   *   *

Over on St Martin's, in their privileged position high on the hill above the Seven Stones pub, Britain's most spoilt piglets are settling in splendidly. There had been a few dramas transferring the hyper-energetic Gloucester Old Spots from Ian's lorry into boxes and then getting them up the hill, perched on the back of Toby's quad, to Colditz, but here they now are, munching away contentedly, as though they'd been born and brought up on Scilly. Thankfully, they have not yet got to know each other well enough to organise any serious escape bid.

Down below, in the steaming kitchen of the pub, Pauly, in a strictly professional sense, has never been happier. People all over the islands are talking about the quality of his food and the pub takings continue to be higher than projected, although there has been predictable sniping over the lack of chips, sausages or cheap burgers. The campsite in the old flower fields below Snowy the goat is full of young families with small budgets and hungry children with voracious appetites, and Pauly is considering an earlier, slightly less demanding menu, though he is determined not to compromise his standards.

While the job is going better than he'd dreamed, Pauly's personal life has become something of a desert. I asked him a few weeks ago if he was looking for a girlfriend and, without a moment's hesitation, he said, 'Always!' There aren't many suitable, available girls on St Martin's—there actually may not be any—and, anyway, Pauly works the ultimate unsocial hours. He has Mondays off and spends them checking out the culinary opposition in the off-island pubs—in particular, the Turk's Head on St Agnes, with its new owners, is a serious potential threat—and mooching about St Mary's, eyeing up the talent, but aware he has to get the last boat back to St Martin's at five o'clock sharp, which certainly limits his horizons. He meets up with the off-duty staff at the St Martin's Hotel, just round the corner and up from the beach at Lower Town, but even though there are some pretty girls there, they all seem to have large, fit boyfriends. There was a

263

barbeque down on the beach at Lawrence Bay—an idyllic evening, except for the slightly painful fact that everyone else seemed to be holding hands.

There had been murmurings from Liz and Darcy about the need for more help behind the busy bar, but Pauly had not thought too much about it until this morning, when Ian arrives in the lorry from the quay with two unexpected pieces of cargo: a large suitcase in the back and a small, sparky girl with laughing green eyes and a cheeky smile sitting beside him in the front. Her name is Thea Charrot-Hickling, and I hope Toby doesn't get in there quick and make her wife number three, lest she becomes Mrs Tobin-Duigan-Charrot-Hickling, a name they'd struggle to fit on the licensees' plaque above the front door.

Thea, it seems, is on the run: from a life in Norfolk, a job in a building society and a failed relationship. The house she bought with her ex-partner has just been put on the market. She's here for a month or two of escape working behind the bar at the Seven Stones, looking for fun wherever she can find it, before deciding on her next move. Pauly says he had to breathe in slowly when he discovered Thea had been billeted in the staff house beside the pub, next to his own room.

All thoughts of romance, though, must temporarily be put to one side. Pauly needs to prepare for an important meeting with Toby, the newly appointed correspondent for Radio Scilly, who, in a moment of divine inspiration combined with shameless self-publicity, is planning on making Pauly, Liz, Darcy, Steve, Thea and the Seven Stones, the subject of his first 'Letter From St Martin's'.

264

Over on Bryher, meanwhile, young Charlie Bennett has already submitted her first report from her home island, which includes a dramatic re-telling of the non-theft of her aunt Kris's fudge-stall honesty box. On the only other remotely interesting issue on the island, however, she is struggling. There's a much-loved goat called William tethered outside the Fraggle Rock pub up by Hangman Island, who, like his opposite number Snowy at the Seven Stones, does a sterling job keeping down the grass and heather on the rocky hillside outside the pub and helping to amuse children bored by their parents' drinking. It was the estimable role-model William who provided the inspiration behind the idea of bringing half a dozen cattle across to Bryher, the famous 'landscape cattle', to graze the heathland and in the process provide a potential additional source of income for the islands' struggling vet.

The move, by a handful of locals, to have them taken away has been growing, however, and there is now a real threat that they will have to go. But before Charlie can instruct Keri to 'hold the front page', or whatever the broadcast equivalent is, she has to persuade someone on Bryher to allow themselves to be interviewed on the subject, and this is proving harder than even she had imagined. In such a small and close-knit society, where everyone is constantly moaning about each other in private, history is littered with examples of the dangers of 'going public' and the consequent family feuds which can last generations. Thus Charlie has met her first 'wall of silence'.

Down behind Porthmellon Beach on St Mary's, the final week of August has seen a frantic Keri assembling an entire radio station. A solitary white van has arrived on the *Scillonian*, stuffed with absolutely everything required: the transmission desk, all the recording equipment, some chairs, shelves, a cream sofa from IKEA for the guests and several large clocks. Engineers have been seen scrambling up the huge radio mast at Telegraph to attach a new transmitter. The technology, including a computerised schedule of daily programmes which almost allows the station to run itself, is now in place. The only remaining obstacle, typically, seems to be the Scillonians themselves. Almost no-one turned up for the initial presenter training session, and Zoe's finding it surprisingly hard to get the lottery started. Everyone is rapturously in favour, but hardly anyone has actually got round to signing the direct debit mandate, most of them stealing one of Fraser Hicks's favourite phrases and declaring that 'it'll be done dreckly'.

The Duke of Cornwall was asked to record the first broadcast when transmission begins at two o'clock next Monday, but HRH, perhaps getting wind of the fact that he'd be competing with the likes of Fraser Hicks, 'Scots' Lorraine and Pete 'The Hat', turned this unique opportunity down. Instead, the honour will go to the chair of the Isles of Scilly Council, Christine Savill, who also runs the campsite below the Seven Stones. Christine's had the same family visiting for forty-seven years, and they've never missed a summer; overall, fifty per cent of her campers return year after year. There's not much about Scilly that Christine doesn't know. She says there will be as many people listening to Radio Scilly in London,

Manchester and Birmingham as on the islands—quite a thought.

Following Christine's opening remarks, there will be a recorded rendition of 'Rule Britannia' by the St Mary's Choir, after which Keri himself will take to the air for the first time in a show made up of very middle-of-the-road music, pre-recorded tributes and 'good luck' messages and volumes of island news and gossip. Later, there'll be a huge party at the Scillonian Club, down by Holgates Green, and, no doubt accompanied by the sound of the boys singing sea shanties, the merry-making will certainly continue well into the night, although it will probably not involve Fraser Hicks, whose first live broadcast outlining the day's boating movements in and out of St Mary's harbour is scheduled for first thing next morning.

Keri says he'll play me the Radio Scilly jingles he recorded in Milan. I stand behind the transmission desk, waiting for him to finish editing a programme on his computer screen. There's a small webcam staring at me from the shelf behind. In a moment of madness, I go right up close to it and gurn the most ridiculous face I can pull.

'When do the cameras go live?' I ask Keri.

'When? You must be joking! They're live now. We're running our test transmissions alongside them. They're going out on the Internet as we speak, all over the planet.'

The jingles sound wonderful, with not even a hint of an Italian accent, and Keri has mixed them with the sound of waves breaking on the sand, which he recorded standing ankle-deep in water on Porthmellon Beach. They make me want to go to sleep, but I resist the urge to tell him this.

*   *   *

The final days of August and the start of September turn out to be an end-of-season bonanza. Not only are there cloudless skies, day after day, but the northerly breezes which have chilled us for so much of the summer have simply disappeared. Scilly has taken on the hazy, humid feel of a group of islands on the equator, where you can watch the sun rise and set without even a moment's interruption; and so you can here.

The pubs and restaurants are once again buzzing, so that finding a free table without booking is impossible, a novel experience. The islanders, raised from the torpor of just a week or two ago, like an ants' nest suddenly revealed beneath a stone, are frenetic in their attempts to get as much cash stuffed under their mattresses as they can. The evening gig races, which over recent weeks have been followed by a mere dozen or so hardy spectators, are now accompanied by almost every available boat in St Mary's, pulling in big nightly bonuses for the boatmen.

There are just two British Telecom engineers on Scilly, who live in cottages up by the Telegraph, which since the Napoleonic era has been the centre of communications for the islands. There are no underwater cables to and from the mainland; telephone calls are made and received through a series of microwave dishes on a mast above their homes. It's a lonely job, and, according to one of the engineers, Stuart Moore, who came here three years ago with his young family, it's not exactly a great career move, but of course there are compensations.

There's a footpath that leads down from the Telegraph to one of Scilly's most beautiful points, Bant's Carn, the remains of an extraordinary prehistoric village, undisturbed by the modern world. It's a remote spot, but a fabulous vantage point to watch the sun drop down over Samson, and on clear and sunny evenings throughout the summer, passing boats have witnessed the strange sight of a lone bagpiper standing just above it, silhouetted against the dying light of the sky. On closer inspection, the figure turns out to be none other than Stuart, who in his ample spare time on Scilly has taught himself to play the pipes.

'I only play out here if it's a lovely sunset,' says Stuart. 'Quite amazing that I'm still here every night. Thought I'd have stowed away the pipes a while back.'

Stuart tells me the bagpipes were created as a weapon of war, intended to scare the hell out of the enemy, and the sound he produces certainly scares the hell out of unsuspecting passers-by, a haunting, almost primal lament that in a gentle breeze drifts right down to Porthloo and across to Porthmellon, as the shadowy blanket of dusk slowly settles over the western horizon.

15

The Waves Hit The Air Too

At last a chance to visit the great Scilly icon that for generations seems to have dominated island life from the western horizon. It's a sublime morning, with a gentle sea breeze taking the edge off the heat, and for the first time in weeks there's not a spare seat on *Sea King*. We are steaming out across the still waters off the northern shore of St Agnes, and Fraser talks us through the history of the sparkling white lighthouse that dominates the islands' skyline, which when it was built in 1680 consisted of an iron brazier containing a coal fire. It hasn't been in use since it was made redundant by the opening of the Peninnis lighthouse on the southern tip of St Mary's in 1911, but its distinctive silhouette makes it still of use to mariners as a daymarker, so it continues to be maintained by Trinity House.

Beside it is a line of coastguard cottages and a tower that turns out to be one of the great follies of Scilly history. Built specifically to keep a twenty-four-hour weather eye on ships heading to and from the maritime graveyard of the dreaded Western Rocks, the cottages appear to have been built the wrong way round, as though the builder had looked at the drawings upside down. The watchtower faces east instead of west, and so any conceivable view of the Western Rocks is blocked by the cottages' chimneys.

It is a fiercely hot morning, and the sexy,

orange-tipped oystercatchers flutter above the dozens of treacherous granite outcrops that scatter our path, while on the lower ledges the shags are lined up in their hundreds, packed together like passengers on a rush-hour tube train, waiting for the tide to turn before setting off in black squadrons, skimming the waves in search of a light breakfast of sand eels.

On one of the outcrops we pass, incongruously perched at an odd angle on the rocks, is a sad, rusting symbol of modern man, completely at odds with the naturally hewn seascape in which it sits so uncomfortably. It's a square container, the only visible remnant of the infamous wreck of recent times, that of the *Cita*, the *Whisky Galore* of Scilly.

Fraser's voyage out to the Western Rocks is turning out to be quite a revelation. Next we pass the little island of Rosevear, guarded by sentries of basking grey seals, the only outcrop so far to sport a modest patch of green grass on it, alongside the gable-ended ruins of small cottages that housed the construction workers who built the astonishing engineering triumph that is the Bishop Rock lighthouse a mile further west, the largest lighthouse in Britain. Suddenly a sea-fog blows up, and as we watch it engulf the base of the lighthouse, the top half of the structure, still in blazing sunlight, appears to be suspended like a rocket in the thin blue sky.

As we sail on, the fog rolls in, in great gusts, and suddenly the air is chilled. Fraser points out a strange, slightly spooky phenomenon: the breaking of waves in the midst of a flat, calm ocean. This is caused, he explains, by the Retarrier Ledges just beneath the surface of the sea, the same ledges that wreaked the catastrophe of the SS *Schiller* and the drowning of over 300 people. With the fog thickening by the minute, an odd silence falls on *Sea King*, and for a moment I start to appreciate what the terror of that moment must have been like, the terrible feeling of isolation and abandonment as the ship slipped beneath the waves on the edge of the world, and not a soul on Scilly aware of the unfolding tragedy.

The lighthouse itself is a breathtaking tribute to man's defiance of the elements. It stands over 160 feet high, yet in gales the sea frequently breaks right over the top of it. The base takes up most of the small rock it sits on; it took the men from Rosevear, who rowed or sailed over every day, depending on the tides and the weather, a year to build. They often had to rope themselves together so they wouldn't be washed away in the unpredictable swell. With the base finished, the tower was slowly built up from the inside, without the use of scaffolding; uniquely, interlocking stone blocks were used, for added strength. It was completed in 1887. The lighthouse was designed to sway with the force of the breakers, and it still does, by up to six inches.

Up until the lighthouse was fully automated, in 1992, the contract to service it was held by Fraser's grandfather, Gee Hicks, and his father, Mike, and as a teenager Fraser would help out on changeover days, when the crews were swapped, often a hazardous operation. The men would spend one month on, one month off, and Gee would take the replacements out and winch them across to the lighthouse by breeches' buoy. They would then make a hair-raising journey, scaling the tower on iron rungs up to about sixty feet, where there is a large door made of solid brass, which has now turned green with age.

Up to this point too, it was the duty of the chaplain to visit the lighthouse at least once a month, to administer to the spiritual needs of the keepers. It's hard to imagine Father Guy being hauled by rope across huge waves and clambering up the soaking stones of the lighthouse now, but who knows? It might have been the making of him.

Later, I bump into churchwarden Sue and her husband Murray, who has a small light aircraft up at the airfield, which he frequently uses to fly friends over to Scilly. I wonder what happens if he hits a sudden bank of fog: does he have instruments that help him get back to the airport in poor visibility? Murray looks at me askance for a moment, then lets out a short cackle and shakes his head.

'You drop down to zero altitude, just above the waves where the fog is usually thinner, then fly towards St Mary's, and when you hit land you zip up over the rocks and plonk yourself down on the runway.'

I tell him this strikes me as extremely dangerous. This prompts Murray to chuckle again.

'On the mainland there are air traffic controllers who will use radar to talk you down. There's no radar on Scilly. You're on your own out here.'

Murray falls silent for a moment.

'Why do you think there are so many graves of Second World War airmen at Old Town Church?'

In 1983, a helicopter came down on the approach to St Mary's when the pilot, disorientated by thick fog, refused to believe his instruments and drove the aircraft straight into the sea. There was no time even for a Mayday call. Six people managed to get to the surface of the sea, where they survived for thirty minutes until they were picked up by the St Mary's lifeboat; twenty were lost, in its day the worst civilian helicopter disaster in the UK. Among the lost were a prominent surgeon and his entire family. Next day, after the news of the disaster had been broadcast around the world, robbers broke into the family home and removed every item they could find.

Maybe the *Scillonian* is not such a bad option, after all; or even, if push comes to shove, the Grim Reaper.

*   *   *

It's not as pretty as Trenoweth Farm, and there are no ducks dozing on the road outside, but the new headquarters of the Ales of Scilly brewery, just around the corner from Radio Scilly, is up and running like a fantasy Toytown factory, all gleaming white paint, glittering industrial steel and steaming vats of hops and yeast topped with big round thermometers, with plenty of extra space to expand. The proximity to the Hugh Town pubs and the quay makes delivering the casks a delight. It's also just around the corner from the Chaplaincy, making it easy for Mark to drop off waste from the vats for Father Guy's garden, and easy, in turn, for Father Guy to drop round and sample the latest fruits of Mark's labour.

Mark has also fallen victim to the persuasive charms of Keri Jones, proprietor of the world's smallest radio station. He is currently in the process of brewing forty casks of a brand-new ale that Keri has talked him into creating to celebrate the station's launch. It's been named, after much debate, MegaHertz, a 4.4% brew made using milder hops, and although it's still a few days off being ready to unleash on an unsuspecting public, Mark tries it out on the chaplain. It's a slightly paler, yellower ale than Mark's legendary Scuppered, which is made from traditional and increasingly rare English hops, and it rapidly gets the full blessing of the Church of England.

The final arrangements for the station's launch are now in place. The day will get underway with an official lunchtime party for everyone involved, which will take place in the council chamber of the Old Wesleyan Chapel in Garrison Lane and will continue right up to the opening transmission at two o'clock.

The Radio Scilly net has been growing ever wider, and now seems to be encompassing almost everyone on the islands. The council dog warden, Maggie Perkovitz, one of the leading lights of the Entertainers, the amateur dramatic team who stage fortnightly shows at the back of the Town Hall throughout the summer, has agreed to write a soap opera, *The Islanders*. As with all the radio station's performers, reviews and criticism will have to be extremely sensitive and very carefully worded. The potential for the unpaid stars of Radio Scilly to take offence is enormous.

As a young trainee journalist on a small weekly newspaper in Kent, I'd consistently been given two onerous tasks to perform, probably the hardest I've ever had to do. The first involved calling round to the undertaker first thing Monday morning to find out who in the village had died, to be followed up by the ghastly business of visiting the bereaved in the hope of gleaning enough information about the deceased to compile a modest obituary. The other regular obligation was to review the local amateur dramatic company's latest production, which in a sense was even trickier. The hours of rehearsal, toil and stress, the sheer blood, sweat and tears invested in these Herculean labours of love could not be lightly dismissed by the flourish of a young man's pen, particularly since this almost certainly would have resulted in a hue and cry and the young man in question being run out of town by an angry mob. On the other hand, to praise their often dubious skills would do little for my self-respect or prospects of a long-term future as the leading theatre critic on a Fleet Street newspaper, something I harboured a secret ambition for. So I soon learned to employ a new and utterly bland vocabulary that allowed me to tread a delicate tip-toe between the two, allowing the participants to glow with pride at their inclusion in the review without at any time compromising my artistic credibility. Thus the theatre set would be described as 'notable', the costumes 'striking' and the performance of the leading lady 'unforgettable'. Other players might give a 'solid' or 'dependable' performance, while the music might be 'intriguing' and the direction 'energetic' or 'highly distinctive'.

This is a vocabulary we will all have to start brushing up on for the contributors to Radio Scilly, and which I soon find myself employing with equanimity.

Later, I see Father Guy's churchwarden Fiona, who's having a particularly stressful few days. As well as grappling with her imminent debut on 'Thought for the Day', Fiona is just back from the mainland, where she has abandoned her sixteen-year-old son Connor in digs in Truro. He'll be studying for his A-levels at the sixth-form college there, and learning very rapidly indeed how to fend for himself.

I find this one of the strangest aspects of life in Scilly. Every September, there's a mass migration of teenagers from the islands, so that, during term-time at least, there are virtually no sixteen- to eighteen-year-olds to be seen anywhere. Andrew, the new headmaster at Five Islands School, has been looking into the feasibility of expanding the islands' curriculum to include A-levels, but on such a small scale it is simply impossible to compete with the range of courses and teaching provisions offered over the water.

The off-island children have been used to boarding at school during the week, so probably fare better than the St Mary's kids when it comes to moving away. After the oddities of island life, some sixteen-year-olds are ready for the outside world, but some are not. Many families find the whole experience very tough; some even quit Scilly altogether.

The tragedy is that most of the Scilly children never really come home. After A-levels, many move straight on to university, travel or the kinds of jobs they could never dream of on Scilly. For those who do return, finding work is hard, finding somewhere to live almost impossible.

That's why the number of Scilly ex-pats listening to Radio Scilly on the Internet will always be far greater than those listening on the islands.

'How are you getting on with your first "Thought for the Day"?' I ask Fiona.

'Wait and see,' she says with a smile.

*   *   *

It's the first Monday in September and Keri and Zoe have been up all night. With the dawn comes news from the airport that there's fog and the helicopters carrying the VIPs for the launch, including the bigwigs from the regulatory broadcasting authority Ofcom, who are in possession of Keri's formal licence to broadcast, are unable to fly.

When I trip up the staircase, past Tim Guthrie's desk at Island Lettings, just three hours before transmission, and stick my head around the door to the studio to wish them a cheery good luck, I sense immediately that I've made a mistake. The atmosphere is taut with anticipation. I ask Keri if all the dignitaries have arrived, and without looking up from the desk, he says, 'You must be joking! How the bloody hell would I know, locked away in here,' at which point I beat a tactical retreat and leave them to it.

At the Old Wesleyan Chapel, they've laid tables with enough wine to intoxicate a small army and a mountain of food from the girls at the Dibble and Grub on Porthcressa Beach is arriving. Steve Watt from the tourist office is joyfully testing the sound equipment, which will relay the opening sounds of Radio Scilly—long sections of Henry V's rallying speech to the troops on the eve of Agincourt.

The bigwigs have arrived on the helicopters at the last moment, along with today's allocation of daily newspapers for the islands, which includes the *Guardian* and a gratifyingly full-page article under the banner headline: MUSIC BY THE TAXI GUY. SOAP OPERA BY THE DOG WARDEN. RADIO SCILLY IS HERE. And beneath: 'Policemen, publican and chef among the stars of the world's smallest radio station.'

The station's future stars arrive, one by one, and stand around sheepishly alongside representatives of almost every island organisation, councillors and even the police. There's Maggie Perkovitz from the Entertainers; Pete 'The Hat'; boatman Phil Culver, who with some mates is writing a comedy sketch show; Charlie Bennett, along with her mother and her aunt Kris, who'll be looking after health and fitness tips; Malcolm Martland, who'll be giving advice regarding ailing pets; and agony aunt 'Scots' Lorraine from the Atlantic, who'll be advising their ailing owners and whose show has mysteriously been named 'A Moan with Morag'. She and Fiona, with her 'Thought for the Day', won't begin broadcasting until tomorrow. Star of the morning show, Fraser Hicks, tells everyone he'll be along to the launch dreckly, then promptly forgets all about it.

Keri arrives wearing his dapper suit, makes a speech of welcome and formally collects his community radio licence from Ofcom before racing back to the studio. Then, after a short, tense period of waiting, during which we all stare blankly at the big, red second hand of a clock on the wall, it's two o'clock and the historic moment has arrived.

Later, at the Scillonian Club, the MegaHertz is flowing and an exhausted Keri manages to escape the overheated little studio at last and joins us.

'How do you think it went?' he asks.

I toy with, 'Just as smooth and well-oiled as I expected,' and 'Can't imagine how you have done it; quite extraordinary.'

In the end, I settle on 'You got it just about right. Well done, mate.'

Keri looks relieved. I do wonder though, whether they will be able to sustain this, month in, month out, year after year.

*   *   *

It's breezy but very clear and bright, so on St Martin's, Toby finishes up quickly in the bakery and hurries over, past a field of huge sunflowers swaying in the wind, to Ganilly. He has an old, very wide-angle Fuji Technorama camera that reproduces a similar letterbox image to the one humans see with both eyes, and he still uses the old Kodachrome film, so his pictures are starkly realistic, with a depth and an almost grainy quality that adds a touch of the fantastic. Then, armed with his ancient tripod, it's off on the quad, with his three dogs in tow, up to the daymark, and the cliffs below. The waves, swirling and breaking with white horses around the rocks of the bay, mirror the puffs of brilliant white cloud scudding across the thin blue sky.

Toby's already taken dozens of photos, but now, with the conditions so perfect and a hint of autumn in the lush heather, he races around the island—Chapel Down and the famous Daymark, to Great Bay bordered by great swathes of what the locals call 'naked lady', the lush pinky-red Bella Donna flower, which used to be cultivated here but now doggedly grows on wild; then to Lower Town for the views across the channel to Tean, then back up to the chapel and the panaroma across Par Beach.

In the peak months of July and August, Toby and Barney need all the help they can get in the bakery. Toby's son Sean has been here for weeks, along with a bevy of three astonishingly beautiful young girls, all unusually photogenic. It's as though he's parachuted in a group of models for a fashion shoot. I'm intrigued to find out how Toby manages to secure the services of such lovely girls to flog their guts out in a steamy bakery kitchen in such a remote location year after year, but he just gives me a wink and says it's an extraordinary coincidence.

So his glamorous team are all photographed in turn, up to their elbows in flour and pastry, or unloading red-hot trays of pasties from the ovens, beads of sweat forming on their tanned foreheads. I'm beginning to think that if Toby can ever get this book published, it could be a runaway bestseller. Then it's down to the Seven Stones, where he and Pauly sit in the evening sunshine over a pint of Scuppered, poring over a mass of paperwork: letterbox photos, schedules, sheaves of handwritten recipes and fading newspaper cuttings.

The idea of a book combining Toby's aspirational 'no-going-back' journey from Soho to Scilly with the secrets of Pauly's inspirational adventures in the kitchen has been knocking around the pub for a while. Now, with a publisher genuinely interested, a real deal may at last be in the offing; they've booked their flights for a meeting with him in Penzance in a few days' time.

After his second marriage to Louise ended, Toby appears to have been very much the single man. He's an athletic guy, what with all that rowing and running, he has an attractive, boyish charm and he could soon be worth a respectable fortune. Even though the island isn't exactly overflowing with suitable women, ever since I met Toby I've wondered just how long his enforced celibacy can last. There's been endless speculation that since they are working together and living close by, surrounded by their children, Toby might get back together with Liz, but that never really seemed likely to me.

After their planning meeting on the pub terrace, Toby roars off on the quad, back up the hill to the bakery, and Pauly and I walk up to the field above the back of the pub to examine the Gloucester Old Spots, who already seem to have doubled in size. If only they could appreciate the view over Lawrence Bay and Crow Sound; as the sun slowly dips down to the west behind Samson, there's a mesmeric combination of glitter and tranquillity all around us. The piglets snuffle around at our feet, happy enough. The pity is that there's still no abattoir on St Mary's, so the pigs will have to suffer the indignity of a trip on the Grim Reaper back to the mainland to be slaughtered.

Pauly and Thea wasted no time getting together. They seem very easy in each other's company. I ask Pauly what drew him to her, and he says that

282

she's short, blonde and available. I ask if they are a couple then, and he says that that's what Thea is telling people. I say, 'What a gent you are, Pauly.' I think he's actually grown very fond of her, although it seems he'd never admit it. As so often on Scilly, there's an intensity to their relationship, brought about by the knowledge that the season is drawing to a close, that soon big decisions will have to be made.

'Tell you another thing, and don't tell Tobes I told you,' says Pauly, leaning against the gate and gently stroking his beard, like an old farmer. 'But he's got a girlfriend too.'

I'm not in the least surprised, just curious.

'Local girl?'

'He's not that daft.'

Pauly pauses for a moment, taking in the breathtaking view. I sense the whole story is about to emerge.

'I wish I had a window in my kitchen.'

Another long pause.

'It happened at the last local produce market over on St Mary's. Tobes and I were both there and suddenly in walks this lovely girl, slim, beautiful, gorgeous, she's an absolute stunner, couldn't take my eyes off her.'

'Get on with it, Pauly.'

'Turns out she's a herbalist, doing some research into unusual recipes and cures for Kew Gardens in London, things that may have been handed down anecdotally through the generations. She marches straight up to Toby and asks him if he's come across any. He looks up at her, and is instantly struck dumb. She repeats, "Do you know any weird and wonderful cures I could include in my research?" And do you know what he says?'

'Get on with it, Pauly.'

'He says, "No." Just like that. One word. I couldn't believe it. "No." Then total silence. Just as well I managed to step into the situation and keep her talking while Tobes regained his composure.'

'What happened?'

'He hasn't seen her since.'

'Is that it?'

'He did manage to get her email address. And they have been writing and calling each other twice a day ever since.'

'Where do they go from here?'

'Who knows. Stay tuned.'

I realise only later that I had forgotten to ask her name.

* * *

The sun still beats down and the boats are busier than ever, but the temperatures are dropping and there's an inescapable shimmer of change in the air. What is it, when the light is still dazzling, the sky is still a gossamer, cornflower blue, and you still discover beads of sweat on your brow after a brisk walk, that tells you that summer is definitely, unequivocally, over? Is it the scent on the wind? Is it the curl of the wing of a shearwater as it contemplates the long journey south to warmer climes? And how is it that summer seems to be over so quickly? Isn't it only a few days ago that the season was just getting underway? Yet now, as the holidaymakers pack their bags, the first of the new crop of narcissi—incredibly—seem

284

almost ready to be picked. Tomorrow, Radio Scilly begins its proper broadcasts. Tomorrow, the boatmen will be busy early on the quays of the off-islands, bringing over the children to St Mary's, loaded down with bags and suitcases, for the first day of term. With the weather holding, the birdwatchers will start to flock to Scilly in large numbers, in their regulation green anoraks and trousers, with long-lensed telescopes and shooting sticks. Most of the islanders never warm much to them, as they never spend any money. Many of the twitchers commit the cardinal sin on Scilly of 'making their own sandwiches', and I'm told that in the rare event of one of them reaching into their pockets and buying a sandwich, they are usually seen to share it with at least five others.

Soon all the restaurants and hotels will start to close, and those islanders who can afford it will leave for their annual break abroad. Down in her terraced house overlooking Old Town Bay, though, Heike has already told Sammy there's no money for them to go on holiday this year, but that next year is a possibility, or if not, certainly the year after.

Heike is planning to commemorate the changing of the seasons with her own celebration. In just over a week's time, it's the Jewish New Year, and Heike already knows exactly what she'll do. She will dress, according to tradition, all in white. Then, she will light two candles, say her prayers and eat a vegetarian broth. There won't be any kosher meat to be had here, that's for sure.

Sadly, though, since Heike is the only Jewish person on Scilly, she will be doing all this entirely alone, which is not the idea at all.

16

A Shore Always To Return To

In a sense the Isles of Scilly saved Donald Marr's life. He'd been the assiduous and conscientious priest of a rural parish in the heart of Cheshire when he was cut down in his prime by a huge and totally unheralded stroke. Donald's wife Margaret held a bedside vigil while he was on life-support in intensive care and was told to prepare for the worst. But Donald wasn't yet ready to shuffle on to his concept of heaven. The stroke left him with no speech for six months, a limp in his right leg and an eternal, boundless gratitude for the gift of life.

On Tresco and St Martin's there are two parsonages, empty from an earlier age when each had its own priest, which are still owned by the Diocese. During the summer months they are rented out to mainland clergy in need of a holiday at a token cost; in return the visiting priest helps relieve the pressure on the chaplain by conducting services in the island church on Sunday.

Fifteen years ago, still unable to say a word and still unable to believe he wasn't dead, Donald Marr and his wife Margaret were offered an intriguing proposition: the old parsonage on one of the Isles of Scilly, Tresco, was vacant through the winter, might that be suitable for a short break to aid Donald's convalescence? It was, and they stayed until the following March. Like so many before and no doubt to come, they fell hopelessly in love with the islands, and have returned to hibernate in their oddly discovered seaside idyll every year since, gladly taking the services on Tresco and Bryher every Sunday, and returning home to their house in Cheshire every March for the summer like a happy pair of migrating birds.

Now, with the summer all but over, the self-styled Revds Bogoff are back, like the US cavalry, and their Skybus plane from Bristol drops soundlessly from a cloudless blue sky onto St Mary's airfield. Father Guy is clearly delighted to see them again.

'A steady pair of hands,' he says, beaming with obvious relief as the little plane taxis across the grass and, noisy now it's downwind, pulls up on the tarmac just outside the terminal. The visibility is unusually good, and from the airport it's possible to make out the dim silhouette of Land's End, twenty-eight miles away, not grim today, but glinting like a distant lighthouse in the sunlight.

I find myself delighted to see them too. Aided no doubt by the backdraught from the Twin Otter, Donald, in sports jacket and jaunty nautical cap, and Margaret, in a fluorescent pink dress, really do feel like a breath of fresh air. Donald and Margaret, masters at diffusing tension, are their relentlessly upbeat selves, and their timing has never been better. Suddenly, I'm not quite sure why, we are all laughing.

Donald is also a craftsman at self-deprecation, which he employs with the skill and confidence of someone who has nothing really to deprecate himself about. When I'd last seen them, back in March, they were planning on joining a cruise which would have taken in Florida and the Eastern Seaboard of the USA. They never made it, says

287

Donald with a flourish. There has been a new crackdown by the US Immigration Authority on visitors to America and, amazingly, the saintly Canon the Revd Donald Marr has inexplicably been turned down for a visa. If he knows why, Donald's certainly not saying, but they will try again for the cruise next summer.

The Bogoffs are exactly what the new chaplain needs: good listeners, dispensers of wisdom, committed and skillful lieutenants who'll offer support, encouragement, a great knowledge of the islands and its ways and, no doubt, a shoulder to cry on.

Down in the Chaplaincy, over coffee, Donald asks how the summer has been for Guy and Kate. There's a long pause. Eventually, after taking a deep breath, Kate says, 'Hard.' And then, after more hesitation, 'It's been a difficult start.' Guy and Kate look at each other. 'But it's getting better.'

Guy seems almost a different man as he talks to Donald and Margaret, that laugh of his booming, reflective but not earnest, able at last to open up, visibly less tense.

'I've made mistakes. I've said things I shouldn't have said, not said things I should have,' says Father Guy. 'In a place like this, small things get blown up in a way they wouldn't on the mainland. And it's been hard, and sometimes lonely, unable to speak face to face with other priests because of the thirty miles of water separating us.'

Later, Donald gives me that jaunty, nautical wink of his, no doubt perfected during the long years he spent in the navy.

'He'll be all right, will Guy,' he says. 'You'll see.'

It's seven o'clock in the morning. I can't believe it's another clinically clear morning, with a fiery sun shooting shafts of light across the Garrison and Star Castle as it rises over the airport. The harbour is like a mill pond, and for the first time since I've been here, the boats on their moorings are all pointing in different random directions.

It's the first day of Radio Scilly's broadcasts proper, and amateur meteorologist Steve Douglas is informing us that the high pressure is due to dominate the islands for some days yet, and that later we'll be cooled by nor-nor-westerly winds, force two to three, and that the next high water will be at 10.22 a.m.

At 7.11, a familiar voice hits the airwaves.

' "Man cannot discover new oceans until he has the courage to lose sight of the shore." ' This is churchwarden Fiona, delivering Radio Scilly's first 'Thought for the Day'. She's chosen the one subject many of the islanders will be preoccupied with in this first week of term. Her voice betrays scarcely a hint of the worry and heartache that many are going through, as she is, with her son Connor just beginning a life without her in strange digs across the water in Truro. With no flights or ferry in or out of Scilly on a Sunday, there'll be no weekend trips to meet up; she has no idea when she'll see him again.

'For sixteen years they have been part of your life, and now you must let them go. It won't be you calling them for breakfast, checking they have everything they need for the day ahead . . .'

Fiona's voice has a flat, stoical, almost Churchillian tone to it; this could be nerves.

'. . . the correct clothes, the right books, pens, pencil, rubber, ruler, maths set, PE kit, lunch money. How will you, how will they cope? It is just this point in time that the last sixteen years have been leading to . . .'

The Grim Reaper slips effortlessly away from the quay, and heads up past Porthloo to Crow Sound. This must be one of its most comfortable voyages ever across to Penzance. In a few weeks' time, when the *Scillonian* stops its summer schedule and the autumn gales begin, this will be the only way of getting cargo in and out of the islands.

'. . . the examples you have set; the rules and boundaries you have made and stood by; the care you have taken; the love you have shown. Have faith in those. Have faith in them and let them go, to discover new oceans, confident that one shore will always be there to return to.'

Then Keri's giving us some island news about a bench being 'borrowed' from the Strand and there's a trail for Charlie Bennett's item from Bryher, about the non-theft of her aunt Kris's fudge cash tin. There's news that it looks like the council's planning committee will give permission for three pairs of low-rent cottages to be built on St Agnes, Bryher and St Martin's; staggeringly, each pair will cost the equivalent of twelve new houses on the mainland. They probably won't be much help to the likes of young Charlie or Fraser's daughter Rebecca, but I guess it's a start in the right direction.

Then there's an announcement about what's

being served for lunch today at the school on St Mary's, a key piece of information that will be phoned into the station daily by the bursar and broadcast at a carefully timed moment, so that parents and their little dears can pack up some home-made sandwiches if they don't like the sound of it.

The main news from London sounds utterly bizarre on Radio Scilly. The British government is asking China why so many Chinese-made weapons are being found on captured Taliban by British troops in Afghanistan. In Finland, of all places, representatives of the warring Iraqi tribes of the Sunnis and Shias are meeting for negotiations under the chairmanship, of all people, of Sinn Fein's Martin McGuinness.

'Nice day for boatin', I'd say.' The reassuring tones of Fraser Hicks brings us tumbling back into the real world.

'You've bought Sally into the studio with you, Fraser. Is she going to bark out the boating times?'

'I'm trainin' 'er up,' says Fraser. 'Now, as I said, it's a nice day for boatin'.' Fraser always says it's a nice day for boating, even when it's bloody tipping it down. 'We've got a lovely trip out to Bishop Rock and to see the seals on the Eastern Isles. Perfect conditions . . .'

Across on the quay, I can see the first of the off-island boats, bright flashes of the low sun catching the glass and steel handrails, like machine-gun shots, as they bring in the secondary school children, weighed down by backpacks, for the week's stay on St Mary.

Andrew Penman will already be behind his desk in the headmaster's study at Carn Thomas for this first day of the new term. But that will soon be changing, rather faster than even he had imagined.

Quite how large a role Bishop Bill, and divine intervention, played in it all, Andrew will probably never know, but it was certainly the Bishop who was the inspiration behind the recent renewed efforts by the school to persuade the government to find the funds for a brand-new school building.

It was he who suggested that the school contact HRH the Duke of Cornwall to enlist royal support for the campaign; and it was the Bishop who press-ganged into service the genius behind the Eden Project, Tim Smit, the ultimate mover-and-shaker, who managed almost single-handedly to raise £30,000,000 for the transformation of an old clay pit in a little-known corner of Cornwall into one of the best-known and commercially successful enterprises of its kind in Europe.

On the rare occasions government ministers or influential members of parliament visit Scilly, they tend to leave pledging generous help with this or that project, only to be then instantly subjected to what the islanders call 'helicopter amnesia'—i.e. the moment they touch down on the mainland, they forget Scilly even exists. In this case though, something must have been beating frantically away behind the scenes. A meeting was called in Truro of all the parties involved in any potential school-rebuild project, including those holding the purse strings at the Department of Education, and Bishop Bill, Andrew and Tim Guthrie, the chairman of the school governors, now working quietly away in Island Properties while Radio Scilly bangs out in the attic above.

Everyone was aware that the Truro meeting was

probably a once-in-a-generation chance to set in motion the biggest single improvement for life on Scilly in years, but no-one seriously expected much to come of it. An hour and a half later, they came stumbling out into the daylight £9,500,000 richer. With the sale of the land at Carn Thomas, with its great views over the harbour towards Tresco and Bryher, probably for a luxury hotel, this is enough to build a brand-new school, incorporating secondary and primary units and, with luck, Andrew's dream of an international centre of excellence for the study of marine biology, which could revolutionise the islands' economy.

After such unexpected bounty, Andrew and his team don't intend to loiter, lest someone in Whitehall changes their minds. Advertisements for a project manager are now appearing in trade magazines, designs for the new building will be completed next spring and the school, on its new site hidden away just behind Old Town Bay, making it even less of a walk for Heike and Sammy, will open its doors for business in three years almost to the day.

This morning, down the road in the vet's house, Leo is in a very grumpy mood because he's been kicked out of his bed by the surgery to make way for an injured tabby cat from Tresco called Daisy. Daisy had been missing for eleven days and then turned up with her chest inexplicably ripped open, so that it's almost hanging in two halves. Heike has done her best to sew Daisy back together again, and the prognosis is looking better by the hour. She's also injected two rabbits against myxomatosis (there's a large, growing population of wild rabbits on Scilly). Business is definitely picking up.

Heike is beaming. She is waving a crumpled piece of paper at me, like Chamberlain after the Munich crisis, as she shoves a burning-hot mug of coffee into my hand.

'Have you any idea what this is?' she asks.

When I shake my head, she says, 'It's a cheque! For £45 pounds! From a client!'

'Why does it look as though someone's screwed it up?'

'Because someone did! Me!'

It turns out that Heike had discovered the cheque at the bottom of her kitchen bin, among a ball of bacon rinds, tomato skins and some old pickled onions.

'You pay your Duchy rent twice every month,' I say, 'you don't charge your clients, and even when they do pay you, you throw away the money.'

'Crazy! More coffee?'

'I'm going to miss you, Heike.'

Later, at the radio station, Zoe is busy recording programmes, not least for Tuesday evening, when it's fire brigade practice around the islands and the deafening siren at the main fire station on St Mary's, just feet away from Radio Scilly, goes off with a howl like an air-raid warning.

'Scots' Lorraine hobbles in on crutches for her agony aunt slot and takes her place, like the Queen of Sheba, on the IKEA sofa opposite Keri. They've had very few letters, which Keri explains is because the islanders, understandably enough to my mind, seem reluctant to share their intimate personal problems on the airwaves with a famous gossip who runs the Atlantic Inn, one of the most popular island pubs.

'Write your problems on a piece of paper and slip them under the door for us in the middle of the night,' purrs Keri. 'That way we'll never know who you are.'

I suspect Lorraine has invented her first correspondence.

'My first letter today comes from a six-foot-four gentleman who says his missus is always going on about his "small man" problem,' says Lorraine, or rather Morag, as she is now inexplicably known.

'Well, I'd say to you, darlin', that unless she's seven foot, you've got a whole lotta satisfyin' to do!'

I'm not sure whether Lorraine has missed out a critical section of this story or I misheard it, but judging by the cackles coming from the studio, it's gone down rather better than I might have predicted.

Solicitor Louise Southwell arrives from the airport for her first 'Legal Eagle' broadcast, a little flushed with nerves.

'I'm not used to public speaking, I'm actually a private client solicitor, so I've never done court work,' she confesses breathlessly. Her hands are trembling slightly.

'You've been interviewed before? Done a broadcast?'

She leans forward, conspiratorially. 'Never. I'm actually petrified.'

Under the beating sun, the studio, even with all its windows open, is like an oven, but Louise, a rosy glow shining through the tan on her cheeks, admirably retains her composure and delivers an intriguing diatribe about inheritance tax, which, it seems, is quite an issue on Scilly.

295

Although most housing is controlled by the Duchy, there are some freehold homes, mainly as a result of the Duchy's need to raise cash by selling off property in Hugh Town in the 1940s. There are also council houses. When the Thatcher government gave council tenants in England the 'right to buy' their homes, the Isles of Scilly, with its tiny housing stock in one of the most expensive places in the country, pleaded special circumstances and asked to be exempt, a request that was promptly turned down. Tenants bought their houses and within a year or two, as property prices on Scilly continued to rocket, they found themselves sitting on fortunes way beyond their wildest dreams. Consequently, anyone lucky enough to own property here and many who have long leases will automatically be liable to a substantial inheritance tax bill and, according to Louise, many have made no provision at all for it. She also believes many Scillonians haven't even made a will, in which case their assets may well drop straight into the hands of Prince Charles and the Duchy, a gift most would be reluctant to make to the heir to the throne and one of the world's richest men were they aware of the legal position.

I predict that Louise's show will be one of the first unexpected hits on Radio Scilly.

*   *   *

There is really only one place to have lunch on such a perfect day. I walk down past the Parade, where there's a bustle at the back of the Town Hall as the RNLI craft sale gets underway, and down Hugh Street, past the tourist office and headquarters of the Steamship Company towards the quay. The blackboard outside informs visitors that the entertainment highlights for today include a guided wildlife walk on St Agnes; a run, jog or brisk walk with the Scilly Hash House Harriers, starting at the Old Town Inn; and a whist drive at the Scillonian Club. There's also an advert for the World Beetle Drive Championships being held on Tresco in a couple of weeks. On the quay I bump into Fraser. In a few weeks' time Sea King will be coming out of the water over at Porthloo for a refit. 'Try and be a bit better prepared for next season,' he says sheepishly.

His daughter Rebecca has fallen on her feet. She and Fraser made friends with the rich French owner of a magnificent 82 foot yacht which called in to St Mary's in July. 'He's invited Rebecca to join him as crew on the boat dreckly,' says a proud Fraser. 'She'll be flying down to Antibes, and they'll take 'er across to the Canaries, and then across the Pond to Martinique, where she'll be worked as a charter boat through the West Indies until March. Then maybe home. Can't be bad!'

Then it's on to the next boat to St Martin's. There's still no wind whatsoever, which is spookily unusual, and we roar past a becalmed, solitary yachtsman who has given up the struggle, rolled up his sails and is rowing to Tresco, sweating in the September heat. The water is the clearest I've ever seen it, and as we cross Crow Bar I can see the turquoise shards of seaweed, hovering, almost stationary, a strangely static foreground to the crystal-clear, miniature sand dunes below. It's like flying over the Sahara desert.

I've come full circle; in a few weeks' time, it'll

297

once again be a very low tide, the lowest since the spring equinox, and following the tragic deaths of the summer, a walk has been organised from St Martin's to Tresco and on to Bryher and Samson, to raise funds for the local emergency services.

At the Seven Stones, where the windless terrace is already bouncing the heat back into the body so that it feels like being in an oven, the glamorous island post lady is arriving with a sack full of letters; amazingly, she's barefoot.

Pauly feeds me like a king: a huge portion of gravlax to start, cured with whisky and honey by Toby, a Polish recipe given him by Krzys; then roasted, locally caught rockling fish with a hazelnut crust on crushed baby new potatoes, grown in the fields just down below.

Toby's been up in the bakery since six, making croissants and pain au raisin. He's slightly hungover following a farewell meal with his bevy of lovelies, who are leaving St Martin's tomorrow to return to their lives on the mainland. Will they be back next year? Toby gives a faintly salacious smile and says he hopes so, but if not, he'll have no trouble finding plenty more where they came from.

As with most of the islanders, the start of Toby's new week is a watershed. Last week, he was taking £1,000 a day at the bakery. Now, with the new school term starting, Christine Savill's campsite beneath the Seven Stones has emptied virtually overnight, so that the old flower fields are an empty patchwork of pale-green shapes, where tents have been pitched for so long. Today, he'll be lucky to clear £300, which is why he can afford the time to share a pint with me and Pauly in the blazing sunshine.

At his feet, Galty and Shima are looking restless.

'I've been cleaning my shotgun,' says Toby. 'The new shooting season starts in a day or two.'

The big news, though, is that Toby and Pauly, after a meeting with the publisher over in Penzance—who was greatly impressed with Toby's photographs and Pauly's recipes—have a book deal. It'll be launched at the Eden Project and will go on sale early in the New Year.

Thea, all smiles, brings out a tray of more Scuppered and skips back to work. We toast the new book.

The whole pace of island life, in just a few hours, has somehow cranked down a large notch. Pauly, for example, has been hoping for months to find the time to experiment with shark steaks, and now one of the local fishermen has hooked him a five-foot blue shark just out by the Seven Stones reef, which is hanging, decapitated and with its fins and tail ignominiously removed, in two halves in his fridge.

'Never worked with it before. Its skin is like rubber, half a centimetre thick,' says Pauly, shielding his eyes with one hand and stroking that gingery beard with the other. 'Had to take a serrated knife to it rather than a flexible filleting knife; nearly took my hand off.'

'What will you do with it?'

'I ended up using two pairs of scissors and five different knives. A typical fish knife is very flexible as well as sharp, but just bloody hopeless for a shark.'

'How will you cook it?'

'Even ended up using my bread knife as well as

299

the big fish shears, but they were just too powerful, which is why I had to use the ordinary scissors. I didn't really have a clue what I was doing.'

'Get on with it, Pauly.'

'I roll the fillets in clingfilm and cut them into round steaks, like a kind of tournedo. Then I season them with salt and pepper and dust them with a spice mix of cinnamon, star anise, madras powder, garamasala, cumin, cayenne pepper, chilli powder and Chinese five-spice. Then I dip them in toasted hazelnuts, sear them and bake them in the oven for six or seven minutes. All I need to decide now is what the hell to serve with them.'

'And who to,' adds Toby.

Pauly's clearly a genius; I have no idea what it'll taste like but the inventiveness of the recipe, which is based on his winter roamings around Far Eastern eating dives, is mouth-watering. In a few weeks, he'll be off to India, but this time, it'll be different.

'I always travel alone, so this is a big thing for me,' he says, lowering his voice and nodding towards Thea, who is now emerging with yet another tray of Mark's finest.

'I've asked her to come with me.'

'Thea? Brilliant! And?'

'I thought she'd say no. How wrong was I?'

'Wow!'

Toby's poring intently over piles of paperwork and photographs from the Internet.

'Have a look at this,' he says.

It's a beautiful converted Italian farmouse called Poggio Covili, which stands atop a solitary hill in dramatic countryside, near the village of Celle sul Rigo in the heart of Tuscany, just south of Sienna. There's an avenue lined with Cypressus trees sweeping up to the stone building, which has been converted into four luxury apartments, and a burning-blue pool. The views are breathtaking.

'Wow! What's this?'

'It's where I'm taking Juliette, the girl I met at the Farmer's Market. Ten days in October.'

'Wow!'

Pauly gives me a wink and mouths, 'It's true love, matey, believe me!' It takes me quite a while to decipher his message.

There must be something in the Scilly air. WPC Nikki Green is on her way back to the islands from the headquarters of the Devon and Cornwall Constabulary, having just sat and passed her assessment for firearms training. She'll finish her secondment in a few weeks, and is now ticking off the hours, like a prisoner due for release after being banged up for years, until her final escape to freedom on the mainland. Recently, anytime anyone so much as mentions the word 'Andrew', Nikki dissolves into paroxysms of giggles, which I guess is a severe symptom of the terminal stages of a shot from Cupid's arrow. She and her young gardener are already looking for a cottage to share near his home in St Erth, just down the road from the lovely harbour at St Ives.

In many ways, it's been a tormented summer for the islanders emotionally; but how have they fared financially? As always on Scilly, finding a consensus of opinion is impossible, doubly so since it involves the delicate subject of money. Beneath the bland, non-committal expressions, though, I detect a huge sense of relief that, thanks to those glorious, sun-drenched weeks of our Indian summer, a disastrous summer has been upgraded to the loftier category of 'well, it could have been worse', sometimes said with the merest hint of a smile at the corner of the lips.

There's also a sense that, emotionally and financially, this summer is already history, gone and forgotten almost as quickly as it arrived. There's an innate knowledge amongst the islanders that survival depends on always looking ahead, planning and plotting the future. They may be reluctant to analyse these past few months, but are ready to point out that every self-catering cottage and apartment is already booked for next July and August. The question, 'Are you making a go of it?' will always be met by, 'I'll let you know next year.'

I look out across the growing flats of Crow Bar. *Marauder* is on her way home after three days at sea, her sparkling wake churning the flat water, speeding her to port. A huge flock of seagulls hurries behind, diving and swooping into the sea; perhaps Martin and Joel have had a bumper catch. I hope so.

I can hear Toby and Pauly chattering away behind me, planning their book launch and discussing the exciting romantic adventures that lie ahead for them both. Thea calls out, asking whether I want more beer, and I turn, shaking my head and blinking in the sunshine, and smile.

Could I ever live on Scilly? Could I really be happy here?

I could, I guess, if I had been born here and was a true islander—they say you need to be at least third generation to claim that elevated status. I could live here if this was home. And so I could, perhaps, if I were rich and could afford to escape. Frequently.

So that effectively rules me out.

The question less easy to answer is this: can I ever, after this extraordinary summer, be truly content and settled living anywhere else?

Out on the Sound I can see the tiny silhouette of the little, yellow Atlantic rowing boat, *Scilly Boys*, the blades of its oars flashing in the light. They'll have to put in much hard labour before they are ready to set off next spring, from beneath the Statue of Liberty, on that epic, incredible 3,000-mile race home to Bishop Rock.

A new set of hands has been found to replace Nathan, but his spirit will be there. The soul of the islands, they had called him, and the soul of the islands will indeed be in that tiny boat, now just bobbing out of sight around Tobaccoman's Point, along with the hopes and aspirations of two thousand hearts.

As Fiona might have put it: have faith in the care you have shown, in the love you have known. Have faith in those and let them go, to discover new oceans, confident that one shore will always be there to return to.